Roosevelt's Forest Army
A History
of the
Civilian Conservation Corps
1933—1942

Roosevelt's Forest Army

A History
of the
Civilian Conservation Corps
1933-1942

BY PERRY H. MERRILL, 1894-

200 Elm St.
Montpelier, Vermont 05602
802-223-2697
Published by Perry H. Merrill
1981

First Printing, 1981
Second Printing, 1983

Other Publications by Perry H. Merrill

  Vermont Under Four Flags

  A History of the Green Mountain State, 1635-1975

  Montpelier The Capital City's History, 1780-1976

© Copyright Perry H. Merrill 1981

ISBN: 09605806-0-3
$8.95

Published by Perry H. Merrill
Typeface: 11 Point Times Roman
Designed and printed by Northlight Studio Press, Inc., Barre, Vermont

Dedicated to
The Late Robert Fechner

Director
Civilian Conservation Corps

FOREWORD

The Civilian Conservation Corps was born from the despair of the great depression: the soup lines, the Hoover villages, and the conditions which spawned "The Grapes of Wrath," in short, a nation in desperate need of help and action.

In 1933, President Roosevelt faced a nation bankrupt in money and spirit. In his first Hundred Days he took many bold actions. Passage of the Emergency Work Act in March authorized several programs, one of which was the Civilian Conservation Corps. It was a program to recruit thousands of young men in a peace time army to work in forests, parks, lands and waters which constitute our basic resources.

The President called for action from Congress and he got action. Senate Bill 598 was introduced on March 27, 1933, cleared both Houses of Congress and was on the President's desk for signature on March 31. The first camp was opened on April 17 in Virginia, and by the first of July there were 275,000 enrollees in 1,300 camps across the country.

It was an amalgamation of agencies. Recruitment was done by the Department of Labor. Transportation, camp construction and management was done by the Army while the Departments of Agriculture and Interior selected the camp sites, planned, designed and supervised the work projects in cooperation with the State Departments of Forests and Parks. Through cooperative arrangements the Corps worked on national, state and metropolitan lands and projects. The team work and cooperation between the many organizations was nothing short of a miracle.

Robert Fechner was appointed as National Director by executive order 1601 on April 5, 1933. He established an Advisory Council of the Secretaries of War, Labor, Agriculture and Interior. It was an unusual organizational structure but one which worked, probably due to the dedication and the integrity of the director.

The CCC program had an immediate economic impact. Supplies of all kinds from food to lumber, trucks, axes and shovels were required. The enrollees were required to send $25.00 of the $30.00 monthly wage home. These expenditure and allotment checks, which look small now, were felt in the cities and towns across the nation.

There was a social impact. Young men were taken off the streets, they traveled far from home, and they performed useful work in a healthy environment. They learned to live and work together and 40,000 illiterates learned to read and write. By 1935, over 600,000 enrollees were working out of 2,650 camps. By the time the program was disbanded in 1942, nearly three million men had engaged in this productive and popular program.

These men built fire towers, truck roads, firebreaks, planted millions of trees, reclaimed thousands of acres from erosion, built countless Federal and state parks and campgrounds, salvaged timber from the

New England hurricane blow-down of 1938, and improved fish and wild-life habitats.

By 1940, due to the growing threat of war and improvement in the nation's economy there were fewer than 200,000 men in about 900 camps. The need for the program was rapidly diminishing. The corps was never abolished. Congress simply failed to provide a budget for its continuance and by July, 1943, the entire program was liquidated.

Many articles have been written about the Civilian Conservation Corps, but to my knowledge there has been no definite history of the Corps. Perry H. Merrill has done the job. As State Forester of Vermont and then Commissioner of Forests and Parks he has been involved in the leadership and administration of the program in his state. As a forester, a legislator and an historian he is admirably equipped to tell the story of one of America's great peace time successes. He not only captures the despair and emotion of the depression but also the thrill of accomplishment in the rehabilitation of both human and natural resources.

DeWitt Nelson

Mr. Nelson was with the U.S. Forest Service 1925-1944, The CCC Liaison Officer, Ninth Corps Area, U.S. Army, Presidio, San Francisco, 1935-1936. From 1944 to 1953, he was State Forester of California being advanced to Director of the California Department of Natural Resources and Conservation where he served well from 1953 to 1966. Ed.

PREFACE

No one can write a correct history of the Civilian Conservation Corps' Director's report for the period of 1933-1942 without using some of its material in whole or in part. There are many other Federal reports from the Federal Security Agency and the Departments of Labor, War, Agriculture and Interior which have been freely used to get the right slant and intent of the entire program.

Since the author was employed by the State of Vermont for 47 years beginning in 1919 and ending in 1966, he is well informed about the beginnings and work of the CCC. Since 1929, he served as state forester and then Commissioner of Forests and Parks. For the first CCC Period, he represented the Secretary of Labor as state selection agent for Vermont youths. He was in the first group of state foresters who were called to Washington to meet with President Roosevelt, Rexford Tugwell and Henry Wallace and learn of the President's proposal to put the nation's youth to work in the forests. Thus much is written in this book which is an intermixture of Federal reports and the state forester's experiences with the administration of the work of 4,000 youths in 20 Vermont CCC camps.

There has been omitted from this publication all references to the interdepartmental differences between the departments of government and members of the Advisory Council and also Mr. Fechner. The real history of the CCC is wrapped up in the heads of former CCC enrollees, officers and technical personnel. Several hundred letters have been received from these persons from every part of our country. The letters herein touch on the interesting experiences and history of the localities where the enrollees were located. Many letters mentioned what a help the CCC had been to them and their families in their time of dire need. Many letters ended with a statement that the CCC should be reactivated due to the serious unemployment in this country.

There are many more details which could have been included in this book; however, the interesting history and stories of the CCC at work and play should suffice. This history could not have been written without the wholehearted support of the state foresters and state park directors, who furnished xerox copies of their biennial reports and other special information. Thanks are also due to the officials and personnel of the Departments of Agriculture and Interior for information which they furnished. Especial thanks are extended to Robert L. Griffith, Executive Director of NACCCA, and to Frank J. Harmon of the U.S. Forest Service and John Helms of the General Services Administration, who have gone beyond the call of duty to fill our requests.

Table of Contents

LIST OF ILLUSTRATIONS

PART I

THE CIVILIAN
CONSERVATION CORPS

PERIOD OF PROSPERITY

America was prosperous in the early 1900's, yet farm prices were greatly depressed. America at that time was a debtor nation, selling her industrial products and agricultural produce abroad. European money bought the goods that our industries produced and the crops which our farmers raised.

When President Woodrow Wilson's administration broke with the old American policy of isolation from the rest of the world, it did nothing to slow down the boom. At Fort Knox extra large holdings of gold were kept safely for the Europeans. To increase the operation of American factories, the United States loaned back to Europe her money at interest. Liberty bonds were issued to fund these loans. Then, on April 6, 1917, we became embroiled in World War I.

The entire picture was changed following World War I. America changed from a debtor nation into a creditor one. It was necessary to change our ways if we were to regain our international trade. Every citizen soon went on her merry way expecting that the situation would continue forever. Soon, however, Europe could no longer purchase American products and the boom was over.

PERIOD OF DEPRESSION

The stock market crashed on October 29, 1929. Hundreds of people lost their life's earnings. Many committed suicide. Some banks paid off their depositors at a few (in some cases, as little as five) cents per dollar. The rise in installment buying eroded the purchasing power of the consumers so that the domestic markets for all types of goods shrank. President Herbert Hoover offered a number of programs to get the economy of the country started again, but he had a Congress which was not receptive. Then Congress passed the Smoot-Hawley tariff, which halted the flow of goods from abroad, with the result that we lost those markets for our own products.

1

Farmers let their crops of wheat, apples, cotton, and other foodstuffs rot in the fields since they could not get back a new dollar for the old one. The rash expansion of credit has been assigned as the greatest single cause of the disaster which followed the serious crash of 1929. The huge amount of national debt was caused by the reckless spending of government officials, which was not well known nor realized by our citizens. The over-expansion of individual credit which occurred through installment buying was little noticed. The credit system, which led to time-purchasing of clothing, automobiles, homes, and almost everything else that you can mention, continued.

Large industrial combines such as we see today were formed. Youths left the farms to take jobs with more attractive wages in industry. Problems were caused by the overproduction of agricultural products in World War I. Factories were turning out goods faster than the people were able to purchase them.

Relief rolls expanded as a result of the increase in unemployment. With every closing of factories there was a corresponding slowdown in business and another increase in unemployment. Following every reduction in the number of hours worked, businesses failed, providing even further reduc-tion in employment. People became hungry since they were unable to find work. In the cities people searched refuse piles at public markets to find food. Farmers burned their grains which they could not sell, because it was a cheaper fuel than coal. Wages averaged $18.00 per week for men and $9.00 for women.

PREPARATION FOR THE TASK

Franklin D. Roosevelt, after winning the Democratic primary in 1932 from John Nance Garner and Alfred E. Smith, carried the November election with 472 electoral votes over President Hoover, who had received 59.

Congress, finally realizing the seriousness of the situation, supported President Roosevelt in his requests for far-reaching changes, and a bank holiday was proclaimed which, on March 6, 1933, closed all the banks in the United States. During his first hundred days in office, the President, and many banks as well, sent repeated requests to Congress to support his proposals for alleviating the situation. In the spring of 1933 Congress acted quickly, passing the Agricultural Act (which provided the farmers with subsidies) and the Farm Credit Act (which, through the Farm Credit Administration, aided farmers with their mortgage payments). The National Recovery Act (N.R.A.) was established to aid industrial recovery. Industries which cooperated with the Act were allowed to fly the Blue E flag. The Public Work Administration (PWA) advanced funds to provide jobs for the unemployed. The Works Progress Administration (WPA) provided funds locally to give employment to those out of work. Though some "leaf-raking" jobs occurred, it was through no fault of the unemployed.

THESE INEXPENSIVE MAN PACK PUMPS AFFORD REAL PROTECTION

STEEL FIRE TOWER
TOWNSHEND STATE
FOREST

FIRES LIKE THIS ONE

LEAVE RESULTS LIKE THIS

FIRE LOOKOUT TOWER, ALLIS FOREST

TWO MEN CAN CARRY IT

THIS PORTABLE GASOLINE PUMP THROWS 150 GALLONS OF WATER PER MINUTE FOR 1½ MILES

Forest Fire Protection, Vermont.

To provide faith in the banking system, the Federal Deposit Corporation insured individual banks against losses. In recent years, depositors have had their savings insured up to $100,000.00.

A Conservation-Minded President

As Governor of the great state of New York, Franklin Delano Roosevelt had pushed a grandiose plan for reforestation of idle lands in the state. His success in this and many other endeavors brought his name into the national limelight. Previous to his election as President, he invited a group of foresters to his Hyde Park home where he very proudly showed his own forest plantation.

An Act for the Relief of Unemployment

In March of 1933, the President sent to Congress a message on unemployment relief in which he proposed to put persons from cities and elsewhere to work in our forests. Within eight days Congress had passed the Emergency Conservation Work Act (ECW). That was the beginning of the Civilian Conservation Corps (CCC). (See Appendix).

Little delay occurred before the President on April 5, 1933, issued an executive order which gave effect to the law.

All state foresters as well as officers of the United States Forest Service and the National Park Service were called to Washington for instructions on April 6, 1933. This meeting was presided over by Vice-President Henry Wallace and Rexford Tugwell. A large group was present and listened to many speeches. We raised the question as to how the camps were to be administered, what kind of work would be done and permitted, how the financing was to be handled, etc., but no definite information was forthcoming.

A committee of three (including Austin Hawes, the state forester of Connecticut) was appointed to meet with Major R.Y. Stuart, Chief of the United States Forest Service. At the meeting the next morning we discovered that the Chief was as much in the dark as we were in regard to details of the plan. Apparently, the President had not appointed anyone to work out the details of this great undertaking. It appeared later in his administration that this was one of Roosevelt's faults.

It had been suggested that the enrollees be conditioned at army camps and then assigned to work camps operated by foresters. Our committee recommended, among other things, that the work camps should be administered by the U.S. Army to relieve the state foresters of innumerable details and allow them to concentrate on the work projects. This recommendation was adopted, and the President finally decided to follow this course. Whether our recommendation had anything to do with his decision, I do not know. Although some of the Army officers were not efficient and sometimes required more men for camp details than seemed to be necessary, the arrangement as a whole worked well.

Park Buildings, Vermont.

Robert Fechner Appointed Executive Director

The Honorable Robert Fechner of Quincy, Massachusetts, was appointed by the President as Director of the Emergency Conservation Work (ECW). His salary was set at $12,000 per year.

It was quite fortunate that Robert Fechner was selected as director. He had been a successful labor leader and had two objects in his mind in regard to the youths under his charge. These aims were to give employment to the youths and assistance to their families. His practical experience and knowledge of how to deal with people, and his ability to beat down proposals which varied from sections of the law as established by Congress led to a very successful administration.

Since Vermont was close to his home, he was able to make a number of trips to Vermont during which I drove him to the camps and communities where he spoke. His interest and sincerity are expressed in letters which he sent me, excerpts from which appear below.

Letter of December 9, 1933 - "This is the first opportunity that I have had to write to you to express my personal appreciation for the many courtesies extended to me by you on the occasion of my first visit to Vermont.

"I had looked forward to this visit for some months and I am glad to say that a realization of my hopes carried with it a greater satisfaction over what was being accomplished by our camps than I had really expected.

"Under the fine cooperation and supervision by yourself and all others connected with this work, I am convinced that the entire program in Vermont is fully justifying itself.

"I hope that I may have the opportunity to again visit with you before this work is completed."

Letter of March 15, 1934 - "I want to say that I fully approve of splendid cooperation that you have given in our CCC work, and I think that Vermont benefitted as largely in proportion as any other State from the program. I only wish that it were possible to have given every state all of the camps that they asked for."

Robert Fechner died on New Year's Eve, 1939. He was succeeded by James J. McEntee, his deputy, who did a remarkable job as director. Mr. Charles H. Tayor succeeded to the assistant director position.

Advisory Council

The law established an Advisory Council composed of the Secretary of Labor, the Secretary of War, the Secretary of the Interior, and the Secretary of Agriculture, each of whom was authorized to appoint a representative to work with the Director of ECW. The original representatives on the Advisory Council were:

W. Frank Persons, Director, U.S. Employment Service (Labor)
Col. Duncan Major, Jr. (War)
Arno B. Cammerer, Director of National Park Service (Interior)
Major R.Y. Stuart, Chief Forester, U.S. Forest Service (Agriculture)

Following Major Stuart's untimely death, Mr. F.A. Silcox, Chief Forester, became the representative. In fact, several personnel changes occurred, as indicated below.

Department of Labor	1933	W. Frank Persons, U.S. Employment Service
	1939	C.W. Bailey, Veteran's Administration
Department of War	1933	Major Duncan K. Major, Jr.
	1934	George B. Tyner, Brigadier General
	1941	J.A. Ulio, Brigadier General
Department of Agriculture	1933	F.A. Silcox, Chief Forester, U.S. Forest Service
	1934	Major R.Y. Stuart, Chief Forester
	1935	F.A. Silcox, Chief Forester
	1939	Fred Morrill, U.S. Forest Service
Department of Interior	1933	Horace Albright, Director, National Park Service
	1934	Horace Albright, Director, National Park Service
	1935	Arno B. Cammerer, Director
	1939	Conrad Wirth, Director

The Advisory Council was, as its name implies, purely advisory in nature, but it established a medium where the numerous views about the operations of the ECW could be resolved. Under the law, Director Robert Fechner had full authority, subject only to Presidential veto. The Director in his wise judgment, listened to the advice of the Council.

It was quite natural that there should be differences of opinion between the administrators of Federal departments. Major Stuart, who had many years' experience in handling men and directing the successful technical management of America's forests, was listened to by the other members of the Council.

Appropriations

The Executive Order of 1933, established in the Treasury a fund of ten million dollars by the transfer of an equal amount from unobligated balances of the appropriation for the emergency construction of public buildings contained in the Act approved on July 21, 1932...."which fund shall be subject to requisition by the said Robert Fechner as Director of ECW on the approval of the President." The director was also authorized to make requisitions of supplies from several government departments for which they were to be repaid.

Cooperating Federal Departments

No new agencies of government were established under the Acts to execute the President's program. The duties of the *Department of Labor* were to administer the enrollment of the youths into the ECW. Enrollees were selected locally by the county or local organization (such as the overseer of the poor in New England towns and cities) and then referred through the State Selection agent to the War Department.

The *War Department* was charged with accepting the enrollees at the induction centers where they were given the necessary medical examinations. Those who were rejected received their fare back home. Enrollees were organized into companies, clothed, equipped, and conditioned for work in the field. They were then dispatched to their work camp. Later, many were sent directly to camps where the Army cared for their needs as stated above. The War Department was also charged with the construction of camps and their operation and maintenance, including the housing, feeding, clothing, and welfare of the enrollees. Some camps had Army work projects.

The Departments of Agriculture and Interior, through their several divisions, had charge of the direction of work projects in the field as well as the coordination of the programs on state and private lands. These Federal departments were divided into divisions, as follows:

Interior Department: National Parks and Monuments; General Land Office; Office of Education, Territories, and the Bureaus of Indian Affairs and Reclamation; and the Division of Grazing.

Agricultural Department: U.S. Forest Service; Soil Conservation Service; and the Bureaus of Biological Survey, Plant Industry, Animal Industry, Entomology, Agricultural Engineering, and Chemistry and Soils.

The *U.S. Forest Service*, in addition to performing work on National Forests, coordinated and checked the work on state and private lands under the state departments and performed work for the Tennessee Valley Authority, Alaska, Puerto Rico, and the Bureau of Plant Industry. The *National Park Service*, in addition to executing work on National Parks and Monuments, supervised the work for Hawaii and the state parks.

The *U.S. Veteran's Administration* selected veterans for the program. The Department of the Treasury through the Bureau of Public Health, looked after the enrollees' health.

No new organizations were established within the states. Work there was executed by the respective forest and park departments, while Federal projects were confined to programs on public lands or on private lands for such projects as erosion control.

Reserve Officers

On January 4, 1935, the President sought funds to put 350,000 people to work. As of June 30, 1935, the Civilian Conservation Corps was expanded to 600,000 enrollees, to be housed in 2,916 camps. To accomplish this the army requisitioned the selecting agencies for 328,000 men to be certified to it during the period July 15-August 31, 1935.

To meet the need of officers with the increased enrollment, an early graduation was ordered at the military academies. Officers were taken also from the Marine Corps and Navy. Later orders were given to fill the positions as far as possible with reserve officers and warrant officers. At the end of 1935, there were 5,900 reserve officers and 70 warrant officers in the CCC program.

Approved Work Projects

The types of work carried on varied from state to state, and from park to forest. A glance at the list of approved work projects gives one a quick insight into the numerous tasks which could be undertaken. All tasks needed some kind of previous legislative approval.

There were up to 300 differing types of work projects so that every enrollee had an opportunity to learn at least one new skill. Work project types approved by the director fell into ten general classifications, as follows:

1. Structural Improvement - including bridges, fire towers, service buildings;
2. Transportation - including truck trails, minor roads, foot trails and airport landing fields;
3. Erosion Control - check dams, terracing and vegetative covering;
4. Flood Control - irrigation and drainage, dams, ditching, channel work, riprapping;
5. Forest Culture - planting trees and shrubs, stand improvement, seed collection, and nursery work;
6. Forest Protection - fire fighting, fire prevention, and fire presuppression, insect and disease control;
7. Landscape and Recreation - public camp and picnic ground development, lake and pond site clearing;
8. Range - stock driveways, elimination of predatory animals;
9. Wildlife - stream improvement, stocking fish, food and cover planting; and
10. Miscellaneous - emergency work, surveys, mosquito control.

CARETAKER'S CABIN—AITKEN STATE FOREST

TENT PLATFORM—MT. PHILO   PICNIC LOGGIA—NORTHAM

COMBINATION CARETAKER BUILDING AND LOGGIA—GIFFORD WOODS

Park Buildings, Vermont.

FEDERAL DEPARTMENT FUNCTIONS
Department of Labor

The Department of Labor was now given a new task which was to enroll the youths in this new project. Instead of creating a new agency to do this, the Department of Labor operated through the local or county relief organizations which did the selecting of the youths in accordance with the conditions established by Federal law. Secretary of the Interior, Harold Ickes, appointed W. Frank Persons to serve on the Advisory Council; every department of government worked with great speed and red tape was forgotten.

Representatives of 17 of America's largest cities were invited to a meeting in Washington held on Wednesday evening, April 5, 1933. At this meeting the group was informed about the procedure in enlisting 250,000 youths. State foresters and state park directors, together with similar officials of the Federal government, were called into Washington where we met with Henry Wallace and Rex Tugwell, who explained the President's program. The Vermont State Forester attended this meeting and others later on in Washington.

Enrollment of Youth

Originally, the number of young men between the ages of 18 and 25 to be enrolled was established at 250,000. They must be physically fit, unemployed and unmarried, have dependents, and be willing to make allotments home to their families. In 1935, the age limits were reduced to 17 and increased to 28 years. The first enrollment was filled by July 1 with 55% of the enrollees coming from rural areas.

As of April 1, 1939, the enrollment had increased to 507,782. Due to the training experience they had received, about 12,000 enrollees had left the camps to accept employment elsewhere. Through the 1936-1937 period 644,692 had enrolled, and at the end of six years, the number with experience in the CCC camps had reached 2,500,000.

About 45% of the inductees had never been employed, and those who had graduated from high school numbered only 13%. By July 31, 1941, many young men were joining the army, so 266 camps were closed and more enrollees left camps to accept employment in Army installations.

The enrollee received $30.00 per month, $25.00 of which was sent back to his family. When single men with no dependents were enrolled, the $25.00 monthly pay was held in escrow by the Army Finance Officer who paid the enrollee the collected sum at the time of his retirement. Enrollees who showed an aptitude were advanced to leaders and assistant leaders at a higher rate of pay, which was $36.00 for assistant leaders and $45.00 for leaders. Qualified leaders had a further opportunity for advancement, with increased pay, to nonenrolled supervisory and technical positions.

Enrollees were also furnished with suitable clothing to fit the location, type of work, and time of year. This issue included heavy woolen clothes, work jackets, heavy shoes and overshoes, gloves, and mittens for winter. A comfortable bed with sufficient warm bedding, including a mattress, woolen blankets, sheets, and pillow case, was provided.

State Selection Agencies

The Department of Labor chose a state selection agent for each state to certify the selected enrollees to the Department of War. During the first six months the writer also served as the selection agent for Vermont. As a rule, the names of agents in all the states changed after the first six-month period. The State Selection Agencies as of June 30, 1933 were as shown in Appendix E, page 202.

Local Enlisted Men (LEM)

Since thousands of young men would be turned loose in the woods having never used an axe or other tool, it was decided that some local experienced men should be recruited to teach the enrollees and assist the technical staff. Until 1935, the selection of these local experienced men was handled under the direction of the Department of Labor, and thereafter the representatives of the states were granted that authority. The technical foremen knew where to locate these LEMs locally, and this change operated very successfully.

Enrollment of Indians

There had been a great deficit in rainfall in the midwest for a number of years previous to 1933. (See Shelterbelt.) A large proportion of the Indian lands had been lost by erosion so they had not enough land for food production. Much work needed to be done to make these Indian lands productive again.

The President directed on April 14, 1933, that 14,000 Indians be inducted into the CCC. Many rules and regulations had to be modified or dropped in order to fit into the Indian's situation. Many of the Indians were married, and they were needed at home to care for their families and raise their food. Previously, there had not been any opportunity to allow much work on Indian lands, but now the need was there.

The tribal councils had charge of the selection of the Indians for the CCC. The work was carried out on parts of 50 million acres in 23 states. The types of work accomplished were the same as those in the junior camps. The Indians lived at home, and in some cases worked on their own lands.

Veterans

Many veterans of World War I (to be known as the "Bonus Army") marched on the Capitol in Washington in 1932 seeking pay for their bonus for wartime service. This group of our population (then around 40 years

PARKWAY CONSTRUCTION UP BURKE MT. ON DARLING FOREST PARK

PARKWAY, MONTPELIER CITY FOREST

ROUGH GOING ON TRUCK TRAIL, PROCTOR-PIPER STATE FOREST

WELL MADE BRIDGES LOWER MAINTENANCE

PARKWAY, BEFORE AND AFTER, PROCTOR-PIPER STATE FOREST

BEAUTIFUL PARKWAY, ELMORE STATE FOREST PARK

Road Building, Vermont.

old) was hard hit by the depression. Another march was held in 1933 with high hopes that President Roosevelt would aid their cause. The Veterans' Administration contacted the President, as a result of which, he initiated an executive order on May 11, 1933, which directed that 25,000 veterans be enrolled in the CCC. Enrollment began at once and increased to 32,924 in 1935 and 36,741 in 1937. The primary function of the Veterans' Administration was to determine the eligibility for membership in the veterans' contingent and to certify such selectees to the War Department for physical examinations and enrollment.

Work Schedules

The work schedule in the camps was as follows:

6:00 AM - Rise
8:00   - Turned over to the technical work agency, where each enrollee was assigned to a group of six to 12 under an LEM as an instructor.
1:00 PM - Lunch brought to them.
4:00   - Returned to camp.
5:00   - Supper from 5:00 to 5:30. Following supper, the enrollee had the choice of athletics, attending classes by the Educational Adviser, or reading in the library.
10:30   - Lights out.

Each enrollee was required to spend a part of his time at camp cleaning up the barracks, policing the grounds, aiding the cook, and assisting in the maintenance of equipment and structures. Others were selected as clerks both for the Army and for the technical service.

War Department Functions
Corps Area Operations

As stated elsewhere, part of the success of the War Department was due to decentralization of the project into nine Corps areas, each of which was given authority to fulfill the mission assigned to it.

The youths who had been certified by the Department of Labor to the War Department were sent to the nearest Army Recruiting Station for acceptance. Here they were given a physical examination, and those rejected were provided with their transportation home. Veterans certified by the Veterans' Administration received the same treatment. Those who were accepted were sent to the nearest Army post, which could have been the same station where they had just been accepted. Here they were enrolled, organized into companies, clothed, equipped, and conditioned for work in the field. The enrollees were then sent to work camps either as companies or as smaller groups.

The plan of the War Department for assignment of personnel, assembly of supplies and equipment, and the establishment of a maintenance system was intended to conform to the rate at which the Department of Labor certified applicants for enrollment. Beginning on May 12, 1933, an average of about 8,500 men had to be enrolled daily in order to meet the request of Director Fechner to have the entire Corps established in camps by July 1, 1933.

Such a goal required speedy selection and preparation of all forest camps for reception of units. Emergency methods were required. This plan called for the prompt approval by the director of about 300 work projects, immediate transfer of necessary funds to the War Department, removal of certain restrictions applying to the purchase of supplies, and issue of appropriate instructions to the Department of Labor concerning the selection of applicants.

Regular Army activities were temporarily relegated to second place so that priority could be given to the execution of this emergency task.

Mobilization Accomplishments - Enrollees. On May 16, enrollment jumped to a total of 64,450 men; the next day added 8,100 men, and the next, 10,100. On June 1, a peak daily enrollment of 13,843 was reached. By June 29, 270,000 men occupied 1,330 work camps.

The task also included the transportation of 55,000 enrollees in 335 companies from eastern Corps areas to the far western states. The CCC gave employment to many others besides the enrollees. Before the expansion there were 5,900 reserve officers, 70 warrant officers, 410 contract surgeons, 160 nurses, 1,468 teachers (Educational Advisers), 18,000 technical advisers, and about 3,000 artisans hired on a day-to-day basis.

The War Department was confronted with the task of administrating and providing for the needs of a suddenly created army of 300,000 men. Immediate needs included food, clothing, shelter, transportation, education, and religious services. This was a larger undertaking than the Army had encountered in the Spanish-American War.

Work Camps. Every state in the Union (including Puerto Rico and the Virgin Islands) had one or more camps. The number of camps in a state depended upon many factors, including the number of enrollees from that state and the number of projects which a state had readily available. Since there were not enough projects in the east to take care of all the eastern men, many eastern youths were sent west.

On April 10, 1933, the first quota of 25,000 was called up, and on April 17, the first camp, Camp Roosevelt, was occupied on the George Washington National Forest near Luray, Virginia.

The total number of camps varied during the eight-year period; as an example, there were 2,069 camps - of which 1,493 were under the technical direction of the Department of Agriculture, 506 under the Department of

Interior, and 70 under the War Department. About 77 camps were located on Indian Reservations. The average yearly enrollment (which included enrollees and other personnel) in 1937 was 374,000.

It is evident that there was considerable government waste in building camps which were never used, such as the one at Ripton, Vermont, and those which were used only a very short time. The experience stories by enrollees included in this publication, show that some companies were moved up to a half-dozen times within a state and/or to other states as well. Camps in Connecticut and some other states were operated a short time and closed before the work projects were completed.

Each company was assigned a number by the War Department. The operating agency usually had a name for a camp as well as a letter to designate the type of land ownership. Thus, P indicated private land, S stood for state forest land, SP for state park land, F for national forests, DG for Division of Grazing, and SCS for Soil Conservation Service.

The number of buildings within a camp varied from one state to another. The size of the main buildings was usually about 100' x 24' and included four 50-man barracks, a mess hall, a recreation building, quarters for Army and technical personnel, an infirmary, educational and library buildings, small garage, tool shed, and machine shop.

When a company arrived at a site which had been established by a cadre of 25 enrollees, tents were used as quarters until wooden buildings were built. On some occasions in the north, barracks were not constructed until snow had arrived with accompanying 30-degree-below temperature. By 1935, prefabricated buildings were shipped into the northeast.

Side Camps. The state foresters soon made a request for the use of side (or spike) camps in locations where there was too much travel time to and from the main camp. Such side camps had the approval of both the Chief Forester and the Director of the National Park Service, and they were finally authorized over the objection of the Army. These camps were run very successfully by the technical personnel without army personnel at the camp.

The original 1933 Act extended the period of the camps for two years. By succeeding acts the camp periods were again extended, and in August of 1939, the period was extended until July 1, 1943. However, much of the CCC work was closed out in 1941 when the camps were carrying on projects useful to the war effort.

Under the 1937 Act, the title of the project was changed from Emergency Conservation Work to the Civilian Conservation Corps. The 1939 Act placed the CCC under the Federal Security Agency.

Army Quartermaster

The general supervision of procurement devolved upon the office of the

ORIGINAL TENTED CAMP
S54: BELLOWS FALLS

CAMP SP3: ELMORE STATE FOREST PARK

MT. MANSFIELD CAMP S60: UNDERHILL

DOWNER STATE FOREST CAMP S56: SHARON

CAMP SP4: SANDBAR STATE FOREST PARK: MILTON

WINTER CAMP S61: NO. SHREWSBURY

CAMP SP5: PROCTOR-PIPER STATE FOREST

CAMP S55: WILLOUGHBY STATE FOREST

CCC Camps, Vermont.

Assistant Secretary of War. The Quartermaster Corps with its widely-dispersed local purchasing agencies and its depot organizations, strategically located in producing centers afforded the flexibility needed. The procurement of perishable items of subsistence, and such items as coal, gasoline and oil, were decentralized to local purchasing agencies, and in many cases, down to a single camp who would be actually consuming the supplies. These local purchases spread expenditures throughout the entire country, making a contribution to many small local businesses. Many supplies and pieces of equipment had to be ordered through the central office.

The purchase of a balanced ration of food sufficient to feed the members of the CCC camps to June 30, 1936, was estimated at approximately $96,300,000. Clothing and equipage added another $120,800,000.

Adjutant General

The CCC enrollees' records of location and other pertinent information were kept in the office of the Adjutant General. All communications to and from the field were handled through this office. The Adjutant General was also charged with the initiation and supervision of the welfare and educational programs. The Office of Education in the Interior Department served in an advisory capacity to the Army concerning educational matters. (See Educational Adviser)

Army Medical Department - Surgeon General

The medical corps was suddenly faced with the problem of providing health care for four individuals where it had formerly provided for one. It had also become responsible for eight humans where it had looked after only one.

All selectees were examined under Army Medical Corps supervision. Accepted LEM's were given protective vaccination against smallpox and typhoid fever. Enrollees were instructed in personal hygiene and given periodical physical checkups. Emergency dental treatment was provided. A medical officer was stationed in nearly every CCC camp.

Some remote camps were 50 or more miles from camp or hospital, so 400 ambulances were provided. Rigorous inspections of food, water and vigilance against epidemics assisted in keeping a healthy CCC corps.

Chief of Finance

The task of acting as fiscal agent for nearly all branches of the ECW was delegated to the Chief of Finance of the Army. The major disbursement problem was in connection with the allotment to the enrollees' families. Nearly 7,760,000 allotment checks were prepared and forwarded by the Chief's office, in addition to the thousands of other accounting and disbursing transactions. The coast-to-coast army pay-net assisted greatly.

Chief of Chaplains

Spiritual needs of the enrollees were not neglected, and religious services were provided regularly to all enrollees. Every attempt was made to get enrollees to attend the religious services of their preference. In addition to taking enrollees to nearby churches, clerics of the several denominations were brought to camps to conduct services. Spiritual ministrations of the chaplain, priest, and rabbi did not stop with the collective religious service; the chaplains talked over with the young men their deeply personal and disturbing problems and did, in a large number of cases, aid them to adjust themselves better in the world in which they live.

Educational Advisers

One of the most significant features of the CCC was its educational program. Director Fechner, as he traveled from camp to camp during the first six-month period, found that camp commanders and camp superintendents in many camps had organized a wide variety of educational programs. What he saw so impressed him that he brought the matter to the attention of the President, who was quite enthusiastic over the idea of educational programs.

In addition, the National Association of State Foresters at their annual meeting in Indiana in 1933, had passed a resolution urging that planned educational instruction be given in the CCC camps.

When the educational program was first proposed, the Office of Education (which is in the Interior Department), wished to have full charge of education. The War Department maintained that they should have full charge of everything that occurred within the camps. Though the placing of the responsibility of the educational program under the direction of the Army met strong opposition, it was finally agreed to. Responsibility was then placed in the hands of the Corps area commanders assisted by a corps area adviser selected by the Office of Education.

The Office of Education selected and appointed the educational advisers for all camps. Over 60% of the enrollees took part in the courses presented. In addition, several thousand attended night school in adjoining communities. At the end of the school term in June, a large number were granted eighth grade and high school certificates or diplomas.

The educational program also included on-the-job training by the technical staff in the field and the handling and care of food by the camp chefs. Many youth on leaving camp obtained employment in hotels and restaurants. The educational program was held outside of the work hours, and both the Army and technical service personnel aided the educational adviser.

This education in the field and in the camp aided many enrollees to be advanced to leaders, assistant leaders, and foremen.

Educational facilities at the camps varied from camp to camp, but usually included books, projectors, and moving pictures with classrooms equipped with desks, blackboards and other educational material.

Educational Advisor
Objectives of the program as established by the Office of Education were:

1. To develop in each man his powers of self-expression, self-entertainment and self-culture;
2. To develop, as far as practicable, an understanding of the prevailing social and economic condition, to the end that each man may cooperate intelligently in improving these conditions;
3. To develop pride and satisfaction in cooperative endeavor;
4. To preserve and strengthen good habits of health and mental development;
5. By such vocational training as is feasible, but particularly by vocational counseling and adjustment activities, to assist each man better to meet employment problems when he leaves camp;
6. To develop an appreciation of nature and of country life.

District Educational Advisers
In the beginning, advisers built their own programs. Educational advisers in the state of Louisiana made the following reports. From Company #255: "Typing is the most popular course. Classes in cooking and baking taught by a former army cook from a nearby veteran's camp, improved the company morale". Enrollees at Montgomery, near Louisiana State University, received the services of the college faculty and staff. College instructors gave night classes in English and mathematics, as a result of which enrollees received college credit for a complete course in Freshman English. Another camp near Polluck, instituted a course in motor mechanics and also (since this camp was near the Stuart Tree Nursery) forestry, surveying and electricity.

The greatest problem in the negro camps was the elimination of illiteracy. At Acadia Camp #7, night classes were taught by four persons from Acadia High School. (Louisiana History, Vol. 1)

Gino A. Carmolli of Barre, Vermont writes: "My first assignment as an Educational Adviser to Company #1217 at Ricker's Mills, Vermont was on April 28, 1934. That was the beginning of a totally new experience in education for me, as well as for many thousands of boys between the ages of 17 and 28 who came from families on relief rolls during the period of severe economic depression in the early 1930's.

"You may be sure that I approached this assignment with a great deal of trepidation since there were no guidelines to follow. The Camp Educational Adviser, while basically responsible to the Camp Commander, was in complete charge of the educational program of the camp and also responsible for the general supervision of all educational and recreational activities of the camp.

"The Educational Adviser had to develop an educational program suited to the educational needs and interests of the boys; secure supplemental educational facilities from nearby schools and colleges available to the camp; supervise the work of his assistant; recommend to the Camp Commander opportunities for coordinating the educational programs with the work and recreational programs of the enrollees; and advise and counsel the enrollees on their educational program as well as their future vocational adjustment.

"A separate building similar to the barracks where the boys lived, was designated as the Educational Building. Here in the evening the boys attended sessions ranging from very simple reading and writing—including most traditional school subjects—to typing, mimeographing for the camp newspaper, photography, woodworking, auto mechanics, forestry, leathercraft, metalworking, safety, cooking, canteen management and a host of other subjects.

"Most enrollees did not remain in the camp for much more than a year, so courses were short and reorganized for each new group of enrollees. Instructors were recruited from the forestry staff as well as the staff of the company commander, and at times, outstanding enrollees were used as instructors.

"Much instruction was also given "on the job", depending upon the work being done by the particular camp. In some instances, the work was predominantly conservation, general forestry, road building, construction of recreational buildings in state parks, or development of camp sites, beaches and picnic sites.

"Personnel from nearby schools were recruited either for lectures or class instruction, and educational film programs were frequently used.

"The responsibilities as outlined above appear not to present many problems; however, it soon became apparent that very little money was available to the adviser for use in the program. Thus considerable ingenuity and resourcefulness was needed by the adviser. Needless to say, the adviser looked to and received a great deal of help from the forestry personnel and the camp administration.

"Each enrollee had to be interviewed in depth to find out what his interests and capabilities were, and a program of instruction was developed around these interests, which were many and varied. Each program lasted as long as the enrollee showed interest. Then new interests were developed.

"All of these activities had to be tied together by the camp Educational Adviser, and coordinated so that a learning process resulted. Without doubt, most of the tangible, worthwhile and lasting learning resulted from "on-the-job" training. Added to these activities were all types of sports and recreational activities which kept the boys occupied so that time would not hang heavy and lead to discontentment.

"What made for continuing interest was the fact that regular enrollment periods brought new boys to the camp, and the process of interviewing and setting up of new programs adapted to new interests started all over again.

"This was a period of my life that I am sure provided much more personal satisfaction to me than an equal period spent in the traditional school system as a teacher. It was not an easy period—but it was novel, interesting and fulfilling, and I feel that we were able to be helpful to many less fortunate than ourselves during a period in our lives of severe economic depression."

Detail: Log Cabin Construction.

Dean B. Fraser on July 15, 1933, reported for duty in Montpelier and was assigned to Co. 1112 then encamped on a hill above Montpelier, Vermont.

"The enrollees were engaged in the construction of a flood control dam down on the Winooski. Later we were moved to a camp at Wrightsville on the North Branch. Here the Army was responsible for both the construction projects and the supervision of the enrollees. Our part was to furnish food, clothes, shelter and pay the men. You had responsibility but little authority over the men. You could discharge a man if he was a trouble maker or refused to work, but discipline was enforced by moral persuasion. That was the most valuable lesson I learned from the experience.

"The 1112th company was made up of WWI veterans. Some came from Veterans' Hospitals; some were skilled craftsmen. We even had a professional strong man. My striker was an ex-tobacco farmer. All had been unemployed and near a state of desperation. I, myself, was on a furlough from my company which is why I accepted the appointment. In general, they were a good bunch of men. Some of them I remember to this day. I never had any insolence or disrespect from any of them and many acts of kindness.

"Snow hit us about the 12th of October. When I awakened in the morning, the roof of my tent was sagged in and my car, parked under a fly at the rear of the tent was completely drifted over. From then on until we got into barracks, the living conditions were pretty rugged. Until that time the men, who were quartered in the army hospital tent, had two Sibley stoves in each tent. So far as heat was concerned, they were practically useless. Tar clogged the park arrestors and there was more smoke than heat. Bathing facilities had been provided for the camp by showers rigged in a shack on the camp site. Of course there was no hot water. When icicles began to form on the shower heads, those of us who decided that we needed a bath, used showers kindly offered by the YMCA downtown.

"Quarters were ready for the men in Wrightsville sometime before Thanksgiving, but the officers' quarters were not ready until shortly before Christmas. I had a wood floor in my tent and a Sibley stove, but temperatures were as low as minus 30 degrees while I slept in that tent. I slept in pajamas, wool socks, a sweater pulled over my head, and seven warm blankets over me and two folded under me. A trip to the latrine on those mornings, which was protected by only a canvas windbreak, was something to be long remembered. Once in the barracks, things were fairly comfortable. Food was reasonably good and barracks were well heated. As mess officer for part of the time, I planned the menus, bought the food supplies, and kept the mess accounts. I think the daily allowance per man per day was 54 cents. Officers messed with the men and paid for it."

Timothy Cleary of Southern Pines, North Carolina served as a reserve officer for the flood control camps in the Winooski Valley. "When F.D.R. took office, the bonus marchers were in northern Virginia and were sent to Vermont to build the dams. The War Department expected the bonus marchers to give continued troubles. Though many of them were alcoholic, they possessed more skills and actual field experience than the soldiers (NCO's and junior officers) assigned to their camps.

"Congressmen had been unable to get companies assigned to them so finally the veterans were moved and replaced by juniors. Quality of life in the Winooski camps suffered. With the veterans there had been experienced plumbers, carpenters, chefs, any job that you can name, putting their civilian skills to work.

"In late 1937, I commanded a junior company. They appreciated very much anything that was done for them, like a truck on Sunday to carry them to the base of Camel's Hump Mountain and a guide to direct their way. There was a large chapel in the Waterbury Camp. Father James H. Doyle who had been a Walter Camp All-American playing on Cavanagh's teams at B.C., was the Catholic Chaplin. He said several masses every Sunday morning.

"Every camp had its canteen or post exchange and the large camp of eight or ten companies would have an outdoor beer parlor in summer. Bottled beer was delivered from a brewery near Troy, New York. The officer of the day made rounds every evening. The beer parlor area on Saturday night after pay day was a lively place. Beer was not sold in the junior camp canteens, and in the Winooski Valley camps, juniors were not allowed in beer parlors.

"An old farm house had been converted into the district school and the educational advisors (one to each company) were all together on one faculty. A program was offered each evening similar to a typical community college of the 1970's. Besides cultural, foreign language and other courses, there were vocational courses. The experimental farm was under the supervision of the educational advisors and the district veterinarian. In addition to the veterinary's duties, he assisted in the raising of hogs, sheep and other livestock on the farm. In addition to all these activities, there was a large movie theater and a hospital with dental chairs.

"In the spring of 1936, there were flood conditions which could have been as disastrous as the 1927 flood if it had not been for the flood control dams built by the Bonus Army in the Winooski Valley."

Army Engineers
CCC, A Great Help in the 1927 Vermont Flood Disaster

October, 1927, in Vermont was a very wet month with the rainfall 50 percent above normal. The ground was so saturated when the rain started on November 2, that it ran off into the streams as fast as it fell. Through November 4, almost nine inches of rain fell, filling the Winooski Valley deep with flood waters. In some of Montpelier's low lying areas, the flood waters reached a height of 12 feet.

The cause of the flood was the meeting of a storm coming up the Atlantic coast with another from over the Great Lakes. The storms met over Vermont. The storm was held over Vermont for three days due to a high pressure area extending northeast from the state of Maine.

The damage amounted to over eight million dollars, with the loss of 1,200 highway bridges, road washouts, and buildings washed away carrying people to their death. Hundreds of homes and businesses received heavy damage from dirty flood waters which in many places reached to the first floor ceiling. The loss of life in the Winooski Valley alone was 55.

Soon after the flood, Vermont Governor Stanley C. Wilson, interested the U.S. Army Engineers in making a study and plans for flood control under the Rivers and Harbors Act. They made a report which stated that dams should be built at East Barre, at Wrightsville above Montpelier, and on the Little River, a branch of the Winooski a couple of miles above Waterbury, as well as a movable dam in Montpelier, known as the clothespin dam.

In 1933, when there was trouble in Washington with the Veterans of WWI marching on the Capitol to get their war bonus, Governor Wilson contacted President Franklin D. Roosevelt and informed him that Vermont had a place and plans ready where the Bonus Army could be immediately employed.

Action was very rapid. By June 7, 1933, the First Corps Area with headquarters in Boston quickly enrolled 10,000 youths and had them in forest camps throughout New England. A new District, the Sixth, was created by General Fox Conner with Montpelier as its headquarters. Col. Clement A. Trott was placed in command of the Sixth District. The pioneer camp of the district was Camp Wilson, being the 1351 colored unit, composed in the main of the original Bonus Army marchers. They detrained in Barre City on July 2, 1933, while the native Vermonters looked on with awe. By the 11th, companies numbered 1105, 1106, 1107, 1108, and 1111 and two days later company 1352 from Maryland and 349 (colored) came up from the 3rd Corps Area, Virginia. The last two outfits, which completed the tent city at Camp Wilson, were the 2214 and 2215 second corps companies arrived in the city. These ten companies started work at once on the construction of the East Barre Dam.

The East Barre Dam. The Camp was established and the men went to work clearing trees and brush from the dam site. Four companies of 200 each were engaged in the construction of a 600 foot trench in a location where a concrete tunnel under the dam was to be built. Six hundred wheelbarrows with picks, shovels, sledges and drills were the hand tools used to construct the dam. The dam required 172,000 cubic yards of earth and 4,500 yards of rock fill. The granite for the dam facing was taken from the waste piles at the granite quarries.

The completed dam measured 1,500 feet long with a spillway 100 feet wide. The maximum width at the base was 400 feet with sides sloping up to an 85 foot crest. This was located 60 feet above the old grade of the stream. The completed dam required 308,000 cu. yds. of earth, 84,000 cu. yds. of rock fill, 200 cu. yds. of concrete, and 1,300 tons of steel.

The Wrightsville Dam. At Wrightsville, an entire settlement of houses had to be moved since they were nearly in the center of the fill. A small stream flowing into the North Branch had to be diverted. A cemetery had to be relocated. Old roads were relocated and new roads were built. The first ground was broken by the 2201 Company in the latter part of July, 1933.

Hand labor was used almost entirely until machinery arrived in September, 1933. On October 24, 1933, a heavy snowstorm of unprecedented severity brought down tents and caused general delay and discomfort.

On a plateau overlooking the North Branch a short distance above Montpelier, Camp Weeks was established with four companies. Camp Cushing with six companies comprised of New York Veterans arrived shortly. The expansion continued with the establishment of Camp Greene with five more companies.

The dam, which is used as a highway, extended across the valley a distance of 1,500 feet, of which 100 feet is the width of the spillway. The width of the dam crest is 160 feet, which is 90 feet above the old river bed. The maximum width of the dam's base is 750 feet and the spillway is ten feet deep. Over 1,115,000 cu. yds. of earth fill and rock, over 5,000 cu. yds. of concrete, and 1,200 tons of steel were used.

The Waterbury Dam. In order to cooperate with the Federal Government, the state of Vermont purchased 10,000 acres from the Green Mountain Power Company and others in the Little River Valley. The road through this valley was thrown up and all the houses in the small settlement were razed.

The Waterbury Dam is among the largest earth fill dams in New England. Over two million cubic yards of earth were required to make the embankment forming the dam, which is over 2,000 feet long. It has a maximum width of about 900 feet and a maximum height of 175 feet. One hundred and sixty trucks were used to transport the earth to the dam from the borrow pit up the valley. There the earth was excavated by 12 large power shovels. The center portion of the dam comprises 500,000 cu. yds. of selected gravel placed on each side of the slopes. Heavy rocks were placed by the enrollees on both faces of the upstream and downstream sides of the dam.

The Waterbury (Little) River is diverted through a nearly semi-circular concrete conduit 14 feet wide and 10½ feet high. In the two steel pipes under the dam, two 48 inch regulators, needle valves, were installed at the outlet. The flow of water can be controlled from nothing to 1,500 cubic feet per second. The dam is protected by a concrete spillway in case of a flood of great magnitude.

Camp Charles M. Smith, which eventually housed over 3,000 men, was located on a mile long plateau. The ten veterans' companies went to work at the dam in April, 1935. They were later increased by junior companies from Elmore, Jericho, Bellows Falls and West Compton, New Hampshire.

Waterbury Dam Construction, 60 CCC Buildings in Background.

Waterbury Dam, Vermont.

Some of the first soil was turned during a visit by Governor Charles Smith and Director Robert Fechner. An outstanding event occurred when President Franklin Delano Roosevelt paid a vist to the Dam. The dam was completed in 1938.

Camp McKee was located in a cornfield on the height in Berlin overlooking Montpelier. Two veterans' companies arrived here in July, 1933, and lived in tents until December's frigid weather, when they moved into barracks at *Camp Greene*. They worked in riprapping the banks of the Winooski River and the construction of the clothespin dam in Montpelier. The purpose of the dam was to increase the channel flow of the river through Montpelier. The work was started in the fall of 1933 and completed through the severe winter of 1933-1934. The dam was dedicated on Monday, November 31, 1934, with Mayor Perry H. Merrill in charge of the exercises. He introduced the former, Mayor William McKee, and Lt. Col. Raymond E. Lee, who addressed the veterans and others present. Governor Stanley C. Wilson gave the main dedication speech. Director Robert Fechner praised the Veterans for their work.

Camp Mead enrollees in Middlesex village, moved to Camp Smith when the Winooski River channel work was completed.

Department of the Interior

The Department of the Interior consisted in 1933 of six bureaus and offices. These agencies included the National Park Service, the Office of Indian Affairs, the Bureau of Reclamation, the General Land Office and the Grazing Service. The Department had an average of 309 CCC camps, 71 Indian Units, and an average of eight camps in Alaska, Hawaii and the Virgin Islands. By July of 1941, there were 262 continental camps operating under the supervision of the National Park Service, 20 under the jurisdiction of the Army and Navy, 83 on National Parks and Monuments, 21 on Recreational Demonstration areas, 113 on state parks and 25 on county or municipal parks.

National Parks and Monuments

As of October 1, 1980, there are 41 National Parks and 90 National Monuments.

The Great Smoky National Park in North Carolina and Tennessee was established exclusively by the CCC. It included a foot and horse trail system.

Road systems were constructed in the Shenandoah National Park in Virginia and on the Colonial National Parkway. Improvements and developments were made on the following National Parks: Mammoth Cave in Kentucky, Lassen, Yosemite, General Grant, Sequoia, Crater Lake, Oregon Caves, Glacier, and others.

Historic Areas

Skillful restoration and repair work was accomplished at several historic shrines and battlefields of four wars, namely: Fort Pulaski National Monument in Georgia, Fredericksburg and Spotsylvania County Battlefields, Memorial National Park in Virginia, Chickamauga and Chattanooga Military National Park in Georgia, Mammoth Cave in Alabama, Acadia National Park in Maine, Gettysburg National Park in Pennsylvania, Vicksburg National Military Park in Mississippi, Rocky Mountain National Park in Colorado, Carlsbad Caverns National Park in New Mexico, Painted Desert in Arizona, Grand Canyon and Mesa Verde National Park in Colorado, Platt's National Park in Oklahoma, Hot Springs National Park in Arkansas and Big Bend National Park in Texas.

Historic Sites, Battlefield and National Cemeteries

The work done by the CCC included the construction of buildings, the building of roads and parkways and developments such as areas for camping, picnicking, swimming and just enjoying the environs. Many shrubs and trees were planted not only to enhance the beauty of the area but also to provide shelter for birds and animals and to stop erosion. On areas of historical significance, over 400 buildings were restored. Acquisition of property by gift and purchase was speeded up. Examples of this action include the Big Bend International Park in Texas and the Mammoth Cave National Park in Kentucky which were gifts.

State Parks

The National Park Service gave aid to state, county and municipal parks in their development by the CCC. In 1933, the following 13 states had no state park system and about half of that number, mostly in the south, possessed no park properties at all: Alabama, Florida, Georgia, Mississippi, Maryland, South Carolina, North Carolina, Tennessee, Virginia and West Virginia. Ten of those states without park lands, had developed parks with CCC aid by 1939.

Over 300 state, county and municipal parks in the region east of the Mississippi River were developed in whole or in part by the aid of the CCC. See the section on states for descriptions.

Recreational Demonstration Projects

Perhaps the most remarkable collateral product of the CCC days was the series of recreational demonstration projects in 24 states. This project involved government purchase of nearly 400,000 acres of submarginal land and the use of CCC camps and funds of the Federal Emergency Relief Administration (FERA) to plan and develop the areas for recreational purposes, under the supervision of the National Park Service. The RDP program started in 1934, with what was known as the FERA

Land Program, an effort by the Roosevelt administration to solve the vicious problem of submarginal land.

Countless farmers were in a hopeless situation on such land since it was below marginal productivity to make a living and no one wanted to buy it. These lands were bought and the farmowners were resettled on productive lands.

Park enthusiasts saw a chance to obtain some of these lands for recreational development. The RDA areas were usually within 50 miles of urban communities. Pennsylvania with five areas, had the largest number. Others were in Tennessee, Missouri, Indiana, Oregon, Virginia, Maine, and West Virginia.

By 1942, Congress authorized the transfer of these RDA areas to the states and Federal agencies. By 1950, there were 29 of these areas which had been transferred to the states and listed as state parks.

Gravel for Road Surfacing.

Bureau of Reclamation

The Bureau of Reclamation, which was created in 1902 in the Department of Interior, provided irrigation to arid and semi-arid lands so that they could be used and settled. The chief tasks were the construction of earth dams, the building of levees to control stream erosion and larger canals, the clearing and cleaning of irrigation water ways to allow for the economical delivery of water to the farms, the concrete lining of irrigation canals to prevent water seepage and canal breaks, the laying of pipe lines and conduits, and the elimination of destructive rodents whose tunneling results in water losses.

Office of Indian Affairs

This office was under the jurisdiction of the Interior Department, which for years had given little, if any, assistance to the Indians. There was much work which needed to be done on their lands, so the CCC brought the first opportunity to protect and improve them.

Work was done on a portion of the 50 million acres of Indian lands on over 200 reservations in 23 of our states. The projects carried out by the Indians were the same as others used. The Indians were allowed to work from their homes since the head of the family was needed to provide food and care for his family.

General Land Office

The General Land Office of the Department of Agriculture operated five CCC camps in Oregon, Wyoming and Alaska. In Oregon, the enrollees worked on the conservation, protection and development of the 2,500,000 acres of Oregon and California (O & C) Revested lands. This area is an important reservoir of commercial timber being developed on a sustained yield basis.

An unusual CCC project was an attack on coal-bed fires in Wyoming, where they were kept busy trying to suppress out-crop coal fires. These were threatening with destruction of an inestimable amount of the nation's coal reserve in the vicinity of Thunder Basin, Wyoming. One of the jobs was the control of a fire 2,000 feet long mentioned by the Sawyer expedition in 1865. A bridge with a 64-foot span was constructed to reach the fire. The other coal beds were 25 to 45 feet in thickness, and the fires in some cases were 1,000 feet or more in length along the outcrop. Thus an opportunity was provided for the first time to develop and test large scale techniques of controlling coal-bed fires.

Grazing Service

This bureau was established in the Department of Interior in July, 1934, to administer the Taylor Grazing Act, which regulates the grazing on the public domain. About 45 camps were authorized in 1935 to carry on the projects as suggested and approved by the local advisory boards of the grazing districts. The work was spread over 58 grazing districts in the ten western states of Arizona, California, Colorado, Idaho, Montana, Nevada, New Mexico, Oregon, Utah, and Wyoming. These districts cover 142,000,000 acres of range land and provide forage for the seasonal use of 11 million head of livestock.

In July, 1941, there were 63 CCC camps working on the grazing districts. The enrollees were used to construct stock water reservoirs, spring developments, wells, windmills, storage tanks, and water troughs for the range animals. Truck trails and stock driveways were built from range to range and range to market. Fences, corrals and other structures were built for better range management. The extermination of insects and pests, the eradication of poison and noxious weed, the control of rodents and the elimination of predatory animals were other CCC accomplishments. Hundreds of acres were treated to retard erosion and conserve water run-off, which areas were then sown with seed to revegetate the areas.

The Grazing Service camps contributed many man hours in fighting forest fires not only on grazing lands but on adjoining National Forests.

Territory of Hawaii

Emergency Conservation Work was established in the Territory of Hawaii and the Hawaii National Park by authority granted on December 11, 1933. The entire program was under the control of the Governor of Hawaii for the territorial program and of the National Park Service for the work which was done in the Hawaii National Park. The participation of the Army was limited to the disbursement of funds.

The work carried on in the Hawaii National Park was very similar to what was done in the continental parks. The program for the Territory of Hawaii was under the supervision of the technical forester of the territory. Projects were carried out on the four islands to conserve the water resources.

Originally, 200 enrollees were allotted to the Hawaii National Park and 577 for the use of the Territory. During a later period, the number for the Territory of Hawaii was increased to 1,212.

Virgin Islands

Enrollment for the conservation work on the Islands of St. Thomas and St. Croix, Virgin Islands was authorized on December 6, 1934. For the two islands, 100 enrollees were assigned to camps there. Typical conservation work carried out by the native enrollees under the supervision of a forester included the development of windbreaks, propagation of mahogany and bay trees, and the development of springs.

Department of Agriculture

The United States Department of Agriculture had the majority of the CCC camps under its jurisdiction from the beginning of the Emergency Conservation Work. As of June 30, 1935, the Department had 1,231 camps which were divided as follows: 517 on National Forests and other Federal reservations administered by this department, 463 on state and private lands, 210 on erosion and flood control, mainly on agricultural lands, 19 operated for the Tennessee Valley Authority, and ten for Federal game and bird refuges, three on mosquito control, and one for the Bureau of Plant Industry. In addition, the Department had the sole responsibility for the CCC work projects and the administration of the camps in Alaska and Puerto Rico, where the camps were small, varying in size, and operated very informally. The Department worked with the 48 states and territories.

U.S. Forest Service

The Forest Service had under its administration, the national forests in 38 states, Alaska and Puerto Rico with a combined acreage of 170,000,000 acres. Under the old Weeks Law of 1911 and the Clarke-McNary Act of 1924, the Forest Service cooperated with the states in forest fire protection, forest management including reforestation, and later, recreation.

National Forests. In 1935 there were 154 National Forests located in 43 states and territories with the main objective being timber production. The following states, in 1935, had no national forests: Connecticut, Delaware, Iowa, New Jersey, New York, Maryland and Pennsylvania.

For administrative purposes, the United States was divided into nine regions: Eastern at Milwaukee, Southern at Atlanta, Northern at Missoula, Montana, Rocky Mountain at Lakewood, Colorado, Southwestern at Albuquerque, Intermountain at Ogden, Utah, California at San Francisco, Pacific Northwest at Portland, Oregon, and Alaska at Juneau.

As a result of the CCC, Federal land purchases were made in the following states: Florida, Georgia, Illinois, Indiana, Louisiana, Michigan, Ohio, Iowa, Kentucky, Minnesota, Mississippi, Missouri, New Hampshire, North Carolina, Oklahoma, Pennsylvania, South Carolina, Tennessee, Texas, Virginia, West Virginia, Alabama, Arkansas, Puerto Rico and Wisconsin.

Experiment Stations. The U.S. Forest Service carries on research from experiment stations at Berkley, California; Ogden, Utah; Fort Collins, Colorado; St. Paul, Minnesota; Upper Darby, Pennsylvania; New Orleans, Louisiana; and Asheville, North Carolina. The Forest Products Laboratory at Madison, Wisconsin, is where research in the uses of wood is carried out.

The National Forests provide range for many thousands of cattle and sheep. Rodents do an untold damage to young forests. Over grazing has necessitated revegetation of thousands of acres on the western forests. Much work was carried on to improve the forest conditions for wild life as well as range animals.

The protection of the forests was the project of prime importance. This work required the construction of truck trails, water holes, and sites for water supply. Insect control and that of diseases such as white pine blister rust, beech scale, Dutch elm disease and the control of beetles which eat needles, bore into trees including the bark, and moths such as the gypsy moth, all needed immediate attention.

State and Private Forests. The work accomplished on state and private forests was similar to that which was done on the national forests. A record of these accomplishments begins on page 108.

Soil Conservation Service

The Soil Erosion Service (predecessor of the Soil Conservation Service) was established as a temporary organization in the U.S. Department of Interior without a formal order. Pursuant to a resolution adopted on July 17, 1933, by a special Board of Public Works, the Federal Administrator of Public Works by memorandum of August 25, 1933, advised the Secretary of Interior that in accordance with the provisions of the National Recovery Act of June 16, 1933 (48 Stat, 195), an allotment of $5,000,000 had been made to the Department of Interior.

These funds were for soil erosion prevention work on public and private lands. Actual operation of the Soil Erosion Service began on September 19, 1933, when Hugh H. Bennett was transferred from the Department of Agriculture to the Department of Interior, as Director of the Soil Conservation Service. Walter C. Lowermilk entered on duty as vice-director soon thereafter.

It was not until April 27, 1935, that the Soil Conservation Service was established by Public Law 46 of the 74th Congress. On March 25, the Soil Erosion Service had been transferred to the Department of Agriculture by order of the Federal Administrator of Public Works and immediately approved by President Roosevelt.

On April 1, 1934, 22 ECW camps were transferred to this service in the states of Alabama, Arkansas, California, Kansas, Louisiana, Georgia, Mississippi, Missouri, North Carolina, Nebraska, Ohio, Oregon, Oklahoma, Texas, Virginia, South Carolina, West Virginia, and Wisconsin.

On May 11, 1934, the first great dust storm originated in the Great Plains and swept fine particles of soil over Washington, D.C. into New England and 300 miles out over the Atlantic Ocean. Another storm followed, carrying great clouds of top soil from the fields of Kansas, Colorado, Texas and Oklahoma over about the same areas and again out over the ocean. This storm evidently spurred on the construction of more camps in Arizona, California, Colorado, New Jersey, New York, New Mexico, South Carolina, South Dakota, and Pennsylvania. By December, 1935, the SCS was operating 498 camps. Although more were assigned, this was the largest number in operation at any one time.

To prevent the agricultural lands from serious erosion, the control measures adopted included agronomic, forestry, engineering and soil management practices, based on the variations of the soil types, gradient, erosion condition, and the uses.

The better part of the work was restricted to gulley control and terrace outlet construction. Other work of a particular nature included the quarrying of limestone in West Virginia, Iowa, Missouri and Illinois. Crushing plants were established from which the lime was carried to demonstration farms where it was spread. This work was carried out from 216 camps.

The main work from these camps may be summarized as building check

Road Building, New York.

dams, bank sloping, planting and seeding, ditches and channel clearing, and teaching the landowners and enrollees how to do strip cropping.

By June 30, 1936, the SCS had in operation 11 regional offices, 147 demonstration projects, eight nurseries, 23 experiment stations and 343 camps. The Prairie States Project which previous to September 1, 1942, carried on the shelter belt work under the USFS was transferred to the SCS. (See chapter under Shelterbelt).

Oren W. Wright writes "I enrolled in the SCS-CCC camp #2942 at Soda Springs, Washington in late 1938. I was the Educational Advisor and later a mechanic when the camp was transferred to Waterville, Washington. The CCC produced the large proportion of trained equipment and construction men for World War II and many as superintendents and engineers after the war.

"We had a very good camp and the army officers did an excellent job in teaching the rudiments of discipline to a green bunch of kids who were a great help to the war service. In Waterville, I worked with an engineer who taught me surveying which I followed for 25 years, having traveled all over the world on construction jobs."

The CCC and the Shelterbelt

The birth of the shelterbelt occurred on July 11, 1934, under an executive order of President Roosevelt, allocating $15,000,000.00 from the Emergency Act of June 18, 1934, to be used for emergency relief in the drought stricken area. The action was objected to by the Budget Director and the Controller. A million dollar compromise was agreed upon, which sum was considered sufficient for one year's operation. Vigorous opposition to the project came from the commercial nurserymen.

In the fall of 1933 and the spring of 1934, the dust storm in the Great Plains accelerated: in fact, it has been stated that in the spring of 1934, the worst storms to date occurred in Tulsa, Oklahoma, and in Kansas. The writer recalls that in the spring of 1934, the snow in Vermont had a brownish tinge from the dust carried east by those storms.

Previous Planting Experiments. Tree planting in Kansas and Nebraska started in the 1850's due to the early settlers who loved the trees in their homelands in the east. Wood was considered necessary for fuel, construction material, and furniture. They soon learned that the planting of groups or belts of trees prevented the wind from blowing away their soils in storms.

The Nebraska State Board of Agriculture was encouraged by Governor John Morton to establish Arbor Day on April 10, 1872. This idea of planting trees on a specific date spread to all states.

In 1886, Dr. Bernhard E. Fernow, a graduate of the Prussian Forest Academy at Munden, Germany, became the third Director of the Department of Forestry in the U.S.D.A. His knowledge and experience greatly assisted in the establishment of the shelterbelt.

Shelterbelt Action. The operation of the shelterbelt project received its final approval on October 10, 1934. The proposed shelterbelt area included a strip of land lying between the tall grasses of the east and the short grasses of the west, extending from North Dakota's northern boundary to northern Oklahoma. The western boundary of light rainfall coincided with the 80th meridian where the tall grasses start.

There were many questions to be solved before the shelterbelt planting could be started. These included: Can the shelterbelt be successfully established?, Where would it be most favorable and where will it accomplish the most good? The first job was left in the hands of Raphael Zon, the Director of the Lake States Forest Experiment Station. Many answers had to be forthcoming, which included, what kinds of grasses and shrubs should be planted, what age and kind of planting stock should be used, the development of technical staff to oversee the planting in the six states of North and South Dakota, Nebraska, Kansas, Oklahoma and Texas. The fieldwork of technicians included obtaining information about the soils, climate, natural vegetation, and the examination of former plantations which had been made on the 1,000 mile zone of dry land. The width of the zone to be planted was set at about 100 miles.

The problem of land ownership had to be settled. Should the Federal government buy the land outright, or obtain a lease or an easement for a certain period? After the settlement of these questions, the first plantings were established as windbreaks around the farm buildings and later extended to larger areas as the farmers and settlers realized the value of the plantings.

The next problem was where would the nursery stock come from? Agreements were finally made with nurseries such as those at Freemont, Nebraska, Enderlin, North Dakota, and Hutchinson, Kansas, either to procure the seed and/or raise the nursery stock.

Experiments were made with many species, some native to stream beds and others which had been successfully planted. The early settlers had planted Osage orange, locust, elm, pines, and red cedar. The CCC nursery in South Dakota furnished 181,200 trees in 1935. Most of the conifers were obtained for the Forest Service nurseries at Bessey site in Halsey, Nebraska and Monument, Colorado, and wild plum seed stored at central extractory at Norfolk, Nebraska, and a three acre block of Siberian Elm seedlings from a nursery at Baltic, South Dakota. The great need for the collection of seed for the shelterbelt project enlisted the aid of the CCC, the SCS and the *Bureau of Plant Industry*.

Prairie States Forestry Project. On July 1, 1942, the Prairie States Forestry project was turned over from the USFS to the SCS. The planting of shelterbelts then became a part of the SCS complete farm plan.

Shelterbelt Planting, 1934.

Bureau of Biological Survey

The area administered by the Bureau of Biological Survey covered about 6,000,000 acres, including Hawaii and Puerto Rico, comprising 95 game refuges. The accomplishments of the CCC include the work on land and water areas which were purchased by the then authorized funds. The work on migratory wild fowl and big game areas consisted of miscellaneous construction including truck trails, fire lines, telephone lines, planting for food and cover, clearing ponds and channels, construction of bridges and dykes and small dams to make fresh water ponds. All of these projects were concerned with the improvement of the physical features of the refuges.

Bureau of Plant Industry

Two CCC camps were assigned to the bureau with one for the preliminary improvement and construction work for a national arboretum. The other at Cheyenne, Wyoming, was for work at a Federal horticultural field station, which was started in 1936.

The CCC enrollees did a large amount of permanent work, all essential to the main purpose of the arboretum. The construction of the roads, drainage, water system, and fencing of the 400 acre tract have been of primary importance.

Camp NA 2 completed seven years of work at the Cheyenne Station in the construction of buildings, irrigation system, sewerage disposal system, pipe lines, erosion control, drainage and landscaping.

Bureau of Animal Industry

During the CCC period, help was given to the Bureau at Auburn, Alabama; Brooksville, Florida; Dubois, Idaho; Jeanette, Louisiana; Beltsville, Maryland; and Miles City, Montana. These research stations were devoted to finding better practices in breeding, feeding and the management of domestic animals and poultry and in disease prevention and control.

All the buildings except one, were given to the government and were in need of repair. Roads were run down and the other facilities needed adaptation to new processes to carry on the needed research. As an example, a new project at Dubois, Idaho, was added to the Bureau's appropriation for sheep research. This made it necessary to increase the expansion of the research facilities. With the aid of the CCC, land was cleared and graded, roads and trails built, water and sewage system extended and landscaping carried out around the new building. At the Range and Experiment Station at Miles City, Montana, a CCC camp proved very successful. At all the research stations, the bureau was well equipped for the research at hand.

Bureau of Agricultural Engineering

Organized drainage districts have an acreage which exceeds the combined area of Indiana, Ohio and Iowa. Due to the depression, many of these ditches were not maintained, and they soon became filled with drift, debris, and vegetation. This work was formerly done by the county drainage officials. In the spring of 1935, 46 CCC camps were established to carry out this work in Delaware, Illinois, Indiana, Iowa, Kentucky, Louisiana, Maryland and Ohio.

Puerto Rico and the CCC

Of the total land area of 2,000,000 acres in Puerto Rico, about 500,000 acres are largely unproductive. With a dense population of nearly one person per acre, the island badly needed forest products. The steep mountain slopes are subject to heavy rainfall. The sugar cane areas of the plains have a scant rainfall.

The U.S.F.S. handled both the camps and the direction of the work with the Army acting as a disbursing agent only. One of the first jobs of the enrollees was the expansion of new nurseries to furnish the needed planting stock.

A total of 2,100 enrollees was authorized and generally there was a waiting list. The number of CCC camps varied, but generally there were 12 of varying sizes; six in national forests and six on insular forest land.

The principal activities were tree planting, operation of forest nurseries, road construction, soil erosion control, and public recreational development. Other projects included trails, bridges, fish hatcheries, fire towers, and landing fields. Millions of young trees were planted including

WINTER TROUT REARING POOL. STOWE

DAM. SHOWING POOL BUILDING ACTION

IMPROVED STREAMS MEAN BETTER FISHING

SMALL LOG DAM CREATING POOL

PLANTING WILD BARBERRY FOR GAME FOOD

DOUBLE RIFFLER FOR CONTROLLING STREAM

PLANTING WILD CRANBERRY ON AITKEN STATE FOREST

Fish and Wildlife.

mahogany, teak, eucalyptus and mesquite on Federal lands, while much tree planting was accomplished on municipal watersheds.

Alaska

In the then Territory of Alaska, the CCC work was under the direction of the U.S. Forest Service. The only function of the Army there was that of a paying agency. In 1935, there were 325 enrollees, all middle-aged men and not handled in 200 man camps, since the work projects were so widely scattered and relatively small. The work consisted chiefly of truck trails, campground development, and timber estimating.

The number of men in the camps varied due to seasonal employment. The largest number of men in CCC camps was 1,200. In some letters written by enrollees they tell of their stateside camps being transferred to Alaska for summer employment.

Tennessee Valley Authority

The U.S. Forest Service directed work of about 188 camps in the Tennessee Valley under the direction of TVA technicians. The major projects were erosion control, reforestation, forest protection, work in the large forest nurseries, and activities relating to fisheries and wildlife management on TVA lands.

Insects and Diseases

The work of the CCC in the control of insect pests and plant diseases was carried out on both public and private land under Federal laws. An effort was made to suppress the white pine blister rust disease which threatened the white pine stands on five million acreas. From this area over 300,000,000 Ribes plants (currants and gooseberries, both wild and cultivated) were removed and destroyed.

The CCC helped in the efforts to suppress the Dutch Elm Disease which killed the American elm in Connecticut, New Jersey, New York and New England. During the period in which this work proceeded, 275,000 dead or dying elms were cut, removed and burned.

Since 1906, the Federal Government has cooperated with the states concerned in an effort to control and prevent the spread of the gypsy moth. This insect attacks and defoliates forest, shade, and fruit trees eventually killing the trees. The CCC examined trees in the above states on 3,250,000 acres in their search for egg clusters of the moths.

Another activity of the Bureau of Entomology and Plant Quarantine was the effort to eradicate the major insect pest of cotton, the boll worm or weevil. The insect, which infested wild cotton in south Florida, was attacked by enrollees from camps in that area. Approximately one million cotton plants were removed from that large area.

Mosquito Control

An important contribution to mosquito control was made by the CCC in New Jersey, Maryland, Delaware, Florida, the Gulf and Atlantic Coasts, the states bordering on the Pacific Ocean, and in Iowa and Illinois. An outstanding example of control was performed in Delaware where 12,000,000 feet of drainage ditches were built.

THE VALUE OF THE CCC TO THE NATION

This section of the history treats of the assistance which the CCC gave to the Departments of Interior and Agriculture.

The work accomplished by the CCC for the Divisions of the Departments of Interior and Agriculture was taken from printed reports submitted by the bureau representatives of those departments and are for the period 1933 to June 30, 1942.

Department of the Interior

The following information is quoted from the Federal Reports.

National Park Service

The Civilian Conservation Corps advanced park development by many years. It made possible the development of many protective facilities on the areas that comprise the National Park System, and also provided, for the first time, a Federal aid program for state park systems through which the National Park Service gave technical assistance and administrative guidance for immediate park developments and long-range planning. Of approximately 3,114 CCC camp years of work under the supervision of the National Park Service, 880 or 28 percent were on National Park Service areas, and 2,234 or 72 percent, on non-Federal park and recreational areas. It is believed that the work accomplished in the park conservation field in the 10 years of CCC was equal to what might have been expected in 50 years without its assistance.

The National Park System benefited immeasurably by the Civilian Conservation Corps, principally through the building of many greatly needed fire trails and other forest fire-prevention facilities such as lookout towers and ranger cabins. During the life of the CCC, the areas received the best fire protection in the history of the Service. Over 414,000 man-days were spent on the work of fire prevention and over 250,000 on fire suppression. The value of the man-days spent in fire protection and suppression in the great scenic areas of the Nation cannot be overestimated.

The CCC also provided the manpower and materials to construct many administrative and public-use facilities such as utility buildings, sanitation and water systems, housing for its employees, service roads, campground improvements, and museums and exhibits; to do reforestation and work relating to insect and disease control; to improve the roadsides; to restore historic sites and buildings; to perform erosion control, and sand fixation research and work; to make various travel and use studies; and to do many other developmental and administrative tasks that are so important to the proper protection and use of the National Park System.

The CCC made available to the superintendents of the national parks, for the first time, a certain amount of manpower that allowed them to do many important jobs when and as they arose.

The State park program received a tremendous impetus through the CCC. Without having had any previous official relationship with State park organizations, the National Park Service was asked to supervise CCC work on non-Federal park areas. This required the setting up of a supplementary organization on a regional basis. Many states were not prepared to utilize effectively the manpower and materials that were suddenly available to them—in fact, the majority of them had practically no state park system or organization.

General Land Office

During the life of the Civilian Conservation Corps, the General Land Office operated a maximum of six CCC camps and carried on a program of work in the Territory of Alaska. This participation was but a small part of the entire CCC program.

Among the first of the CCC camps to be established was one for the control and suppression of outcrop fires in the coal beds on the public domain in the Little Thunder Basin, Wyoming. In the early years of the program the work was suspended during the winter periods and for a while two camps were assigned to this project; but in realization of the fact that the work could be more economically carried forward on a year-around basis the number of camps was reduced to one which continued work throughout the year until the closing of the entire CCC program.

Some of the fires in these coal beds had been burning since the earliest recorded history of that area, destroying and endangering a mass of coal measured in terms of billions of tons. Using special techniques developed in collaboration with technical experts of the Geological Survey, approximately 25 of these fires were completely suppressed or extinguished and several others brought under control to the point that they will probably burn out without material damage; yet there are other fires which were not touched up to the time the CCC program terminated which will continue their destructive forces. The immense coal deposits in this area lying in the public domain constitute a fuel reserve of immeasurable value, as large-scale production can be quickly accomplished through strip mining in case production in the Eastern states should be curtailed. These deposits on which the fires have been extinguished or brought under control have been saved for future generations by reason of the magnificent work of the CCC.

In 1938, three CCC camps were assigned to the General Land Office for work on the O. & C. lands in Oregon.

The many miles of access and utilization road constructed by the CCC through the O. & C. timbered lands are today proving their value. The CCC truck trails penetrating the hitherto unbroken forest wildernesses make it possible for the forest fire fighters to reach remote areas and control fires which otherwise would rage unchecked for days. These same truck trails make it possible to reach stands of high-quality timber necessary for aircraft construction and other special war needs. Trained CCC fire-fighting crews controlled numerous forest fires quickly and efficiently. Had it not been for these highly trained mobile crews, many fires would have devastated unknown thousands of acres of forest land and destroyed huge quantities of highly valuable forest products which are now in use and vital to the progress of the war.

Many other activities of less tangible value were conducted by the CCC on the O. & C. lands, such as perpetuation of our forests by planting small trees on denuded areas; the control of forest-destroying diseases and insects, and the education of the public in the need for conservation.

CCC activities on the 325,000,000 acres of public domain in Alaska were transferred to the General Land Office in April, 1940. Since the impact of the war prevented the employment of the planned number of whites, the employment was chiefly Alaskan Indians and Eskimos, and the program was directed mainly for the benefit of the native peoples. The projects worked on during the year were in villages scattered from Wainwright on the Arctic coast to Atka on the Aleutian chain, and Eagle on the Upper Yukon River. In this vast area, sanitary facilities and community water-supply systems were constructed. Debris within and in the vicinity of the villages was cleared and burned. School houses were erected and remodeled, roads and trails constructed and maintained, and reindeer corrals were constructed for the benefit of the native inhabitants. Probably about 100 villages were benefited by this program.

One of the greatest problems in Alaska is transportation. CCC personnel maintained and staked winter sled trails and maintained winter landing fields to make mail, freight, and passenger operations possible with a minimum of disruption in service.

Office of Indian Affairs

Emergency Conservation Work and Civilian Conservation Corps activities within the Office of Indian Affairs began June 19, 1933, and ended July 10, 1942.

During that period 88,349 different individuals participated as enrollees. Eighty-five thousand two hundred of these were Indians; 3,149 were whites, most of whom were intermarried. An average of 7,564 enrollees, and 776 employees—8,340 persons in all—were engaged in conservation activities each day during the life of the Corps.

Approximately $72,000,000 were expended—an average of $8,000,000 per year.

The work accomplishments were impressive, and have contributed directly to the rebuilding of the reservations and the National Domain.

They were favorably commented on by numerous officials, including the directors of the Corps.

Careful and adequate planning was insisted upon, and every effort made to insure that each project was completed in an efficient manner with the least possible expenditure of funds consistent with good engineering and construction practices.

The improved economic condition of the Indians has definitely influenced their morale. They were participants in the planning, they did the work, and they directly benefited by the results.

Thousands of enrollees became skilled workers as a direct result of their participation in the Corps and are now contributing to the war effort as members of the armed forces, as skilled workers in war industries, and as producers of food. Training was always a real, if not conspicuous activity.

The program was the first piece of emergency legislation under which the Indians benefited. There was much work to be done on Indian reservations. Heretofore, funds had not been available in sufficient amounts to undertake large-scale programs. There was considerable erosion; millions of acres of forest, range, and farm lands needed attention. Under ECW, funds were given to the Office of Indian Affairs, enrollment for Indians was eased, and thousands, literally, obtained their first steady employment in years.

The program started from "scratch." There were no precedents. It was necessary to undertake a huge program with a new staff of employees.

The immediate objective was to furnish gainful employment for needy Indians, and to improve their land holdings, and the Office of Indian Affairs was thus able to undertake a long-range program to help the Indian become self-supporting. Work was undertaken on nearly 300 different tracts of land—on reservations, rancherias, and other holdings—under 71 jurisdictions, in 23 states.

The program revitalized Indian life; it gave wage work where and when it was needed. It made possible the building up of reservation resources. Indians were taught how to use the land and water conserved.

Bureau of Reclamation

Federal Reclamation is a Government enterprise designed to utilize the water resources of the West in the work of developing the arid and semiarid regions that lie west of the one-hundredth meridian; an area of 740,000,000 acres comprising a third of the land area of the United States. Less than 20 inches of rain falls annually in nearly all of this vast territory, which is incapable of supporting any considerable population or agriculture without an artificial water supply. Through the irrigation of desert lands and the operation of power plants, new opportunities for farms, homes and for cities, for mining and processing the country's mineral wealth and for manufacturing many of the essential tools of a modern industry, are created. It is the task of the Bureau of Reclamation to plan, design, and build the intricate engineering works that provide water for irrigation and generate power and to supervise their operation and maintenance after completion. The water and power users who benefit by these developments are required to repay their cost over a period of years.

Federal irrigation in the Western States began in 1902 with the enactment of the Reclamation Act. In the early years following passage of this act many irrigation projects were built and placed in operation at a reimbursable cost approximating $220,000,000 by 1935. These projects consist usually of a dam and reservoir to store water and an extensive system of Government-owned canals and canal structures to control and deliver the stored water to individual farm units.

The economic depression that began in 1930 made it difficult to maintain the irrigation systems at proper standards and the droughts in the early years of the depression further reduced the available water supply, augmenting the problems of the irrigation farmer. Thousands of control structures built 20 or 25 years previously, became deteriorated beyond repair, canals became silted and clogged with vegetation, and crop yields on the farm lands decreased alarmingly with the decrease in water supply. By 1934 it had become a matter of urgency that some means be found, not inconsistent with the unemployment problem of the country, to overcome these adverse project conditions and to protect the Government's large investment.

A few CCC camps were established on reclamation projects in 1934. In 1935, 50 camps were allotted to the Bureau of Reclamation to undertake a comprehensive program for the rehabilitation of the irrigation systems and the development of a supplemental water supply on projects affected by drought conditions. Rehabilitation was programmed on a basis of permanent improvements designed to avoid difficulties in future years. Deteriorated wooden water control structures in the canals, such as checks, drops, turnouts, etc., were replaced with permanent concrete structures. Canal banks were cleaned of vegetation, reshaped to their original design, and were lined with concrete, rock, or gravel to prevent future erosion and silting. Operation roads for motor vehicles were built along canals to facilitate operation, inspection, and maintenance of the facilities. Telephone lines and fences on Government property were rebuilt to present-day standards. Impounding and diversion dams which had suffered from excessive wave action or wind erosion were rebuilt to their designed lines and grades and were heavily blanketed with rock or gravel.

Supplemental water supplies were developed for several projects by the construction of small reservoirs and the building of feeder canals to bring additional water to existing reservoirs.

Later in the CCC program, camps were assigned to aid in the construction of new reclamation projects.

Fish and Wildlife Service

During the nine years of its existence the CCC has been an extremely influential force in the conservation of our wildlife resources, notably migratory waterfowl and big game animals. Coincident with the establishment of the Corps in 1933, a gigantic wildlife refuge purchase program was begun. In the continental United States, since 1933, approximately 8,000,000 acres of land and water have been acquired for national wildlife refuge purposes, increasing the total refuge holdings to approximately 9,570,000 acres in 257 refuges. These refuge lands compensate in part for the millions of acres of wildlife habitat which necessarily fell before the plow, the ax, and the drainage ditch.

Two thousand five hundred ninety-eight camp months of CCC labor have been directed toward the accomplishment of two fundamental objectives: the improvement of wildlife habitat and the improvement of administrative facilities. In order to improve the refuges to a condition most favorable to wildlife, dams, dikes, and other devices for the impoundment and control of water have been built; food and cover-producing vegetation has been planted for wildlife and as a deterrent to soil erosion; millions of trees have been planted as windbreaks and to provide wildlife cover; stream- and lake-bank protection has been given prominent attention, as has the construction of nesting islands and wildlife shelters. To facilitate refuge management, truck trails, bridges, lookout towers, fire lanes, telephone lines, small but well-built headquarters and utility buildings, and seed- and tuber-storage cellars have been constructed, and to keep out stray livestock and prevent trespass, fences and boundary markers have been erected.

Grazing Service

The CCC camps were distributed uniformly among the 58 Grazing Districts in the ten Western states of Arizona, California, Colorado, Idaho, Montana, Nevada, New Mexico, Oregon, Utah, and Wyoming.

The services of the enrollees were used by the Grazing Service toward the accomplishment of those objectives of the Taylor Grazing Act which have to do with the construction of improvements on the public domain for the purpose of opening up new range lands, increasing the forage on existing range lands, regulating the use of all range lands, and protecting and conserving this natural resource for the benefit of all concerned. Many of these valuable accomplishments on the part of the CCC enrollees are now in evidence throughout the 142,000,000 acres of Federal range administered by the Grazing Service.

Perhaps the most important contributions to the range are the many stock-watering facilities constructed by CCC enrollees. Chief of these are the earthen reservoirs, ranging in size from 2-acre feet up to 100-acre feet in capacity. Included also are numerous small reservoirs and waterholes having capacities under 2-acre feet. Other water facilities consist of spring developments and drilled wells. Although wells render excellent watering facilities, preference was given to the development of springs and the construction of reservoirs with earth dams, because they afforded greater opportunities for the employment of enrollee labor. The materials required for springs and reservoirs were nominal, whereas for wells the cost of the materials was far out of proportion to the labor required. The placing of water in the outer reaches of the range allowed grazing to expand into vast areas of land which were rich in forage but which could not be used until water was provided.

Truck trails, stock trails, and stock driveways constructed by CCC enrollees are also a major contribution to the range.

The Department of Agriculture

The five Bureaus (originally six) in the Department of Agriculture, cooperating in the CCC program benefitted greatly in many ways through the many years of the Corps. Participation by the Forest Service and Soil Conservation Service was outstanding. These two bureaus were able to actually carry out a large portion of their programs and to put many of their plans in use. All of these programs and plans which had for their objective better protection, improvement and development of the forests, soils, waters and recreation of the nation, taught the department people about both the natural and the human resources of this country.

The Department's bureaus have taught these youths how to work, how to use tools and machinery, how to work safely and helped the enrollees by friendly advice and counsel.

Agriculture had the majority of the camps assigned to it, 820 out of 1,500, with the number fluctuating.

The Civil Conservation Corps will go down in American history as a great and worthwhile achievement in conservation of natural resources, in human conservation, and also as an experiment in practical education and training of youth. The Corps was moreover probably the first example, certainly the most successful, of real governmental cooperation between the six Federal departments or agencies.

Forest Service

At the end of the fiscal year 1942, the regional foresters of the ten districts of the National Forests recorded their reactions and conclusions of what the Corps and the three million enrollees meant to them and the 176 million acres of National Forests for which they were responsible.

Northern Region-Missoula, Montana. In WW II when the demand of trained organizers was great, the CCC made a great contribution. A large number of the Forest Service on-the-ground managers came from the CCC with experience and knowledge which they learned there. The fundamental objectives learned in the CCC transcended the physical and economic benefits to natural resources. The spiritual and cultural contribution to the American way of life were incalculable.

Those young, red-blooded Americans who took the first line of defense in forest fire control served valiantly in like positions in distant lands. Conservation projects benefitted the forest lands and also benefitted the members of the Forest Service with experience in handling men.

Rocky Mountain Region-Denver, Colorado. The CCC contributed to the relief of disaster-stricken communities and assisted in the rehabilitation of the damaged regions following the floods. Such an example was the work done in the spring of 1942, at Trinidad, following the Purgetoire flood.

The training given several thousand young men at numerous skills and effective work habits proved to be of immense value to both the war effort and on the production lines. The training given to truck drivers, tractor operators, mechanics, blacksmiths, telephone linesmen, carpenters, masons and others made them directly usable in the armed forces, in the factories, and on the farms as skilled technicians. The close cooperative camp life, the accepting of directions from those in charge of the camps and work projects fitted all CCC men to the kind of team work on a ship, a flying squadron, or any other combat force when faced with the real test.

Members of the Army overhead as well as the enrollees, obtained valuable experience in the CCC organization. Officers who were in charge of CCC camps were cited for bravery during the withdrawal to Batan in the Phillipines.

Southwestern Region-Albuquerque, New Mexico. A generation or more would have passed before the bulk of the nine-year accomplishments of these young CCC men could have been completed on the National Forests.

On the up-building side, mention might be made of some 35 boys in just one camp, who learned to read and write thanks to the educational program. Also, several from a National Forest camp received training that secured for them good paying jobs in South America. These attainments would not have been possible without their CCC training. The monetary assistance has been a life-saver to many Southwestern families whose sons were in the CCC.

Perhaps the most important phase of the CCC during the nine years of operation was the training of local Spanish-American youths from isolated and backward communities in sanitation, the ability to work with others, and to teach primary English to many.

Intermountain Region-Ogden, Utah. Sixty-eight CCC boys were employed from one camp in Idaho by a Boise company in four months. This company had over 500 former CCC's on their payrolls at Pacific Island bases where the Japanese started hostilities in December, 1941.

The winter of 1936-1937 was extremely cold with low temperatures along with deep snow. One million sheep were stranded and threatened with starvation and death in southern Utah. Their loss would have been a blow to the sheepmen of that part of the country. Quick action was taken by the administrative personnel who called out the CCC enrollees and their overhead and equipment into service. A battle ensued with the deep snow drifts that blocked all avenues of approach. Ways were opened up and sheepmen followed with cottonseed cake and other supplemental feed, which saved the lives of the valuable woolies. The CCC's worked against time and spared no effort to reach the stranded livestock in time to save their lives.

California Region-San Francisco, California. It immediately developed that a large number of the projects which were undertaken for peacetime uses, administration, improvement and protection of the forests were potentially and actually of tremendous importance to the war effort. Previously inaccessible forest products, such as timber and mineral products of strategic value, were not within easy reach when needed. There was easier access to forest fire control over the 7,900 miles of CCC built roads. Many streams which would otherwise be serious barriers have been spanned by 550 sturdy CCC built bridges, thereby providing the means of rapid movement of men and heavy equipment. The physical development of these young men, under regulated work and good living habits has been amazing. A great number used their CCC gained knowledge and healthy muscles in the nation's force or in the defense industries.

North Pacific Region-Portland, Oregon. It would be unfair to discount the value of the physical accomplishments of the CCC program. It has developed and conserved natural resources and provided protection and management facilities which are invaluable.

However, important as these may be, though, and far-reaching in their effect, they are subordinated in value and more restricted in their influence than the broadened physical, mental, and social capacities of the enrollee, and the return he will be able to make to society because of what the CCC has done for him. Although a by-product of the program, we feel that outstripping all other accomplishments of the Civilian Conservation Corps and of greater value than any other, is the young man who served in it and the contribution he is hereafter able to make to our national life. They have benefitted by it. Now they are giving back a handsome return on the investment and the government benefits by it.

Eastern Region-Philadelphia, Pennsylvania. The first tangible job on national forests, state forests and on private forest land was to bring to wasted and threatened areas a conservation force that would recapture, restore, or in some cases, stay incipient loss of invaluable natural resources of forest, stream and wildlife. This was well done. It had been a byword among conservationists that the Civilian Conservation Corps had enabled foresters to advance their conservation programs by the equivalent of 20 years of improvement work. But this was not all . . .

These men learned to handle power shovels, stone crushers, trucks, graders, and many other types of machinery. They learned at the same time both the mechanics and the theoretical side of road construction. No job was undertaken without explaining it to them. Here again they were learners. They were learning employable skills in a way in which they would never have been taught to them in civilian life.

The history of nine years is a saga of service in which the largest body of men in the country, working as a single unit, have labored with tractor, truck, pick, shovel and planting tool in rebuilding the resources of a nation.

With no pandering to fetishes or pampered whims, the cultural side of these men's lives was not overlooked. Religious worship was provided for. Hobbies were encouraged-painting, carpentry, bee culture, gardening. Civics were taught-even table manners. These men went back to their communities as well rounded citizens. What they have done for conservation stands as a living memorial to their courage, their prowess, and their will to be good citizens, appreciative of the opportunities afored them. They were a great blessing to American and to the conservation of important resources to make America.

Southern Region-Atlanta, Georgia. Largely through the fire control improvements and facilities constructed by the CCC it has been possible for the state foresters in the southern region to provide fire control for millions of acres of privately owned timber lands that otherwise would have continued to suffer severe damage annually. At the beginning of the CCC program in 1933, there were about 47 million acres in the south receiving forest fire protection. By January 1, 1942, this area had increased to 75 million acres.

The CCC opened the portals to millions of outdoor recreation seekers at a time Uncle Sam wanted every worker to get rest and relaxation necessary to send him back to his job doubly efficient.

The build-up and the education of three million youths proved to the people of the United States that the CCC program was a worthwhile investment previous to WW II. Its tremendous accomplishments in less than a decade serves to remind us that the nation is fortunate in having done so much toward building up the essential resources for our continued existence.

North Central Region-Milwaukee, Wisconsin. Approximately eight billion trees for America's future needs were planted by the CCC in this nine state region on some 800,000 acres left bare by the timber hungry pioneers who built the west. That planting means protection for watersheds, refuge for wildlife, lumber for peace and war, and jobs for local people. Seedlings for planting came for the most part from nurseries seeded and cared for by enrollees in a total of 1,527,453 man-days of labor.

The establishment of the Corps so closely tied into the creation of the Upper Michigan National Forests that it is hard to visualize just what development would have taken place had there been no CCC. The work of fire suppression has been broad and far-reaching. With the exception of three small lookout towers which existed prior to 1933, the entire protection system for the Marquette and Hiawatha forests has been constructed by enrollees. Since the beginning of the Corps in 1933, the enrollees have carried practically the entire load of fire suppression. They have developed truck trail systems which we have today. In addition to reforestation, there have been approximately 50,000 acres of timberland improved by the use of CCC labor. A large number of public camp and picnic grounds have been built, which are enjoyed by thousands of people during the tourist season.

The residents of southern Indiana will never forget the emergency work of the CCC during the Ohio Flood of 1937, when the organized effort of the enrollees saved countless lives and property that would have otherwise been sept away.

Last and most important was the achievement of the CCC with regard to the final crop of any region-its people. Through its camps in the region have passed some quarter-million boys, untrained, unskilled, many of them uneducated. Their earnings in the CCC helped their families over the lean years of the depression, but their own compensation amounted to more than their $30 per month. They found additional returns in strengthened bodies, keener minds and industrial skills.

Alaska Region-Juneau, Alaska. A large part of the work accomplished during the duration of the CCC program in Alaska was of real value to National defense. Air, sea, and land transportation have been materially benefited by the construction of emergency airplane landing fields in remote areas, the installation of docks, floats and breakwaters, and the construction of standard roads, trails, bridges, shelters, and dog trails. Great strides have been made in the improvement of sanitation and living facilities in the Eskimo and Indian villages through the development of water systems, drainage ditches, sewerage disposal systems, hydro-electric plants, model homes and simple walks. Recreational areas throughout the National Forests have been developed by the construction of shelters, cabins, bathhouses, picnic areas and trails.

CCC in Puerto Rico. There were great needs in 1933 for conservation work in Puerto Rico and there still are. With a total land area of nearly two million acres, nearly 500,000 are largely unproductive with a dense population average, nearly one person per acre. Forest products of all kinds are badly needed.

The steep mountain slopes are subject to heavy rainfall. The sugar cane area of the plains has a scant rainfall. The denuded mountains and the improvement of stream-flow conditions are therefore extremely important. One of the first jobs started in Puerto Rico, therefore, was the expansion of existing government tree nurseries and the building of new nurseries to furnish the needed planting stock.

The U.S. Forest Service handled both the camps and the work, the Army acted as a disbursing agent only. CCC work on the island was directed by the forest supervisor at Rio Piedras under the general supervision of the U.S. Regional Forest at Atlanta. The CCC organization on the island differed greatly from that in the States. Married as well as single men were eligible for the camps and there was no top age limit. Most of the enrollees were from the mountain areas rather than towns. Regular and nourishing meals with a liberal use of quinine wrought great change in the health of the enrollees, besides the work, both with hand tools and machinery, gave valuable training to the men. Enrollees proved to be careful, energetic and dependable workers.

PART II

THE VALUE OF THE CCC TO THE ENROLLEES AND THEIR FAMILIES

To obtain information for this section of the History, letters were sent to daily and other newspapers in all sections of the United States. The editors were requested to print my letter addressed to former enrollees, army commanders, camp supervisors and others, asking that they write me a letter giving their experiences during the CCC days of 1933-1942. As a result of those letters, the writer has received over 300 interesting letters of which about 75 are published entirely or in part in this volume. Some of the letters contained little information of interest.

These letters not only tell of their experiences and the history of our country, but also they remind and enlighten many of us about the serious depression days and its toll upon the lives of our people. How many youths could be found today, who would be willing to sign up to work for our country at a wage of $6.00 per hour, as compared with the enrollee's $25.00 per month (which went back to the enrollee's family) and $5.00 monthly spending money?

The following letters are listed under separate headings and reflect history which is better told by the enrollee than by anyone else. Thousands of enrollees were directly benefited. They were trained, fed, cared for and paid $5.00 per month. New arrivals at camp were often scrawny and listless and in a month they responded with renewed spirits. They increased in weight and their complexion was better.

The enrollee felt that he was working to help his family, many of whom were in dire need. Many families were kept from the relief rolls with the small monthly check. They were interested and proud of what their sons were doing.

A wide range of education was received by the enrollees from their part in the CCC programs. They learned of methods to conserve and harvest and protect our forests. They saw the need for and learned how to take care of soil erosion by revegetation and diversion ditches to furnish water for arid areas. They saw the dangerous effect of certain insects and animals upon forest and agricultural crops. A large number of the enrollees learned to read and write and our newer aliens also learned to use our language.

Their close association with each other taught them how to get along and cooperate with their neighbors and fellowmen. Though there was no severe army discipline they soon respected the need of it in their daily life. They were taught to use tools and operate heavy equipment of all kinds. Their entire training fitted them aptly for the many similar tasks which they met later in the armed services.

RELIGIOUS TOLERANCE

In each camp, religious training was made available to all by clergymen of Catholic, Jewish or Protestant faiths who were attached to the camps as chaplains. The enrollee, if he chose, could go to a church of his faith in the community.

Manuel Gomez of Montpelier, Vt. wrote, "This work phase in which I spent two years of my life happened over 40 years ago but the benefits I derived have stayed with me all of this time.

We lived with boys from farms, cities and small towns; every nationality and most religious denominations were represented in our camp. Regardless of what nationality or religion we professed to have, basically we had all the virtues and shortcomings. We had blacks in our camp-this was before integration was accepted in our country.. I got to know these boys in work and play and realized that discrimination had no place in our world. Taking a look at the world today, we certainly got along much better then in the problems of living and working together.

"There was an intensive safety program in the CCCs. We were taught how to carry and use tools safely in all phases of our work. The forester in charge of our safety program did an excellent job in making us safety conscious in the way we worked and lived. This safety training has never left me. This was over 45 years ago when most businesses had not recognized the value of safety programs.

"Working on construction and in the forest did wonders for all of us. Boys coming from large cities and mill towns of Massachusetts came into camp underweight and pale but soon gained weight and healthy complexions. In this outdoor life we learned to do a hard day's labor. We also developed a love for nature and a caring that it not be abused by selfish interests.

"Summing these thoughts up, I don't know if this work phase could operate successfully in this country today but I am sure that in many of the developing countries with problems of unifying and getting along, that it would work very well. Instead of giving these countries more munitions and weapons we should help subsidize programs like the Civilian Conservations Corps- and the world would be better for it."

Hauling Poles.

Irving H. Moore was a technical forestry foreman with the U.S. Forest Service on the Chippewa National Forest at Cass Lake, Minnesota from the inception of the CCC until its termination. "I handled CCC crews in the field under all types of conditions."

FAMILY SUPPORT

The sum of $25.00 per month of the enrollees pay was sent back to his family, and helped to keep many families off the relief rolls. It gave also to the enrollee a sense that he was working to help his parents.

Major Malcolm V. Fortier reported on the history and work of Company 4606 Camp Paul, BR-56 of Rupert, Idaho as follows: "Company 4606 was organized on July 16, 1938 at Camp Eureka, Congerville, Illinois and the cadre moved on to Sparta, Wisconsin where the company was filled and then on to Rupert, Idaho where a camp was set up in the sage brush. The work project, as developed under the Bureau of Reclamation technical staff, consisted of jobs that helped insure the delivery of water to farmers to irrigate their farms. Willows were cut from canal banks to prevent loss of water from the growth of roots in the canals. Canals were lined with eight inches of clay to prevent seepage and loss of water into the sand below. Canal banks that were subject to damage by rodents, wind, live stock or water erosion were surfaced with fitted rock, called rip rap, to insure permanency.

Various activities such as baseball, basketball, music and amateur shows provided leisure time enjoyment. Through the work on the leveled camp area the lonely desert was changed by the CCC into a home atmosphere with flowers, shrubs and trees."

Frank G. Schmidt of 8437 Livingston Road, Coleraine Township, stated, "I enlisted in September 1937. I was 18 years old and went to Yellowstone Park. I went home after nine months and enlisted again in January 1939."

"We had no money. My father worked in a foundry. My $25 came home and paid the rent. It was a good clean life of discipline. Everything was spit and polish. You were outdoors all the time. You slept out under the stars at night. You learned how to get along with people, with the fellows. I think it shaped my life. I learned you don't get anything unless you work for it."

Joe S. Perkins of Willisburg, Kentucky writes: "In 1933 I had no job nor any hope of obtaining one during the depression, like so many others of my age. I was from a large family and there was no money to further my education. It was hard for families to exist in those days of no welfare and no social services. So at 18, I joined the CCC at Hemet, California and was sent to Camp Kenworthy in the mountains, Company 537. Our main duties were cutting fire trails and breaks and fighting forest fires. After a few months I became an army truck driver hauling supplies to camp and taking enrollees on weekend excursions to Long Beach, Catalina Island, San Diego, and Tijauna, Mexico.

"After about 10 months we were transferred to Moran, Wyoming. We lived in squad tents on east shore of Jackson Lake, 15 miles south of Yellowstone National Park. I was the ambulance driver for several camps in the area.

"I came home in 1934, after 13 months in the CCC, returning to my hometown of Willisburg. I got married. I found my first job as a truck driver due to my CCC experience. Later I started working in a general merchandise store at a salary of $1.00 a day. After a few years I bought the store, where I served the public for 41 years until I retired in 1977.

"To me the CCC was a wonderful experience, a great character builder for us and even an education itself. I have always been grateful for the experience."

Louis I. Schneider of Company #772 states, "I came from a family of 12 kids, back in those days when a lot of people were out of work including my dad. I went into the CCC to help him keep food in the rest of their mouths and keep them in school. I got through the 5th grade. I was in a camp at Cascade, Iowa and then moved to Sigourney. To some who came from ne'er-do-well families it meant experience and a pastime. You sure could tell, because they always got the good jobs like truck drivers, while the rest of us hunkeys, either walked through tall timbers pulling hackberry or made water ways of terraces or crushed rock, but, all in all, we had a lot of fun.

"All in all, I believe the three Cs was a very good thing in more ways than one. It made men out of us, we know how to live on very little and that's something most of the youths could not do today. Mrs. Schneider and I have been married for 43 years and we have four daughters to whom we have given a good education. I have been a free lance carpenter all these years. I have never made much money but we have got along OK."

L.J. Millikin, Camp 832, Fox Park, Wyoming: "I enlisted in the CCC in October, 1935. I lied about my age which was 15. I was broke and hungry. I was eventually made an assistant leader. My father got along very well on the $25 per month which was sent him. I worked at several side camps on timber work in the winter; and in the summer it was road work, building picnic grounds, cabins, and buck fences. The CCC was a very good thing for the enrollee and his family and the country as a whole. Due to the determination of today's youth, a program like the CCC could never work. I can't recall a single instance where any one from our camp got into trouble."

J.B. Whittaker of Richardson, Texas writes as follows: "My dad was a farmer and during the depression he lost his farm. He insisted that all six of us kids got a decent education. Had he not been so anxious, I could have helped him and he would not have lost his farm. There were no jobs in those days, so I came to Dallas, Texas to live with my aunt. I had no trade so I could not find a job. I stayed until Christmas and then went home. I had no more got in the house than my dad said, 'Son I am

C.C.C. Barracks

glad that you are back, I want to talk with you.' We went into the bedroom and he began to cry. Only the day before he had gone to the county seat and applied for relief. The lousy bunch of people who were working there (they had been on relief) asked if he was applying for relief. 'Not Harvey Whittaker.' I told him not to take it too hard.

"I joined the CCC and was sent on January 5, 1935, to Brownwood, Texas. We worked like we were getting top wages. We were building some rock steps and boat landing out of great big boulders, building roads and stone cabins. Late in the summer we were shipped to Tucumcari, New Mexico to finish up work on a park. When we finished there we went to Clovis to clean up work there.

"I asked the commanding officer what he thought of us going to church. He gave his assent and I rounded up about thirty who went on the first Sunday at least. We had a good image with the towns people until with the arrival of some local Indians and California replacements. I give credit to the CCC. Otherwise, I shudder to think what would have happened to me."

Robert R. Shaver of Cedar Rapids joined the CCC in 1933 and was assigned to a camp at Archville, Tennessee in the Cherokee National Forest. "In those days there were no truck trails up the mountain so the ranger had to walk or ride horseback. We built truck trails, and cleared the forest of brush, thus making it easier to fight forest fires. We built some dams on the streams.

"Our camp was composed of all types of people including the local men, whom we called hillbillies. They knew the country and how to survive and were in charge of the working parties. They knew how to handle dynamite, fell trees, use axes and cross cut saws. Without them we would have been lost. We had a group from New York, some of whom were unable to read and had very little writing ability. Since I had finished high school I got a job as clerk. I volunteered and built a lean-to on the PX building and stocked it with books and newspapers. I was surprised how many used the place.

"The city slickers each chipped in five cents a week to one of the hardy natives, who was up at five and had a roaring fire going at six when we rolled out. When we went to town there were some problems when the local boys and the city boys would get into a free for all, which was not too often.

"My folks were poor. There wasn't work. I had only a 6th grade education. It meant an income of $5.00 for me and $25.00 sent home to my family. They had an educational advisor with whom you could take up wood working, telegraphy, typing, leather craft. They taught us long enough so we learned them. We built roads for fire protection out through the timber. I drove a truck some of the time but I did not like that job. We learned music and took up boxing.

"I was also a grease monkey on bulldozers in Fly camp. I was on the head end of a road detail where the surveyors and blasters were working. I was a jack hammer operator there."

O.D. Curry, then 45, enrolled in the CCC at Blair, Oklahoma where he lived. He was blacksmith and worked on road construction crews. The drought had dried out the land so, with no farm work, there was no work for blacksmiths. His family of seven was hungry and so he enlisted. He was shipped to Wetumka, Oklahoma where he worked most of the time as a foreman. His major job was the building of stock ponds on the farms. They were scooped out with fresnos drawn by horses, since they had no equipment. He also taught blacksmithing to the youths. They built walls around cemeteries and constructed tables and benches, stone walks, cement benches. Other work was done in the school yards. The farmers were shown how to plow to prevent soil erosion.

James Maloney of Monticello, Iowa joined the CCC on May 27, 1933 and was sent to Brimson, Minnesota to Company #719, in which he served for 13 months.
"The barracks were constructed by the CCC from lumber sawn on the site in an old sawmill from pine logs, which were salvaged from the bottom of a shallow lake. They had remained there for many years and were perfectly preserved. A long, pike pole and chain were the primitive method to retrieve the logs from the mud bottom. When located by a pike pole, the end of the log was raised and a chain fastened around it and pulled to shore by a boat. The other end of the log was similarly raised.

Home Sweet Home to Co. 538

"The camps were heated by wood stoves made of 55 gallon steel drums set horizontally on legs in sand boxes. The sleeping facility in the beginning was on a cot with a straw mattress which you stuffed yourself. When the barracks were built, we had double bunks with mattresses. To wash our clothes, sheets, etc., we were furnished brown chunks of laundry soap. Wooden kegs with homemade plungers consisting of a tin can nailed to a peeled sapling served for the washing job.

"During the 13 months, we planted thousands of white and Norway pine seedlings, fought seven forest fires, built a ten mile road complete with bridges using an old Fordson tractor, dynamite for the numerous boulders, and lots of picks and shovels. We also cut and set many telephone poles, which we dragged out of the cedar swamps. In the winter, we strung 30 miles of telephone lines to two towers. I was picked to act as one of the linesmen. Other jobs included white pine blister rust control (as described in other states), roadside clean-up of dead trees and brush and cutting a large amount of pulpwood on this state forest area.

"We worked in the forest in the winter thinning out pulpwood trees if the temperature was above 30 degrees below zero. There was no gold-bricking, since you kept moving or froze.

"I think that a program like the CCCs would be a great benefit to the youth of today, but I do not think that the young people would be willing to endure the toil and hardships that we took for granted. Most of us came from families hard hit by the depression and had never known any kind of affluent lifestyle. We simply accepted conditions as they were."

James Alfred Miller of Parma, Idaho, who joined the CCC in 1933, was shipped to Camp Remote in Company 757. "They issued us a pair of dress pants, our work clothes, a razor, soap, metal soap box, metal looking glass, toothbrush and paste, a barracks bag to keep our clothes and other things in.

"My folks were poor. There was no work. I had only a sixth grade education. It meant an income for me. Under an educational adviser, we could take up wood working, telegraphy, typing, leather craft and Morse code, after which we had grasped these, we could take up other jobs or crafts.

"We built fire roads out through the timber. I drove a truck some but didn't like the job. I had K.P. for one week in the two years. I stayed in as long as they allowed. Also I was a grease monkey on bulldozers in the Fly Camp. I operated a jackhammer at the head of the road construction. Crews followed us clearing, piling and burning brush. We constructed a road through the mountains to meet up with another crew from Bend.

"In September, 1933 I signed up at Ainsworth, Nebraska and was shipped to Omaha, Nebraska and from there we went to Eugene, Oregon. We were then taken to the Camas Valley CCC. I spent two

Thanksgivings and one Christmas there and arrived home for Christmas 1934.''

Albert W. Frazier, Covedale, Ohio said that he was flat on his back when he joined the CCC in 1934.

"My brother joined in 1933; he was in one of the early companies. It was a little strange at first, almost like going into the army. It (CCC) kept a lot of young fellows from the street or from going to jail. Anyway, making $25 a month at the time was doing pretty well.''

"The first forest fire I went on (in Yellowstone National Park), I almost lost my life. The fire took to the crown of the trees and can travel up to 40 miles an hour. We were in the path.''

"We would get up with revelry and eat a pretty hearty breakfast. Most of the time we worked about eight hours and had weekends off, except for KP. The guys got along pretty well.''

Ivan E. Koehler started his tour of duty in April, 1934, at Bastrop, Texas as part of Co. 1805. From there he was shipped to Camp S 29-T at Ottine, Texas, where he worked in the construction of the Palmetto State Park, which is next to the Gonzales Warm Springs Foundation.

Ivan traveled much being transferred in October, 1935, to Co. 2853 in Tuscon, Arizona at SP-6-A and on May, 1936, he moved to Gillette, Wyoming to Co. 2853, where he was supply sergeant. In October, 1936, his company moved to Lone Pine, California. In July, 1937, we moved up to Mammoth Lakes Camp F-100 until October to work on the Mammoth Lakes State Park. Then they went back to Lone Pine and in December, 1937, to DG-12 at Inyokern, California and then transferred back to Texas.

Arthur R. Merrill was in a veterans camp in western Kansas in 1936. During a terrible dust storm on one afternoon, they were going by truck out to where they were making water holes. One of the men called "Slats", who weighed 140 pounds and was 6 ft. 4 in. tall got out to open a cattle gate. From out of nowhere a large black bull rushed at him, knocking him down in a furrow in the field. The 25 men in the truck stayed there acting like they were paralyzed. Arthur Merrill grabbed a tiling spade and rushed to "Slats" rescue, giving the bull a sharp cut on the nose with the spade. By holding the bull at bay "Slats" got up onto the truck in safety.

George Beam, of 1728 Dewey Avenue, Priceville, Kentucky and a post office employee, said his experience with the CCC taught him independence and helped him adjust to WW II. "I had never been away from home and asked my father if I could go. I had only been in the Tri-State area. I had never slept on a train, but the boys who were never on a train got sick and tired of the train." The tour of duty took Beam to Kentucky, California, Idaho where he fought forest fires. Fighting forest fires was a terrible, traumatic experience. When it came to the war, however, he said such experiences helped make the transition easier. "During the war, the (CCC) boys had a jump on the other boys. We had discipline, the experience of living in barracks, getting along with others."

"If a fellow did it right, it could broaden his life in many respects. All in all, it was a wonderful experience. It did the country a lot of good and was a constructive thing for all concerned."

Frances L. Waters wrote: "I went into the CCC quite by accident, as I was a replacement for a member who cancelled out. I graduated from high school in June, 1933, and it was impossible to find a job. I did paint two houses and worked for a grocery store for a short time. As I walked up the street past a grocery store, the man in charge came out and asked if I would be interested in joining the CCC. I asked the man when I was to leave, and he said 2 p.m. that afternoon.

"I went home and talked with my mother and then decided that it was best that I go. My Dad was a coal miner working part time and I had a younger sister whom we were trying to put through high school. I then decided that I would talk with my girl friend, who agreed if I was to be gone only six months (I stayed 15 months and she got married before my return after sending me a "Dear John" letter). There were 17 Randolph boys who took the railroad to St. Louis where we had an eight hour layover and went to see Mae West at Lowe's Theater. We arrived in Chicago at about 8:30 a.m. after an all night's ride on a milk train. We spent half a day filling out papers before we left for Fort Sheridan, north of Chicago.

"After arriving at Fort Sheridan, we were fed our first meal in 24 hours, which consisted of a slice of large summer sausage between two slices of bread and a tin cup of black coffee. We were then shown to our quarters which consisted of a tent like a Civil War Sibley one, which would quarter eight persons. There was no wood so we scrounged along the banks of the lake and found only wet wood which filled our tent with smoke. If you have ever slept on the shores of Lake Michigan in a tent in November, you can imagine our comfort. We slept with our clothes on, covered by two blankets.

"After about ten days, we left for Vancouver, Washington, where we roosted again in tents. Then we were taken to a permanent camp, known as Brouden, situated along Lewis River. On the trip, one of the enrollees was hit with an Idaho russet, breaking his glasses. We halted the truck and 150 of us took after the boys and warped their pants real good.

"Our mission was to construct a road from Cougar, Washington to the town of White Salmon, a distance of 22 miles. On our first day of work, it rained all day and all night until we were washed out of camp on Christmas Eve. We were given rain clothes, boots, gloves and hats to use each morning. We had one bulldozer and a dynamite crew and the rest of us felled trees which were small for virgin timber. The following crew bucked up the timber into a length that could be easily piled along the road, and set afire. The last crew dynamited all the stumps and then the bulldozer was used to remove them.

"Shortly after lights out on Christmas Eve, 1933, we heard quite a commotion and the forest ranger opened the door and told all of us to get our rain clothes on, since we were to move out. I noticed water running in the front door and running out the back one. Mud had slid off the mountain back of the recreation hall where it reached the roof. I picked up my toothbrush and a box of cookies, a Christmas gift, and we started single file for high ground four miles away. In the pouring rain, it was pitch dark so you were lucky to be able to follow a man with a yellow raincoat. We came to a small stream called a dry creek, which normally you could jump across, but now it was a raging torrent. The forest ranger had felled three large trees so on hands and knees we were able to cross over.

"When we reached higher ground, we were packed into trucks and taken to an evacuated camp where we spent the rest of Christmas Eve on the floor, hobo fashion (Your head on my shoulder and my head on yours). The next day, we were trucked back to Vancouver, where we remained for three weeks before returning to our old inundated camp. It was a task to clean up our camp and its surroundings.

"We had no power saws in 1933, just two man crosscut ones. The wood was cut for the camp and one man spent the day splitting kindling. Supplies were hauled from Vancouver in a truck which also brought 55 gallon drums of gasoline. One night we had supper of potatoes soaked in gasoline and then made into stew. This action was the cause of a new officer in camp.

"In the spring we moved to a site in northeastern Washington near the Idaho-Canadian line. For our tent, we hewed timbers for a floor and covered them with plank. Here we had a dining room and a nice recreation hall. Our task was to fall timber burned a few years previously and reforest it with young seedlings. This work soon ended since we were called out to fight a fire, which burned 40,000 acres. We spent two months on the fire, sleeping in bed rolls on the ground. Lunches were delivered daily and we used our axes to open the canned goods. A group of us were trapped by a fire one night, where we had to climb the mountain to a clearing and slept there until morning.

"We cleared strips about 40 feet wide ahead of the fire and had men stationed every 15 to 30 feet to make a backfire against the coming blaze. With a wind change, the fire lane was jumped and we had to fall back and start all over again. We worked up to 18 hours some days and we were glad to see rain again.

"We were rewarded for overtime, given a truck and a 55 gallon drum of gasoline with rations for a weekend trip which we took to the

Pendleton Round-up, down the Columbia River to seaside and back through Seattle.

"After finishing our six months at Myers Falls, we were transferred to Seiad Valley in northern California on the Klamath River near a gold mine. Our work here was mostly clearing and building a road. When they found out that I had graduated from high school, they made me a clerk where I did not stay long due to loneliness.

"The immediate preceeding company was comprised of youths from the east side of New York. It took some time for the natives to get used to us midwesterners. They finally opened up their homes and gave us a farewell supper where we had a nice time. This camp was Heaven compared with what we had, and the weather was out of this world."

LEARNING SKILLS

This category includes on the job training and job experience. A large proportion of the enrollees had never had a job. Many had never used, let alone seen, a hammer, ax or saw. Here they were taught how to use tools and equipment including jack hammers, compressors; how to drive heavy trucks and trailers and bulldozers. From the educational adviser they learned to read and write, and many trades; how to use a typewriter and adding machine and do bookkeeping, etc. From the foreman in the field they learned vocations.

Jack Vincent was a CCC educational adviser at a camp in Richfield Center, Wisconsin. He was an unusually successful educator. He stated, "My work was to teach over 150 boys how to read and write. They had to write a letter home and read a newspaper before they got the coveted reading and writing certificate. I also got 182 boys their high school diplomas. The highlight of my career was when I had 22 CCC boys graduate in cap and gown in the Pasedena Rose Bowl along with the rich kids of Pasedena. A millionaire furnished the caps and gowns for me. A judge, Leonard Schaeffer, called me from San Diego not long ago and told me he was one of the 22 I kept after, until he completed high school. If I had not kept after him, he would never realized his ambition to become a judge.

"Also, we had classes in truck driving, mechanics, typing, journalism, cooking and baking. My greatest thrill in the CCC was attending the Worlds Fair with five chosen enrollees from Richland Center, Wisconsin. I met President Roosevelt and interviewed him for the camp paper. Later he sent me his autographed picture at Camp Peanut, Hayfork, California."

J.A. Taylor states, "It has been a most gratifying experience to me assembling some of the important accomplishments and activities of the early years on the Green Mountain National Forest. Admittedly, probably my greatest interest was in the period which the CCC program was operating on the National Forest, since I had been a part of it, as an enrollee from July, 1933 to June, 1934, and for the rest of its life as an employee in the Forest Supervisors offices at Laconia, New Hampshire and Rutland, Vermont.

"I was selected at Bellows Falls, Vermont and started my career at the Weston CCC Camp, Weston, Vermont. After spending only a few days at Hapgood Pond, shoveling muck from the old Hapgood dam site, I was interviewed by Camp Superintendent, Paul Bedard and offered the position of Forest Service clerk at the camp. Through this assignment, I was able to learn much about the Forest Service programs and became quite interested in working for the Agency. After serving about 11 months at the camp, I was offered a position in the Headquarters office at Laconia, N.H. which I accepted without any reservations.

"During 1934, offers of employment in private industry were turned down because I felt that I should devote my efforts toward securing a permanent appointment with the Forest Service. Fortunately, I did secure an appointment in 1936.

"I have never regretted my decision to enter the CCC and feel very fortunate to have had such a gratifying career. Through almost forty years of service no program has ever stood out, in my opinion, as making such wonderful contributions to the development of our National Forests."

An Eureka, Kansas CCCer helped to build Woodson County Lake at Toronto before his Company 4702 was transferred to Burlington, Kansas. Stationed here about a year, he helped to build terraces, outlets, channels and ponds since this was a soil erosion camp. Longing to see more of the country as an assistant leader, he was finally transferred to Co. 4715 where he was made a leader.

When the camp disbanded, he went to Waterville, Minnesota, where he worked building concrete dams on streams connecting lakes, to control water levels in the lakes. He was discharged in July, 1937.

"I believe the CCC was a great thing for everyone, especially for us boys. I learned operating heavy equipment among many other things, and especially the value of discipline which seems lacking in our younger generation today.

"I came out of the CCC and after about one year got married and am still, to the same wonderful woman for over 41 years.

"I hitch-hiked to Co. 1516, Hardinsburg, Kentucky, 30 miles away, where I met the educational adviser, and was enrolled. When he found out that I had high school typing and was a ball pitcher in school plus some ROTC, I was in uniform in an hour with stripes as assistant leader. A cadre left soon to form another company and I sewed on another stripe as a senior leader.

"During the time at this company, the Commanding Officer gave me the authority to operate the company as I liked. I taught the men military discipline and courtesy, close order drill, pride in their uniforms and company grounds. As a result of this, in two years, we were the 5th Corps Area Honor Camp."

"But our good times were not to last. On paynight "Whorehouse Blondie" insisted on spending time in the woods with our men. We had continuous outbreaks of veneral diseases. In 1936 we had two enrollees murdered in town. On a Monday when our men were on their way to the field, they ran down two civilians in town.

"As for the benefits derived from the CCC, I believe the following: Pre-trained men for WW 2, preserved and restored soil and forest land, got boys off the street, fed parents, taught boys how to get along with people, and developed a personal pride and patriotism."

"Company 1825 of Fort Sill, Oklahoma, moved to Wilburton, Oklahoma under a State Forestry Superintendent, Mr. George M. Brown. The enrollees were World War I veterans with the exception of two Spanish American War Veterans.

"The early major projects were building dams on Fourche Moline Creek, planting pine seedlings and building a watch tower on a mountain peak. A complete water system was built, which supplied the camp with water from the famous "Iron Springs" located near the camp. The camp operated its own electrical power plant."

"While the CCC men were fighting forest fires in the rugged mountains in the Selway-Bitterroot Wilderness in the Idaho-Montana border, northern Cascades in Washington, or Eastern Oklahoma, the U.S. Forest Service was experimenting on parachuting men in to fight the fires. In 1935, the Forest Service started aerial fire control experiments using water and chemical bombs. The planes and equipment were the major problems in the early tests. Later in 1939, professional riggers and jumpers were used in an experiment at Winthrop, Washington at Okanagan National Forest. A small group of parachutists or later called "Smokejumpers" made 60 live jumps. Toward the end, a few Forest Service fire fighters volunteered to jump.

"Early equipment was designed by Frank M. Derry. Basic design has remained mostly unchanged today but minor revisions have been made using nylon and silk and modern foam has replaced felt padding. In 1940, two squads of smokerjumpers were organized; one squad at Winthrop Washington and the other in Montana near the Idaho border."

Floyd R. Boals wrote, "On June 20, 1933 I became a mechanic in the NPS Camp SP #11 at Grant City State Park at Makanda, Illinois, about 60 miles north of Cairo. I served until June, 1942. Duties included the servicing of all the working equipment such as tractors, trucks, air compressors and cement mixers. I also had to keep an ample supply of spare parts and select and train operators of the equipment.

"The work of Company #696 consisted of building roads, guard fences, bridges, picnic shelters, cutting stone for buildings and brick laying. In 1937, when the Ohio River went on a rampage (the worst flood in history to that time), we had to go to Cairo to protect it from going under water. We worked day and night carrying sand bags and doing almost everything that we could to save the town."

T. Taplin, now 71, recalls his time spent in the CCC in a Cavendish, Vermont camp. "I worked driving a truck at the East Barre CCC dam job for a contractor until the work was completed. Then I enlisted in the CCC and on one weekend on my way home with a fellow who had measles, I caught them. I reported to my Captain, who placed me in quarantine for ten days. I lived chiefly on soup, for three weeks had passed. Then I had a good meal of baked beans.

"My field work at the camp was the brushing out of road areas, which eventually extended through the forest. It was cold work in January, 1934, with the thermometer hovering around zero most of the time. I had a chance to take K.P. duty since I figured that it would be warmer there. One day two of us were holding a contest to see who could slice a loaf of bread the quickest. I won because he sliced his finger and quit. We invited some New York boys to go on a snowshoe hike on the week end. We had not gone far when the New Yorkers gave up and walked back to camp. We used small wheelbarrows to cart soil. The captain told us to carry only five round pointed shovels full which seemed odd to those of us who were accustomed to more."

Frank Pedneau writes, "My beginning in the CCC was over 45 years ago and it is difficult to go back that far and remember. My first enrollment came from Harvey, Louisiana, a small town across the river from New Orleans. I had been working there on new locks being built for a canal from Harvey to Corpus Cristi, Texas, making two dollars a day and happy to get it. My enrollment was in Fort Barrancas, Florida and moved from there in about 30 days to Co. 1486 at Kratz Springs, Louisiana, a village on the Atxha River. My enrollment ended in June, 1934, and I went to Dallas looking for work, but none was available. Since the C.O. at Flagstaff requested an experienced clerk, which was scarcer than polar bears in the middle of the desert, my extension was approved. We spent 1934 and 1935 between Flagstaff and Camp Verde, Arizona.

"In the summer of 1935 we were sent to Tucson where I spent the best part of my CCC career. The camp had a golf course and the canteen had beer. Being the supply sergeant my work in the morning was brief and much of the morning was spent on the golf course. I was a duffer but my partner was very good so we bought very few rounds of beer.

"From Tucson in 1936, we went to Gillette, Wyoming. The project there was putting out fires in underground seams of coal. It didn't work and the last I heard the fires were still burning. Late in 1936 we came to

Co. 526, Lone Pine, California. We moved back and forth several times from Lone Pine to Mammoth Lake to Kernville to Inyokern. At that time there were about six buildings in Inyokern and nothing at Ridge Crest on China Lake Naval Base. At Inyokern, the company was disbanded and most of the boys returned to Texas. Being married by then, I joined a newly formed company that was sent to Mammoth Lakes. Since I was mess sergeant of the disbanded company I had made a very careful inventory of the mess supplies. This large supply of staples I took to the new mess, needless to say our mess fund got off to a good start. My last camp was in Death Valley where I got a job in a talc mine near the Town of Darwin, California. Since 1968 to 1978, I have been working for the school district in Lone Pine."

Leo D. Thompson writes, "The camp I served in was Co. 526 at Lone Pine, California. We arrived at Lone Pine about 2 p.m. and were met by several Forest Service men and trucks. Lone Pine is about 5,260 ft. above sea level, and we were taken up Lone Pine Canyon about 5 miles right at the foot hills of Mt. Whitney. The camp was about 1200 feet higher than Lone Pine. There was nothing there but some rocks, cactus and rattle snakes. Tent floors had been built by local men and we had from about three p.m. until dark to put up tents for 190 men, new members of CCC. We were some of the first men from the east to be sent to California. I stayed for another six months and was sent to Co. 536 Camp Anza, which is about 60 miles southeast of Riverdale."

Mario William Franck who was in a CCC camp at Guernsey, Idaho wrote: "We went to Cheyenne where we were enrolled and lived in tents. We worked at K.P. duties in the soldiers barracks and cleaning the graveyards and in the barns. Our camp was then established on the west side of Guernsey Lake where we built our barracks first. A Texas company was located across the lake. We kept quite busy building roads and paths. We had a specialized hobby of chipping stone by hand for the "million dollar outhouse".

"There were twenty negroes, who had their own segregated barracks, but we all worked together. On Wednesday nights we staged our own shows. I was later a musical major at Wyoming University.

"Once a flood came down the valley bringing dead horses and cows. This was in 1934-35, when we had the bad dust storms that caused us to stay in our barracks for several days at a time. At times the odor of skunks was so bad that we had to congregate in the bathhouse after being perfumed."

John T. Creaser, Plymouth, Vermont, writes; "The first construction project by the technical service was to cut spruce logs, and construct a two-story building to serve as an office and technical staff dormitory style quarters. To develop a recreational area on a site which had been lumbered for pulp wood, there were acres of slash and windfalls which had to be cleaned up and burned. With the lack of tools and vehicles in the beginning, this was an ideal project. The third project was locating and marking all of the boundaries of the Calvin Coolidge State Forest.

"The winter of 1933-34 was unseasonably cold. One week the temperature did not go above 20° with night temperatures at a minus 35 degrees. The water systems were frozen solid.

"My assignment, with four enrollees, was to survey and stake our truck trails and recreation roads. I was equipped with only a compass, tape and Abney hand level. Curves were laid out by a chord method. Straight lines were run with a staff compass. I also surveyed and plotted a road from Route 100 opposite Black Pond to meet the road being built from Shrewsbury.

"Two forest fire projects were accomplished out of our camp. The steel for the Okemo Mt. tower was drawn by horses on sleds to the mountain top in winter. The steel for the Killington Mt. fire tower was brought to the summit by a tractor and sled. A side camp was erected here to construct it. The supervisor and a dozen enrollees had their camp there destroyed by the 1938 hurricane, but there were no injuries.

"Several times during the life of the camp, it was necessary to assist the Town of Plymouth and the state to clear the road of snow from the camp to Ludlow, about eight miles, to insure the movement of food and mail.

The 1927 Flood, Montpelier, Vermont

"The personnel from our camp developed the picnic area at Gifford Woods State Park. Here a combination stone caretakers quarters with a picnic loggia and toilet building were erected.

"In the spring of 1935, I was reclassified as Truck Trail Locator and began to work on assignments out of the camp area. Then we were supplied with transit, level, rods and other surveying equipment and a station wagon. An enrollee was assigned to help me.

"My succeeding duties included the surveying, designing and laying out roads, parking areas and buildings at Shrewsbury, Killington, Aitken Forest, Thetford Hill, Sandbar, Mt. Mansfield, Underhill, Maidstone, Roxbury, Allis Park, Groton Forest, Woodford, Sharon, Grafton, Paul Stream and Fayston.

"When the 1936 flood occurred, I was detailed to the Bellows Falls Camp to assist in reopening that camp for flood sufferers. I offered CCC assistance to a Westminster farmer who had 200 bales of hay covered with water. Instead of letting us spread out the hay to dry, he gave me a verbal lashing. He said in no uncertain terms that he did not want any assistance from a "gang of Roosevelt pups". Perhaps if he had, he would have saved his hay when his barn burned from spontaneous combustion a few days later.

"With engineer, Charles Lord, we worked on a survey of a proposed parkway along Lake Champlain for a distance of 15 miles from Sand Bar to St. Albans Bay. The end of the CCC terminated this survey.

"As the entire CCC program began to terminate, I was assigned to the Underhill camp to work with the Corps of Engineers to design training aids for various army contingents. These projects included a moving target representing a tank or personnel carrier. The target was to be used for machine gun and antitank practice."

Joe Batistella wrote: "We spent the winter of 1935-36 at Camp Bungalow across the Clearwater River from the Bungalow Ranger Station. In the spring, we moved to Camp Upper Beaver, a summer tent camp. Our project was to fell all trees in a 600 acre tract left standing by a lumber firm which was only interested in trees of commercial value. The theory behind the setting the fire was to set off a huge blaze in the center and when it was reaching its peak, the signal was sent to touch off small fires around the perimeter. The huge blaze in the center was supposed to create huge drafts thereby drawing the flames from the outer edge toward the center. But nobody consulted Mother Nature; a strong wind came up. Sparks flew across the break and soon spot fires were cropping up around. To compound our efforts to curb the raging blaze, the fire crowned in some areas and before we brought it under control, some 1,300 acres had been burned. Fortunately, the extra 800 acres that were burned unexpectedly, had been scheduled to be treated the same on the following year."

"The personnel in my company was distributed among 13 companies in Illinois, Wisconsin and Michigan. I was sent to Camp Crivitz near the village of the same name where I remained until the spring of 1937, when the company was disbanded. I was sent to Camp Echo also in the Dairy State from which I was discharged in June, 1937.

"Early in 1937, while still at Camp Crivitz, a message went out for all CCC volunteers to head to the Ohio River Valley to battle the flooding of the Ohio River which was made up of the Allegheny and Monongahela. I declined. I prevailed on one of the truck drivers to teach me how to drive. In April, word arrived that the company was to be disbanded. The result was that I drove a truck to town with loads of equipment from the camp to be disbanded.

"Among other things at Camp Crivitz, I had charge of a crew working around a fish hatchery, helped plant trees, fought a couple of fires, and did roadside clean-up."

Ralph A. Figuerosa, Co. 1231, Canon City, Oregon states: "In the winter of 1939, I arrived in New York from Puerto Rico. For a 17 year old, I was frail and my biggest problem was the language. In January 1940, I entered the CCC and was sent to Camp Canyon Creek, Canyon City, Oregon. I was there January through December. Most of my work was in the forest. Because the type of work I was doing was extremely physical, I was able to build up my body and, at the same time, I became familiar with the English language. Most of us in that camp were from the east coast; i.e., New York, New Jersey. At the camp, I was known as Ralph or Chiqui (short for Chiquito which means shorty).

"At the end of 1940, I returned to New York City, ready to face the world, thanks to the training that I received in the CCC. I retired from the U.S. Air Force in 1973 after 30 years of service, and today I am working for the Delaware State Department of Labor. I have accomplished plenty in the Armed Forces, and now with the state; however, I will always be grateful for the first break after arriving in the United States, and that was in the CCC."

Bill Gyorfi says: "I was stationed at Fort Ethan Allen, Vermont in January 1935 in the 170th Supply Co. as a clerk taking care of 18 camps in issuing clothing, hardware and other supplies. I enjoyed the stay in the CCC very much. I think it was the best thing that could happen to a young fellow of 18 at that time.

"I took a course in typing and bookkeeping at Burlington High School twice a week. I think in all my life I enjoyed the CCCs the best. There was always something doing. I wish they would start some programs like that for the generation we have now.

"I left the 170 Supply Company in June, 1937, to accept employment with the Vermont Marble Company as a draftsman.

"All the training I got in the CCCs helped me when I went into the army and spent 4 years in England and France.

"As an assistant leader I did sign painting and lettered signs for other camps, too. In 1940, I went to work for the Coca-Cola Company where I worked for 39 years doing all their sign work."

Wendell E. Bulger, #790, Custer, South Dakota says: "I do not believe that the shelterbelts of South Dakota started before 1935-1936. As I recall, the main way to combat drifting soil in dust storms was planting Sudan grass and cane which started about 1935. Then tree belts were started perhaps 75 feet wide every couple of miles to stop dust and the sweep of the wind. Otherwise our sandy topsoil, without water, literally kept blowing across plain states from North Dakota down to the Gulf of Mexico. Or tumble weeds would blow for many miles until they came to a woven wire fence and then pile up. Then the dust would clog in the tumble weeds until finally the entire fence was buried and then dust would blow over it. You could then drive a car or tractor over the buried fence. There was much work done to combat the hordes of locusts. I believe it consisted of destroying their nesting eggs along fences of tumbleweeds, or pits of crude oil, or to drive around and trap locusts."

"Our main job was thinning jack pine stands to seed growth, burning brush in winter. Each CCC boy had a doublebitted axe, one blade for trees, one for roots near racks. We also had a bush hook for small saplings too flexible to chop with an axe."

"Most South Dakota CCC camps were in the Black Hills, and the Lightning Creek fire of 1934 was so severe that every camp in the Hills fought it. We were transferred to Belvidere, South Dakota on the edge of the Pine Ridge Indian Reservation where we built a 1,200 foot earthen dam. We had the dam mostly riprapped with rock when a sudden cloudburst came. Without entire stone riprapping, the water broke through and washed out a 100 foot section of the dam. There were coyotes, Bad Lands and some rattlers there. At the nearby reservation, the common sight was a government wooden shack of about 8 x 16 feet with some cottonwood poles alongside to form a sheltered patio from the sun. It was surrounded by acres of barren waste that could only support 50 jack rabbits and one coyote every 5 square miles. A whole Indian family would have to live there."

Jesse Kirby Camp 160 Hurricane, Utah says: "I was enrolled in April, 1939, at the age of 22 at Fort Knox, Kentucky. I was dispatched to St. George, Utah to a Division of Grazing Camp #45 and finally to Camp 160 at Hurricane, Utah where I worked maintaining and driving trucks, gasoline powered water pumps and electrical generating plants at Short Creek, Arizona. We generated our own electricity. I took typing and bookkeeping at a night school at Hurricane High School.

"I am still impressed with the CCC and what it did for the conservation of the country's resources including what it did for the men in it. It was very educational in many ways. I consider my stay in the CCC as an excellent way to be introduced to the military. I had no problem when I got into the military. I think that the country will have to get back into something on this order before we get control of our destiny. I am in favor of some form of military life for every young person due to my CCC experience and that of the Army."

Manuel R. Martinez says: "I was in a CCC camp in 1934, located in the Stonewall State Park area west of Trinidad, Colorado. We built roads, planted trees, placed rocks, anything to beautify the existing surroundings. In 1935, I was transferred to a soil conservation camp in the Colorado Springs area. After three months of planting trees, grass, contour plowing, I was sent to a cook and bakery school for instruction during a two week period. I was then transferred to the food department as night baker. It was not long before I was promoted to second cook, working days. Very soon I was made a first cook and promoted to Mess Sergeant, which is why my tour of duty lasted for four years.

"During 1938-39 I took a correspondence course with the Lewis Hotel Training Center of Washington, D.C. I was discharged in 1939, with one of the highest commendations a commanding officer could give.

"Our camp had a mixture of Latins, colored and a company of enrollees from Boston, a real hodgepodge.

"I am over 62 and consider the CCC the happiest period of my life, and I have met others who feel the same. We were disciplined and worked hard during working hours but the government took good care of us, and our free time was a happy association with fine youths."

Planting Wild Cranberry for Game Food

"When I went into the CCC, I got my belly filled with the best nourishing food I'd seen in years. I got the first complete outfit of good clothing I had had in nearly nine years. I had a fine doctor for the first time in my life and a fine hospital. I got $5 per months and $25 was sent home to help my family who desperately needed it, and I was taught some skills."

"It is a pity that today's youth can't have the huge Conservation Corps that we had. It would solve youth crime, youth unemployment and benefit the nation, like our forestry work, dams, roads and bridges did in the thirties."

Carl Johnson; Willow Springs, Missouri, Manila Camp F-35 Wyoming. "I was enlisted at West Plains, Missouri on October 7, 1936 and went by troop train to Ft. Leavenworth, Kansas, where we were housed in tents. We went by troop train to Green River and then by truck to Manila Camp F-35 in Wyoming. The barracks were in a canyon above Manila in Utah. While there we did some road work, with jack hammers and dynamite and built a road along side the canyon. We also built a Ranger station and fire tower and constructed 50 miles of telephone line.

"From there we went to Camp F-41 in the lower part of Utah before the year was up.

"As for what the CCC meant to enrollees there were differences of opinion; some thought the discipline was too strong, while others like myself was there for our own benefit as well as our families. We had some good officers as well as one or two who were not so good. The food was fair. We had a good cook. As for the experience, I think it gave the boys a chance some would otherwise never had. I may be wrong but I believe had it not been for the CCC we would not have roadways or parks as we do today.

"One day it was very quiet and we were creosoting telephone poles, when we heard an explosion. Since we were not dynamiting that day I went to learn what had happened. I saw one of the boys on the ground near the infirmary door and heard him say 'he is up there, go get him' and then collapsed. We found an enrollee with a leg and arm blown off. What had happened was they were carrying a box of dynamite and the bottom fell out and it exploded."

Norman F. LaMaster, Camp 1599, Indiana: "I was a member of Camp 1599, a forestry camp at the Clark State Forest at Henryville, Indiana. I started work as a general laborer pulling weeds in the nursery and also gathering seeds and nuts from trees in the forest for planting in the nursery in the spring. I worked at a small charcoal plant for a week or so where there were three kilns. It was interesting but a bit dirty. After it was learned that I was a high school graduate and had had geometry and algebra, I was placed on the surveying crew as an instrument man in charge of the crew. It was a thrilling experience for a 19 year old. And all that money for my widowed mother.

"I came down with appendicitis and during my recovery I helped with the sick call. This led to an assistant leader so I ended up in charge of the camp dispensary.

"We had a fire tower and a fire fighting team. We were dispatched to fight fires in the area. It was a great experience. The amazing thing about the corps was its members were on their honor. You could leave anytime and it was not held against you. There was not much law breaking. The canteen sold beer, but you had to be 21 to buy it. The discipline was excellent, and we had a very high esprit-des-corps. My year in the camp taught me a lot about getting along with my fellow men.

"I am a retired Air Force civilian aircraft maintenance supervisor. I didn't use any of the skills I learned in the Corps, but I will say one thing. I learned early in life to respect the other man and his property and how to get along with my fellow men."

Leroy A. Lewis, Colorado Camp. "I joined the CCC in June, 1933, and was located at Colorado National Monument. That project was mostly a road construction job through sandstone for pioneer work on what is known as the "Rimrock Drive." I worked on the project for a few months and then they found out that I could type and keep records. I was then given work in the office of the C.O. and the Park Superintendent. Some other jobs such as a truck drive that had the high privilege of going to town once a day, plus working in the supply room occupied me until the spring of 1934. I then got a truck driving job to two summer tent camps at Tabernash and Yampa, Colorado for two months. I was selected on return to the Monument as a member of a cadre for a new camp at Norwood, Colorado. My job at Norwood, a Forest Service camp, was supply leader with a $45 per month pay. The work project was road construction and pine beetle insect control in the adjoining Ponderosa pine forests. I met a young lady in town who is now my wife of 45 years.

"After 13 months at Norwood, I obtained a job at Grand Junction taking care of supplies for the camps in Western Colorado which was a civilian job and paid $105 per month. I served for 26 years in the Army and retired in 1963 with a Lieutenant Colonel's rank."

Harry F. Beasley was a member of Camp F3W Company 852 located in the winter on the Tongue River, Dayton, Wyoming. In the summer "we were encamped in the Big Horn Mountains in a fly camp. The work consisted of cutting lodge pole pine trees for telephone poles, peeling them and then dipping them in oil and tar for preservation. We built 30 miles of telephone lines from the ranger station to the mountain. At the fly camp I was the cook. We built a ranger station, horse barn and shed. We cleared up the down timber. We riprapped the Tongue River banks. We constructed the Syblle Dam. We were called out to fight a forest fire and I marvel that none of us didn't get burned to a crisp but everyone held up their end, from swinging an axe (no chain saws in those days), using a grub hoe.

"It was at the same time that a huge fire was burning just east of Yellowstone Park—across the Bighorn Basin from us—that several CCC boys and supervisor were trapped in a canyon and were burned to death."

Luther D. Davis of Casper, Wyoming enrolled in 1934 and was sent to a National Park Service Camp #SP2W at Saratoga, Wyoming. "The first winter we were planting trees in what was to become a state park, which was located around some mineral springs. This park was located on the North Platte River so a bridge made of rock and cottonwood logs was constructed across the river. In the spring of 1935, I was placed in the truck maintenance shop and worked there until the fall of 1936, when I was discharged from the CCC's and was appointed to the job of mechanic for the National Park Service. In the spring of 1937, we moved to a camp on Casper Mountain, where we worked on a city park on the mountain top, building and surfacing roads with gravel, building picnic tables and shelter houses.

"The camp was at an altitude of 8,000 feet and we lived in tents. It was a little rough when some pretty heavy snows, like 3 or 4 feet, fell and the tents collapsed. We were 12 miles from town and sometimes we had to use a Cat tractor to pull our supply truck down and back out of the snow belt. In the fall of 1937, we moved down out of the mountain to a location near "Old Fort Casper", which was originally an Army post on the Oregon Trail. There we improved the roads and the buildings around the fort. In the process of building roads we dug out five skeletons buried in a knoll near the fort. One of the skeletons had 60 arrowheads in it."

W.E. Jackson Company 538, Idaho writes: "I am one of the younger CCC alumni. I dropped out of high school half way through the tenth grade and joined the CCC in the spring of 1940 at the age of 17. In July, 1940, I was shipped from my home in Cincinnati to Rupert, Idaho where I was assigned with a lot of youngsters from southern Ohio and northern Kentucky to Camp Minidoka, CCC company #538.

"I think that the next year and a half was undoubtedly the happiest and most rewarding months of my life.

"Our primary purpose was the building of irrigation systems in southern Idaho. We had gone through probably the worst drought years in history in the west and midwest during the early thirties. So heavy emphasis was placed on developing an irrigation system so such future castrophies would not wreck havoc on the important agricultural sections of our country.

Our secondary purpose was the building of a beautiful park on the bank of Lake Walcott Reservoir, Rupert, Idaho.

"We were engaged in lining the canals already built with rocks to prevent bank erosion. We used lava rocks which were plentiful in southeastern Idaho. The work which we were doing was called riprapping. After doing riprapping for a few weeks I was assigned to a crew which was digging out the lava rocks. By late fall it was getting cold, so I decided to enroll in a driver training course and became driver 'trainee'. At the end of my six months I reenlisted. Shortly thereafter, I was approached by the educational adviser to assist him, which I did for six months. Again I reenlisted and the foreman of the park asked me to join his crew, which I did. I learned how to use a transit and alidade. With one other enrollee we prepared a topographic map of the park.

"Since I had attended life saving and first aid schools in Pocatello, I was offered the position of first aid attendant to fill the place of the enrollee, who had joined the Navy. The doctor in charge was headquartered at our camp and looked after two other camps. We had a dispensary and a hospital consisting of a six-bed ward and an isolation room. The enrollee in charge of the post exchange elected to leave at the end of his enlistment. I was offered the job which I willingly accepted.

"I finally returned to Cincinatti in the fall of 1941 after eighteen months of enjoying everything that I had done. I worked with a company making wooden boxes and then went to the Wright Aeronautical Corp. In 1943 I joined the Army Aviation Cadet program, from which I received my bars and wings on February 5, 1945. Part of my training was at the University of Vermont from 1943 to May 1944."

Canal Bank Sloping

Ray W. Meeks of Anamosa, Iowa stated as follows: "I joined the CCC in 1937 and stayed in until 1939. I helped plant small trees to aid soil erosion. I worked in a stone quarry—it was something to do. I also served as a truck driver. I enjoyed every day of that life. It was a wonderful experience for anyone of that age. It was a paid home away from home. No clothes to buy, no food to buy, all expenses paid. It was a marvelous duty for the young, which should be in effect now."

Glen W. Lane of Campbellville, Kentucky, was enrolled in April, 1937, and stationed in a Bureau of Reclamation Camp (BR) 24, Company 2506 at Caldwell, Idaho. The camp was located on Deer Flat on the shore of Deer Flat Lake. "We were putting riprap on 6,800 feet of the banks of earth and gravel on a dam. After the first six months, I was promoted from a $30.00 enrollee to a $45.00 leader in one promotion, which was the first one in the history of the company. After leaving the CCC I went to raising tobacco, corn and hay, in in 1952 I went into the dairy business."

Arthur E. Victor of Spokane, Washington wrote and phoned me the following information. "During those CCC days I was assistant Regional Administrator of the CCC camps of the Soil Conservation Service in the three states of Washington, Oregon and Idaho. I maintain that the CCC was the best of the New Deal. I wish that it could be started again under much the same administrative set-up with more discipline. My experience was that 90% of those young men responded to discipline and regular hours and accepted responsibility. The news is all bad today but despite all the bad things we are living better than any generation ever lived. We are 'Spoiled Brats.'

"The enclosed book refers to the CCC and the U.S. Forest Service development of the bulldozer. It is quite apparent that the CCC had a great influence in the development of the bulldozer and certainly was a factor in making it visable to the general public and the construction industry. The CCC provided almost an instant market for the manufacture of the machine."

George B. Kibler was in Camp 772, Sigourney, Iowa: "This camp was a SCS (Soil Conservation Service) camp which did everything about soil erosion, planting trees, grasses, and concrete waterways, etc. My job was driving a state truck to haul men to work in the field. I do remember that every morning we rubbed down the pine board floors of the barracks with paraffin and polished them with gunny sacks.

"This camp closed down in 1938 and was moved to Audubon, Iowa. All of the men were replaced except me and a few others. After I got out of the Navy I worked for the Quaker Oats Company for 32 years.

Alden H. Lane, Waterbury, Vermont camp: "I grew up in Boston and being a city boy it meant a great change in my life when I joined the CCC. I didn't know an axe from a pick and I had never seen an axe. I had never driven a car or truck but I soon learned.

"I got a safety citation for running a jackhammer and blasting. I had charge of the tool room, starting generators for lights and maintaining them. Also I served as night watchman. I learned landscaping as our company made many miles of new roads in the Mt. Mansfield area. If it had not been for the foreman being so strict, and making us toe the mark, I would not have learned half what I did. I was taught to save money and to set higher goals for myself. Discipline was the key; if you didn't do as you were told you got a dishonorable discharge, and this made one think twice before breaking any of the rules.

"The CCC's helped when I entered the service because it had taught me how to work as a team with other men and, of course, the routine basic training helped. I do not know if the generation of today could take the strict discipline and hard work we did. They would get a clean place to live, clothes, their meals, and most of all a trade which they could not otherwise achieve on their own.

"My training in the CCC's helped me to get a job before and after I entered the service. I could always find work from my CCC experience. I became self-employed as an electrical contractor in Arlington, Vermont."

Woodruff G. Leel, Vermont camps: "I joined the CCC in January, 1934, and was assigned to the Ricker Mills camp in Vermont where I worked as a clerk until 1935 when I was transferred to the Waterbury camp as a clerk. I worked in the Thetford camp on white pine blister rust control for a short time, and then I was transferred to the Montpelier office where I worked on automobile reports and inventories.

"When the CCC closed down, I transferred to the U.S. Air Force Base at Windsor Locks, Connecticut. From there I went to Mitchell Field, Long Island, New York where I spent 13 years before entering Pratt and Whitney in the purchasing agent's office."

Arlington Kane: "I was in the CCC at two different times, first for six months in 1936. We traveled from Wheeling, West Virginia by troop train to Superior, Montana, to a camp about 15 miles from there.

"We worked on fire trail road and cleared the underbrush and trees back away from the road. Telephone lines were run along the roads to the outposts. We pruned trees and cleared forest areas.

"Our barracks were heated with stoves made out of 55 gallon drums with legs on them. Over the weekend most of the men went to the only show in town. The canteen was open until ten every night. If you ran out of money, you could borrow up to $3 against your next paycheck. When a guy tried to goldbrick, he ended up on the fire wood detail and hauled wood in rain or shine. Where we were, it was nothing to be snowed in for two or three days at a time. I was discharged in June, 1938.

"I enlisted again for eighteen months, and they were not going to let me stay. They made me a leader which position had no limit. This time I was located in Redmond, Oregon where I met a childhood chum. The camp was set right in the prairie with sand, sage brush, tumble weed, lava rock and juniper trees.

"We worked on a large irrigation ditch that would irrigate two counties. The ditch was banked up as much as 20 feet high and you could drive along the banks of the canal which we ripraped with rough rocks. I learned how to operate a jackhammer. Our dinner consisted of sandwiches of peanut butter and jelly, and cheese, or dog meat, which we had to eat along with the dust. There were no such things as coffee breaks. There were many small lizards of which many made pets.

"In June, we were moved up into the mountains where an earth dam with concrete locks was being built. We cleared a large area for a reservoir and burned the brush. Heavy equipment was used on this project and finally I was able to drive a large caterpillar and a carry-all.

"When I left there in 1940, I felt that the 3C's had done more for me than I could have learned in a good trade. Soon I joined the Army and came out as a technical sergeant."

Fly Camp

D.C. Clark of Marion, Iowa: "I joined the CCC in the spring of 1933 and was sent to Albia, Iowa. I was in camp operations, mostly. The field work was reforestation, soil erosion, and building parks with lakes. We went from Albia to Council Bluffs and later moved to Indianola. I advanced from operations guard to cook, second and first, and acting mess sergeant. From Indianola we went to Chariton, then I transferred to Ottumwa."

Hiram Moger-Co. 759, Roseburg, Oregon writes: "I was inducted May 19, 1933, and was sent to Fort Crook, Omaha, Nebraska. There we were supposed to get two weeks military training but due to lack of our WW I, o.d. clothes, we had three weeks there. We went to Roseburg, Oregon by rail. This was quite a trip for some that had never been away from home. When we got to the camp site, we set up tents in the timber on a government reserve. We lived in tents and ate out of WW I mess kits for six months.

"We worked under the Forestry Service building roads for fire protection and also strung telephone lines back in the reserve to lookout stations. There were a lot of people that came out of California at this time, that had taken up timber claims. Some went broke in 1929 and had come up there to live. They were as far as 16 miles back in the timber with no roads or schools. They lived in log houses, and packed all their supplies in by horses or mules. Most had a cow or goat to milk and they had a small garden.

Co. 580

"There were plenty of bear, deer and fish for meat. They would work around Roseburg in fruit harvest or sell wood and fight forest fires.

"This was one of the best things that happened to me. I learned how to work falling timber, also how to cook. Many boys had jobs driving trucks for the foresters, also heavy equipment, such as bulldozers. Many stayed out there.

"I was one that was riding a freight train looking for work when this chance came up. I always said President Roosevelt took me off a freight and gave me a bed, clothes and food and made me feel like somebody. I think that this is what we need today instead of welfare. Everybody should work for what they get."

Woodrow W. Bryan of Clinton, Kentucky: "I enrolled in the 3 C's in April, 1937 at Fort Knox, Kentucky and was shipped to Camp #538 USBR 56 about twelve miles from Rupert, Idaho. The camp was under the direction of the Bureau of Reclamation. The work consisted of the rock paving inside and outside of canals, building parks, parking lots, fencing of desert areas for control of livestock, and road building. A group of us were given 14 pound hammers and bull pricks or pointed bars to wedge out, loosen and remove some rock ledges. In no time, we were out of wind slinging a 14 pound hammer at 4,500 feet elevation.

"It was amazing when in three months or so, due to the good food, regular hours, etc., what a skinny "Hill Billy" (as we were called) looked like on the raw strength that we had developed.

"At the end of the two year term, I was offered a foreman's job but I decided to go home. I was discharged in 1939. Things were dull in Kentucky so I wrote to a superintendent of a BR Camp, and he accepted me. In a year or so I was promoted to a sub-foreman."

Charles E. Britten wrote: "Times were so hard back in the "dirty thirties" so I enlisted in the CCC. My unit left Ft. Riley, Kansas in September 1935, going by train to Schley, Minnesota, where we arrived on Labor Day. It was a beautiful time of the year, but we were in for a real cold winter, being 54 below zero one Sunday morning.

"I worked for the first month in the timber, scalping out hazel brush and then planting trees. Then I spent the rest of my time there working in the Forestry Office, USFS 32. I enjoyed the work which involved a lot of typing and record keeping. Each project had to be kept separate on the reports. I enjoyed the stay there even though the pay was quite small. I was promoted to assistant leader which meant an increase in pay to $36.00 with $25 sent home to my family which were in need of help at that time as money was very scarce.

"I had a chance to help the Educational Adviser in the evenings. I taught typing and also a little class in journalism, having a camp paper monthly, the *Schley Journal*, of which I was the editor.

"I returned home in the summer of 1936, and since there was no work available, I re-enrolled and spent my time in Kansas camps at Camp Leavenworth, Garnett, and Neodesha. During all this time I spent in the orderly room. I recall the army major telling us we had been receiving training in the CCC which would help us to prepare for WWII which was coming in the future.

"I served in WW II for three years in the Southwest Pacific with the 380th Bombardment Squadron as a clerk and discharged as a staff sergeant.

"I retired after 40 years service with the local welfare department."

A Buffalo, Oklahoma lad preferred learning to become a cook to working in the field. "They were needing cooks so I decided to go to the kitchen, which I enjoyed very much. I took some cooks training at Fort Riley, Kansas and also some at Woodward, Oklahoma. To me the CCC meant survival at that time as jobs were really scarce. I think that the state and nation really benefitted by it, as we helped build ponds, terraces and we planted lots of trees for windbreaks and shelter belts here in Oklahoma. We used to have a lot of snow out here. I would not take anything for the experience and help that I received during my five years as a member. I feel that I benefitted from it when I went into the service. I also made a lot of friends over the state."

Edward M. Cummins of Corbin, Kentucky: "I joined the CCC in 1933 and was assigned to Company 512, Camp P 52, Putney, Kentucky. The camp was located at the foot hills of Pine Mountain on the Poor fork of

At Camp Nine Mile with Bean Sandwiches

the Cumberland River. Part of the time I worked on camp grading, planting grass, setting out trees, etc. I also worked on a road to the fire lookout tower. I did a lot of fire fighting. On weekends a movie house or a few beer joints were about all the recreation that we had. We had a pretty good basketball team and played with teams in Cumberland, Lynch, Benham and Harlan.

"I spent three months in a side camp on the other side of Pine Mountain. We built a telephone line from Bledsoe, Kentucky to the Frontier Nursing Mission. We stayed in a four room rented house on Beech Fork Creek in Leslie County. We cut large dead chestnut trees killed by the blight, which were still solid enough for telephone poles. Another group of three or four erected the poles and pulled the wire to the base of them. I was one of the three linesmen. It was fun to climb the 30 foot poles, secure the insulators in place and tie the wire to the insulators.

"Here we had the best of food with two good cooks. We had plenty of meat, eggs, bread, fruit, coffee. This house had a step stove the first that I ever saw. We dug our own cannel coal which you could almost light with a match. One or two nights the temperature plunged below zero. Three of us put our cots together and we selpt crosswise that allowed us to have nine blankets instead of three covering us."

Ralph R. Brown states: "I was in two different companies in the CCCs, one being Co. 771 which was formed in May, 1933, at Fort Des Moines. Then after doing soil erosion work on farms that summer, we wintered at Camp Dodge where we did a lot of useful work in a couple of state parks around Des Moines. The following spring we headed for Fort Madison, Iowa with half of the company dropping off at Mt. Pleasant, Iowa to complete work unfinished by another company. At Fort Madison we did a lot of tree planting and soil erosion work. In July, I was picked to form a cadre for Company 2716, a new company, which was shipped to Maquoketa, Iowa. Here we did soil erosion work, mined limestone, milled it and took it to the farmers for fertilizer. At the same time we worked at Maquoketa Caves State Park."

Robert Hartwell of Lowell, Massachusetts states: "To start with, my father was a blacksmith in the Ricker's Mill camp and was later transferred to the Poultney, Vermont SCS camp #2142. At the time I did not do well in school. So I joined up with the CCC and that started a learning process that still is in force. I was very anti-social at the time, but you cannot live with a whole bunch of fellows in a barracks without getting along. It can get painful. I credit the CCC with starting me out of my anti-social habit. I still like to be alone at times but not like at that time. There is a plus side for anyone who wants to know what the CCC was good for.

"There was a ¾ ton Bay City Shovel there at the camp and through the old man and the mechanic, I learned how to run heavy equipment. I did real well too. So that led to running other equipment. We did a lot of rip-rapping along the stream. Everything was fun for me anyhow even if I was a loner. The food in camp was good. I could eat everything that they put on my tray and go to Poultney and eat hot dogs, hamburger and candy bars from the PX.

"When I got in the army, I worked at the Boston shipyard running a crane, so that is where that little Bay City shovel started me in the CCC."

William R. Dryer states: "I enrolled in the CCC in the spring of 1935 going to Camp #1858 on the west shore of Lake Gurnsey near Gurnsey, Wyoming. This was a Park Service Camp as far as the work detail; they were making improvements in Gurnsey State Park. In the winter of 1935-1936 I transferred to Camp #3848 near Centennial, Wyoming, which was on the Medicine Bow National Forest; this was a Forest Service Camp as far as work detail. The work here was improvement and clean up work on the Medicine Bow National Forest. I left the CCC in the spring of 1936 back to ranch work in Wyoming. I had been raised on a cattle ranch in Wyoming.

"I reenrolled in the fall of 1936 going to Camp #844 on the east shore of Lake Gurnsey, very soon I left there on a detail to setup a new Camp at Devils Tower, Wyoming, the number of this Camp being #3887, this camp was on Devils Tower National Monument. The National Park Service had control of the work detail, which was improvement of the grounds. I left this camp in the spring of 1937 going to Camp #853 near Dayton, Wyoming; this was another Forest Service Camp. The work was on the Big Horn National Forest which was road building and clean up work as well

1934 CCC Camp Road

as building a dam on Prune Creek named Sibley Lake. I was only there a few months when I went to work for a large cattle ranch near there; this did not last long. I reenrolled late in the fall of 1937 to the same camp site which had been changed in number to Camp #1811. This change came about to honor Company #1811 for the work that they had done on a forest fire on the National Forest which cost the lives of a good many enrollees and some technical personnel. The work was of the same nature as was the work of Camp #853. I left the CCC the fall of 1939.''

A Florida enrollee wrote: "In April, 1933, I enlisted in the CCC and was sent to Fort Benning, where I was given a physical examination and work clothes and then shipped to Green Springs, Florida. We were located at a Camphor Farm camp and some of the group was at a side camp at Pico-lata, Florida. The district forester in charge of the camp was H.J. Malsberger, who became state forester of Florida from 1939-1945.

"In a few weeks time, since I was interested in the work and with some woods and farm experience, I was made a leader and supervised a work crew of 6-12 enrollees. I took an interest in trucks, fire plows, construction, etc., and ran and supervised the operation of some equipment. At this time I was earning $36.00 per month and $25.00 was sent home to my family—they were glad to get it. The camp food was nourishing and the work interesting. We had plenty of work to do on the nearby fire control set-ups.''

Walter L. Mallory, CCC Company 709, F.6: "I enrolled in the CCC on October 1, 1933, and after travel on a troop train landed in Two Harbor, Minnesota and then by truck to Grand Morais on Lake Superior about eight miles from the Canadian line.

"About the first of December, the snow began to fall until the camps were covered with about 18 feet. We had to go and come by a trapdoor in the roof. We had to wear snowshoes to get to the bathhouse and mess hall nearby. We had about 15 Indian civilian workers who kept the bathhouse and mess hall fires going.

"I passed the truck driver's test and so was assigned a 1931 pick-up which was used to make a daily trip to Grand Morais to pick up mail and movie film and other needed things...as the temperature ranged from 10° to 20° below the pick-up was not used. Instead, I went with an Indian by dog sled to Two Harbor to bring the mail.

"On January 1, 1934, the temperature dropped to 39° below, so we packed up and loaded the entire company on to 15 dog sleds, and headed for Two Harbor. We boarded the train and after two day's travel, we were held up a day waiting for a snow plow to clear the rails west. On January 16, 1934, we arrived at Camp Gasquet, California, 45 miles west of Crescent City (temperature 60°). I had many experiences fighting forest fires in California and in Oregon in the Siskyou National Forest.''

Arnold M. Rennie of Louisville, Kentucky entered the CCC in 1938 at the age of 17. He was a member of a camp near Snow Hill, Maryland. "The main purpose, or teaching subject, was forest stand improvement. This was pine tree country and we cut out the diseased, old and unprofitable trees. Another job was the cutting of fire trails and access roads. Occasionally we would fight a forest fire, which was always an exhausting and exciting job. I can still recall getting wet from a leaking pressure hand pump with the can attached to my back. I put more water on myself than on the fire. And who can ever forget the one-lick method while dragging a sawtoothed rake across the ground. And I certainly can never forget the first ax encounter with a black gum tree. I remember the falling of huge trees, the scramble to safety and the resounding crash.

"To me, the experience in the CCC was the opening of my world, which, until that time had been limited and poor in so many ways. My parents died when I was six and the grandparents raised me and died not too many months before I went into the CCC. The camp life not only helped me physically but also psychologically. What a wonderful opportunity and blessing it was for young men in those lean years."

R.W. Michaelsen wrote that: "I was a member of the Corps from April thru November, 1934. My first hitch was spent at Meyers Falls, Washington, and the remainder at Yreka, California. My company No. 602 was made up of a contingent from northern Illinois, namely Rock Island, Rockland, Chicago, etc.

"We spent 52 days on forest fire duty, both fighting and patrolling, part of which was terrifying. Part of the fire was in northeastern Washington and the southeastern portion was in Canada. The fire covered 300,000 acres of timberland. It was a great experience and I would not have missed it for anything."

Ralph C. Oliver joined CCC Co. 2808 at Checotah, Oklahoma. "I first served at Camp DG 52, CCC Co. 875 at Worland, Wyoming from October, 1936, to March, 1938. The projects were building earthen dams, (snow) drift fences and roads. Later I served at Camp SCS-26 Co. 2808 from January, 1939 to December, 1939 with the survey crew, the same work I did in Wyoming. The work consisted of soil conservation, terracing and building pond dams."

J.D. English, Jr. joined Camp P-66-O Co. 876 at Nashoba, Oklahoma. He writes: "It has been many years since I was an enrollee and assistant leader of old Company 876.

"I credit my experience in the CCC with my fast promotions when I suddenly found myself in the U.S. Army in 1941. Because of my camp life experiences I was made barracks leader my first day in the army, acting corporal all during basic training and promoted to First Sergeant on the thirteenth month. I stayed in the army for a total of 22 years and retired in 1962 in the grade of Major of Engineers. Then because of my army experience I became the Veterans Employment Representative for the Grand Prairie Texas office of the Texas Employment Commission. Uppermost in my mind, however, I credit any success I might have had in the army and civilian life directly to the training and motivation I received during my tour in the CCC.''

Company 1808, Broken Bow, Oklahoma: "On the morning of June 19, 1933, a weary crew of sturdy Oklahoma boys arrived in Broken Bow being assigned to a camp in the State's Game Refuge. The company arrived from Fort Sill. An advance guard had already arrived at Broken Bow, and had breakfast ready when the special train rolled in. The trip from Broken Bow to the Game Preserve was difficult because of poor roads after leaving Highway 21. One man reports that the distance from Broken Bow was 33 miles. A temporary camp site had already been selected by Captain William Fisk, and on arrival of the company one of the fastest tent pitching exhibitions was demonstrated to a delegation of local people who were on hand.

"Many projects were completed, among them the construction of a bridge across Mountain Fork River, and a road from the highway to camp.''

George D. Deas says: "I entered the 3C's in April, 1939, and became a member of Company 431 at Marietta, Georgia which is a National Park of the Civil War. I worked in a granite quarry, then at the rock crusher to get material to build a road from the highway to Cheatham Hill, where the battle was fought.

"I planted pine trees, fought forest fires, and had a lookout point in a tower on Kennesaw Mountain. On Sunday I served as a guide to show tourists the National Park, tell of its history and location of the battles.

"I was transferred to Company 6440 at Winnemucca, Nevada in 1941, where we had to fight sagebrush fires at times. The main job was building barbed wire fences to contain cattle and horses. We also did plenty of rural masonry work.

"I enjoyed the CCC; had plenty of good experience and was discharged in 1942. I served in Europe in World War II and in Japan from 1950 to 1955.''

Phil Maunsell, Peru, Vermont wrote: "I was indoctrinated about the first of May at Fort Ethan Allen, and issued the old army regulation uniform. After about a month I was sent to Co. 167, Danby, Vermont, where we lived in tents. After about six weeks we were transferred to Peru where we lived in tents until November when our barracks were built.

"I recall the huge three day snowfall around Christmas which we had to shovel out manually since snowplows and bulldozers would not touch the 25 foot drifts. We had some severe weather with temperatures which fell to 50° below. We worked during the cold weather on a road leading to Danby.

"About the middle of January, we moved back to Danby. The barracks had not been winterized, and were just a shell. We had three small officers wood stoves and a field range set in sand to keep us warm. Sometimes there would be two or more inches of frost on the walls and we went to bed with newspapers under our thin mattresses and all possible clothes piled on top of us. In February, 1934, we had two weeks when temperature was 20° below zero during which period we did not go outside except for supplies and mail. We had a GI can for drinking water and that would freeze solid at night. We also had an old style privy and you can bet there was not much dilly-dallying out there.

"By the way of transportation we had an old F.W.D. and a solid tire Libery which was pretty slow going up ten miles of mountain road from Manchester to Peru."

A North Carolina enrollee wrote: "Three very vivid experiences stand out in my mind while at this camp.

"1. The bed bug invasion that swept the camp in 1933. No one was exempted from this and it took about two months of extensive fumigation of both humans and buildings to clear up this problem.

"2. The near lynching of the Mess Sergeant when it was discovered he was buying spoiled meat crawling with worms and serving it at meals. It took the + + + county sherriff force to stop this uprising.

"3. The invasion of the camp on Saturday nights by the "Ladies of the Night" from the "Red Light" districts of + + + *and* + + +."

Loading Telephone Poles

PERSONAL CARE

They were taught first aid, safety with tools, machinery and equipment. They learned good housekeeping by their K.P. chores, how to make a bed and to clean their clothes, themselves and learned about a proper diet.

A.J. Hill, Co. 1806, Fort Sills, Oklahoma wrote: "In May, 1922, I was sworn in at the Federal Building at Dallas, Texas, given a box of fried chicken and put on a passenger train for Fort Sills, Oklahoma, where we were quartered in WW I Army tents. I think it rained every day for the two weeks we were there, being shaped up for permanent camp. SHOTS, Short Hair Cuts, WW I pants and shirts and hobnail shoes, etc. CCC Co. 1806 organized at Ft. Sill, June 1, 1933, entrained at Turners Falls, arriving at Davis, Oklahoma, June 18, 1933. We arrived on a Sunday morning and were transported by school bus to our camp site outside the park.

"Two hundred strong, we cleared the camp site of knee deep weeds and set up several army tents and we were in business.

"Turners Falls State Park was a nice public recreation spot, ideal swimming, camping, hiking, etc. Since it had no regular maintenance, CCC Co. 1806 was assigned to beautify the park with trails, picnic tables, benches, clean out the swimming pools, build dams. We even built stone steps up a vertical cliff from bottom to top, some 350 steps with resting benches on the way up.

"Being 22 years old when I joined the CCC, I soon learned things I never knew; first, self respect, consideration for my fellowman, something you learn quickly living with 200 other guys like yourself. Many of us had never made up a bunk, washed our own clothes or brushed our teeth regularly. One thing your buddies saw to was that you took a regular bath, had your hair cut and used all the articles that were issued to you. Our first few weeks at camp, we took baths in the ice cold waters of Honey Creek which was near the camp. Later we had a real bathhouse built. There was lots of talent among the camp dwellers; musicians, singers, barbers, crapshooters, cooks, K.P.'s (kitchen police) and boxers.

"We had Crows, Kings, Frost, Snow, Days and Knights. We had Indians, Blacks and Whites; we had 'em all.''

WORK HABITS

They learned to be punctual, to take orders from their superiors, to accept responsibility, to be disciplined and learned to cooperate with others.

Charles "Chuck" Krall writes: "I spent a hitch in the CCC in 1937-1938 at Camp Nine Mile, Alberton, Montana (near Issoula).

"During the fall season we worked on range improvement clearing undesirable brush, poisonous plants, and installing rock erosion control structures. The camp cooks brought out our lunch. Their favorite menu was baked bean sandwiches, and my first and last experience of eating baked bean sandwiches. Whenever I eat a picnic lunch, I often think of the CCC grub.

"During the winter months we worked in a mountain logging camp harvesting logs and poles, primarily telephone poles. The foresters in charge would load us in army trucks and take us to the mountain camp before daybreak. We used horses and mules to skid logs and poles to the loading areas. The animals were kept at the mountain camp in a tent for a barn. Axes and hand saws were used for cutting as chain saws were un-heard-of at the time.

"An experience which I will never forget was my assignment to a one-eyed mule used to drag logs and poles to the loading area. Being a farm boy from central Montana, I was experienced in handling animals. Well, this one-eyed mule was big and ornery. She could outpull any of the horses. When you hooked the chain to a log you had better be out of the way because when that chain clicked she was off to the logging area. One didn't need a watch at quitting time or lunch time because the mule would head for the camp right on time...logs and all if she happened to be hitched to one at the time. Well, to make a long mule story short, the boss gave me a promotion to a job at the loading dock. The promotion lasted exactly one day as it seemed that no one else could handle the one-eyed mule. I had to go back to skidding logs. I suppose that being a farm boy raised with livestock, the old mule and I did communicate as one jackass to another.

"While in camp I took some conservation courses. I credit the CCC experience as the main reason for the conservation field and my thirty year career in the Soil Conservation Service. This employment was after college graduation from Montana State University and World War II."

Delmar H. Gilchrist: "When a student, I enrolled in the CCC on October 24, 1933, and was discharged in September, 1934, from Camp SP-a #895 located at Lincoln Park north of Oklahoma City.

"I think it was the most important thing in my life. I was twenty years old; times were hard and this employment gave me an opportunity to work and to realize the responsibilities of life, the value of a dollar, and how it came; also discipline, how to take orders and comply, even when under pressure, and take it under stride. It was a very worthy cause...

"I met many wonderful people, I had the opportunity to learn many trades. I took diesel mechanics and learned to be a mechanic and learned how to cut and lay rock. Later I became a field foreman in charge of over 28 enrollees.

"We built the camp theater in Lincoln Park, also a new bathhouse on the lake there. We riprapped the north bank of the lake with Spooner no-acks, quarried rock. We built shelter houses and picnic areas at the Spring Lake Park and at Hasseman Park. We planted trees and shrubbery.

"I think it was one of the most beneficial things for young people in my time. We learned responsibility, beautification, and landscaping. All of these things were worth thousands of dollars to Oklahoma City at a very small cost for labor. We need it today and should never have closed it out.''

Eugene T. Squillace, Idaho and Plattsburg, New York wrote: "I remember well the good old days in the CCC. It was a good life as that was depression time and thanks to President Roosevelt for making it possible for helping save many young boys from the poverty and suffering we had to endure during those times. It made men out of us by having to leave home at an early age (I was 17 at the time). You could say that it was like being in the Army. The only difference then was that we were recruited to, and what we did all over the country was build dams, plant trees, fight forest fires and cut down trees. We did a lot of good work in those days and the pay was not much, $30 a month and $22 of that was sent home to the family. We received $8 which had to last for a month, which most of us were able to do, as you know. Then you went to the canteen and bought a pack of Bull Durham with the paper for a nickel and rolled your own cigarettes. You bought a big *O Henry* bar or *Love Nest* candy for a nickel, so with your canteen book worth a dollar, you managed pretty good."

Walt Godfrey, Underhill Center, Vermont stated: "First I think it was a great thing to take young men and teach them the different things to do. I was a leader on a road job working in the woods. I also worked on ski trails and operated all kinds of trucks and tractors. At last I worked in the garage, which I liked. I have worked for the past 38 years in a garage in Underhill. I do not think that I would have had garage work, if it hadn't been for the CCC. I think that they should have something like it today."

Jackhammer Use

Gerald Allard, Afton, Wyoming: "I joined the C's on August 18, 1935, and helped build the Forest Service Camp #3848 which was thirty miles west of Laramie, Wyoming. We cut timber and made "buck fences" to make a forest barrier. During the winter I was on a snowshoe crew of eleven who cut and burned what we called "bug trees." I returned home to Afton on August 4, 1936. I graduated from Star Valley High School in 1937 and in 1938 I rejoined the CCC's."

C.P. Bradford, Manchester, Maine writes that he began his hitch in the CCC as an enrollee and ended as assistant superintendent of the Alfred Camp P 52 (USFS) Company 130. "The two major projects were blister rust and gypsy moth control. In addition I drew the assignment of developing several picnic sites for the State Forestry Department. In the spring we were transferred to Baxter State Park where we were put on the fire line of a bad forest fire, which was out of control. This was quite an experience for the boys of east and south Boston. They, however, proved out and received commendation from the old time lumberjacks."

George Trebert of Wallingford, Connecticut related his experiences as follows: "The day's routine started at about 5:30 to 6 a.m. with a good hot breakfast, after which we rode in a covered army truck to the work area. I learned to drill holes in ledge rock for dynamiting while building a road in a state forest. I operated a bulldozer for moving the rocks and clearing the state forest boundary line.

"Some of the crews were burning the gypsy moths out of the trees with long bamboo poles with an oil soaked rag tied to the end of the pole. For lunch the forester would build a fire, make a large pot of coffee and we had a half hour for lunch, which consisted of two sandwiches—one of peanut butter and jelly and the other of plain peanut butter. Then we would be glad to get back to work in order to keep warm. The ride back to camp was always exciting—everyone trying to guess what was for the evening meal. I must say that after being outdoors all day and coming into a warm building a hot meal was grand to me. Believe me, when I say, I think that I could have eaten a 2 x 4 with gravy.

"I do believe we learned a great deal while in the CCC. My six months stay in the CCC ended, and not too long after returning home I joined the Navy and made a career of it, retiring in 1957."

Peter Swol, Ricker's Mill, Vermont Camp says: "I arrived at Camp Ricker in October 1935. I worked building a camp in the Groton State Forest. I was then assigned to a group cutting and burning timber in the forest for a road. After that I became the camp baker due to my previous bakery experience and worked at it for about six months. After I left camp I got a job in a factory where I worked until 1942 when I was drafted into the Signal Corps. At first I was a cook then a meat cutter, probably because of my experience in the CCC. I held this job until I was discharged in 1935 and then went to work in a factory.

"I have thought a great deal about what the CCC was to me and the experience that I gained from it. After I was drafted it helped me to get along with people, socialize and be comfortable with people.

"We now have four children; one has worked in a factory for ten years, one has a bachelor's degree in Social Science, one has a master's in French and English, and the fourth has a masters in English and Spanish. The latter two are working on PhD's."

CCC Company 1803 was organized on May 31, 1933, at Fort Sill, Oklahoma and on June 11, the men entrained for Eaglet, Oklahoma. Their new home was a logging camp back in the mountains about nine miles from town. During the following month their time was spent mostly in improving the camp site due to the fact that, as yet, they had not received any tools or equipment. The 3Cs lived in tents until about November when the barracks, mess hall, recreation hall and other buildings were completed. Their work was building roads, fire trails and bridges. Soon the regular officers were replaced by Reserve Officers.

William H. Oliver entered the CCC Camp Co. 876 at Nashoba, Oklahoma in 1935 and stayed three years. "My personal opinion is that the CCC provided a lot for boys and their families. I believe the work experience was one of the best training programs. It taught some of us what responsibility

CCC Co. 1803 Tent Camps Ready on Arrival

meant and how to associate with others. Although many were from different backgrounds, we soon became a family.

"I worked in various capacities in the CCC. I drove a truck and most of you will remember that the speed was controlled by a governor, which was set pretty low. I had a truck load of boys and couldn't get up enough speed to make the top of the mountain. Needless to say we started to roll back.

"Another assignment was working in the forestry office. I was also a cat skinner and hammer operator.

"One of my fingers was almost cut off when a buddy who did not stop when I told him to hold it. We were cutting a bolt, getting ready for a new bumper on the truck. I guess I must have been lucky because I was only 50-60 miles from my home town. One reason, the day before my company was to move to Colorado, I came down with the mumps, so I stayed my three years in the same camp at Nashoba. I can still remember many interesting and some frightening experiences. Also we had a lot of fun pulling jokes on new arrivals. We sent a new man out with two large pails to milk the cows. Anyone in the CCC knows we did not have any cows in the CCC.

"Some of the major projects, while I was in camp, were building roads, trails, bridges and fighting forest fires. This was the most hazardous and tiring of all the work."

Mt. Hood, elevation 11,245 ft. is called the Queen of the Oregon Cascades. The CCC and WPA cooperated in developing this area. The CCC blasted out the road to the site of the proposed Timberline Lodge. The men, working with the Mt. Hood Recreation Association and the Federal Forest Service, built a lodge to house 230 guests. It was an architectural dream made of massive glacial scarred rocks.

Joseph Aebisher states: "My first assignment was the CCC Camp at Waterbury, Vermont where I was a Technical Foreman. There were some veterans twenty-five to thirty years older than I who used moonshine as the drink of the day. In order to get them on my side I stood on a mess table and told them that they knew so much more than I did and I would appreciate it if they taught me some of the things that they knew. They cheered me and from then on I had it easy in directing their efforts.

"One of the first projects was when we went to Stowe and built a ski jump. Later, I was assigned to operate a logging camp at Camel's Hump with sixteen enrollees and six horses. This was quite a job for a fellow who had been raised on the sidewalks of New York City. In January, 1934, it was the coldest weather that had hit Vermont in some seventy years. The thermometer did not get above minus 30° for twenty-six days. It was so cold that we bunked and ate next to the horses by keeping the stable door open in the same building. Anyway, our crew cut a lot of logs which were loaded and taken down to the mill.

"My next assignment was at Mendon Mountain near Rutland where I designed and built a picnic area with water lines and a parking area. Here on one day I slashed my forearm while pruning a tree and tied a tourniquet around my arm. After walking three miles to my car, I drove six miles to the Rutland Hospital. I asked to see the doctor and the gal at the desk said I would have to wait because the doctor was busy. The blood started to drop on the floor through the towel that I had wrapped around my arm. When the lady noticed this, she rounded up a doctor in a hurry.

"When the CCC camp closed I stayed there for a while until the superintendent of the Shrewsbury camp, Signey Ruggles, rescued me, and I was transferred there. Here I did everything from cruising timber, running a crew that cut brush in summer, logged, shoveled snow and finally assisted in building what I still consider the most scenic recreational area in Vermont, Northam. I taught myself how to use dynamite, did surveying for the road which was built through the Coolidge Forest from North Shrewsbury to the Plymouth Union Road.

"In retrospect, the Civilian Conservation Corps, in my case, gave me the job experience that I've built on during the rest of my life. On no other job could one be thrown into the responsibilities to the extent which one received in the Corps.

"While at Shrewsbury, I passed the U.S. Army 10-series examination and received a commission as a Second Lieutenant in the U.S. Army Reserve. I entered the Army in 1940 as a construction engineer. Later, since I spoke fluent German, I was placed in Counter-Intelligence in charge of special agents in Germany and retired from the Military in 1962 as a Lieutenant Colonel."

O.W. Strange of Douglas, Wyoming states that he served in CCC company #858 which originated in Willette, Wyoming and was transferred to Tucson, Arizona.

"We built parks and roads within the park. Our camp was just behind the left field fence of Randolph Park, Tucson. We had the opportunity of seeing lots of National League baseball teams work out as that was the training ground of two National League teams.

"Our company was made up of Texas boys other than a few local enlisted men (LEMs) from Arizona. In June, 1935, our company was sent to Casper Mountain, eight miles south of Casper, Wyoming, elevation 8,000 feet. Some snow which fell in May was still on the ground in protected spots. Only the mess hall and the headquarters building were completed when we arrived.

"I was 24 years old when I enlisted so I was older than the average and had truck driving experience. Due to an accident the former truck driver was busted and I got the job, which turned out to be permanent, so that is all that I did while in the CCC.

"The CCC got me off the farm. Being the only child I learned fast to get along with people. Being on the army truck, I guess the big thing I learned and through Lt. Trumbull was to be a man among men."

Wayne Foster of Kansas City, Missouri states: "I joined the CCC on April 12, 1933, and became a member of the first contingent to arrive at Fort Leavenworth that day. They asked for men who had previous military experience. Having been in the National Guard I raised my hand and was promptly delegated to take out a squad and drill them. Soon General Heintzelman drove by, stopped and asked, 'What the hell was I doing'? He told me to forget drilling, check out some equipment and cut down a certain tree about two feet in diameter. Since I had been in the combat engineers, I knew a bit about what I was supposed to do. The rest of the fellows from Kansas City had never seen an axe or saw, let alone use them. The tree was properly cut. The next day a call was made for some one who could type and I became the first chief clerk of headquarters company. I supervised the enrollment of over 10,000 men. Then I had my choice of going anywhere, California, Oregon, etc., and I chose Richmond, Missouri, 40 miles from Kansas City, because I liked Captain J.E. Wharton.

"While in Richmond the town boys decided that they did not like us and started a riot. Since the captain was in Kansas City, an Army sergeant, another guardsman and myself strapped on our 45's, went to town and brought our boys back. The town was put off limits and three days later the Mayor, sheriff and other big shots came to camp and promised that there would be no more trouble. After that we had only one serious fight when one of the enrollees got into a fight and sent five of the town boys to the hospital.

"Company 734 was first located in a City Park in Richmond. Next we were in Big Springs Park in Van Buren, Missouri doing forestry work, building construction, fire towers, roads and park work. From there we moved to Deer Run State Park where we continued similar work. Company 3735 was in Ellington for a very short time. From Ellington we were

A Vermont Side Camp

transferred to Centerville, Missouri, where we were engaged in forestry, fire fighting, soil erosion and road building. We had a side camp at Greenville, of which I was in charge.''

Paul McKinley, as an officer, had his first assignment to a Bureau of Reclamation Camp at Denver, Wyoming. ''When the commanding officer was on leave I gave a less than honorable discharge to the first sergeant for using a quarter of beef at the Fourth-of-July barbecue for friends somewhere away from camp. He was a very proficient operator and a likeable fellow, so I wasn't welcome around there after that.

''Early in the summer of 1937, I was transferred to Cheyenne to the arboretum camp where I took over command after the C.O. left.''

Captain LML reports: ''I came on duty with the CCC as a Reserve First Lieutenant, Infantry in 1935 and was assigned to the Petrified Forest camp twenty miles outside Holbrook, Arizona, as fourth in command. I had been commissioned at Oklahoma State University (ROTC) in May, 1929. The company was in a state of flux-as was about all of my CCC career proved to be. Within two weeks I was commanding the company.

''I was ordered, after one successful year there, to the District Headquarters in Phoenix to be Motor Transport Officer, but before I arrived there the Corps Area Commanding General was retired, so I was shifted to the command of a company at Superstition Mountain. There the drivers of several trucks had been killed in accidents and there was a car stealing ring working among the enrollees. We moved that company to Papago Park, Phoenix. An accident with a drunken driver flipped my car down the highway resulting in a broken back bone. When Uncle Sam decided to send me with the company to Colorado, I decided that I had had enough and went on inactive duty.

''After working for the State of Kansas Income Tax Department for a time I received a telegram asking me if I was interested in coming back to Phoenix. I was, after all the snow and ice of Kansas.

''I was assigned to Safford, Arizona where I had a company of Pennsylvanians, mostly from South Philadelphia. There were all types of people in that company from coal miners to some 42 who had been in reform school in western Pennsylvania, as I understand. I had to send one boy home in a box, as had happened to me before at the Petrified Forest Camp.

''After about a year at Safford I hauled a troop train of 25 Pullmans and two kitchen cars back to New Cumberland Post near Harrisburg, Pennsylvania. This was an interesting trip, as we had a stowaway whom we never located on the entire trip. I stayed back there two months helping the doctors inoculate kids to go west and finally took another train back to New Mexico and Arizona. On this trip one of the enrollees had a nightmare, raised up and went right out through the window. He was found wandering in Plymouth, Ohio, little hurt, put on a train and sent west the next day.

"I took two companies plus mine to Montana and finally was released. In February, 1941, I was called to active duty but because of my back I was released again and had charge of shipping troop trains east and west. I was called up in July, 1941, but never got beyond the Fort Bliss Hospital and given a job to audit books of the companies, investigate, fires, wrecks and murders. So I had quite a varied CCC experience."

Howard C. Peck 167th Co.: "We reported to Fort Ethan Allen, Vermont where we were assigned to the 167th Company and sent to Danby in May, 1933. The 166th company was assigned to Peru, where they were located to build the other end of the road through the Green Mountain National Forest working toward Danby from Landgrove.

"We were quartered in pyramidal tents, eight to each, and a canvas city was born in Danby. During the summer wooden barracks were erected and we moved in from straw filled mattresses to regular cotton felt foundations, a welcome transition.

"In addition to the road project, a side camp was established near Griffith Lake from which trails and recreational sites were constructed.

"While in Danby the members of the 167th took an active part in the social life of the community with parades to the mid town statue on Sunday evening and sing-a-longs with the local people. We had our own baseball team which competed with the local outfits. There was a general integration into the village life of the families, who received us warmly, and I believe contributed to the general rebirth of the community.

"At that time in history the Army was allowed 27½¢ daily for each man and, believe me, we ate well. The mess was excellent, if sometimes repetitous, but a well balanced diet was provided and no food riots ever erupted. Working conditions were hard and primitive with the tools provided for the work. Most of the road layout was made with hand held transits and performed by an enrollee, a Norwich graduate, Peter Molinari, an excellent engineer.

"I served as company clerk and received the magnificent sum of $45.00 per month due to my early training and education in the business college field, which was a satisfaction.

"Late in the fall, we received word that we would move to a site on the Harold Parker State Forest in Massachusetts, near Andover. Work here consisted of construction of recreational areas, ponds for boating and fishing, picnic areas.

"A number of romances developed here and some marriages resulted, including mine, to a local girl.

"I then went on to the 2nd CCC district located at Fort Ethan Allen, where I became a clerk-typist in the Quartermaster office. Later I was assigned to a position at the Boston Army Base.

"I felt that in the CCC we were doing something constructive, a benefit to the community and to future generations to come. I regret now that the program was not continued and most of the constructive innovations that occurred, have been left to fall in disrepair. Impact on my parents was good in that I was away from home and earning my own living, sending some money home, which they really did not need, but they saved it for me. In a larger capacity I was put on my own, learning respect for my ability and gaining a confidence in my ability, that was sadly lacking in that period in history.

"In August, 1938, I resigned to go to work for the old Vermont Savings Bank of Brattleboro, Vermont. This career I pursued until 1942 when I became associated with the First National Bank of Springfield, Vermont to cover over the years as an employee, Officer- and Director-relationship, retiring in 1977 after 35 years service."

Francis Thumma of Phoenix, Arizona joined in April, 1935, a CCC camp near Onondaga, Michigan. "Our first project was to clear fire roads in the forest. Later I was sent to Sault Ste. Marie for a short session on operating power units for new camps. After returning to my home camp, a group of us were shipped across Lake Superior to Siskiwit Bay on Isle Royale. Here we helped open a new camp. We cleared the area near the shore to make it ready for the new CCC contingent. A water line was laid far out into the bay.

"During the early 20's it was very cold and the lake froze over so the moose migrated to the island. The island was overpopulated and it was our task to catch them and take them to the main land. After our scouts were looking for suitable sites to set moose traps, several of the men were treed for the night by an angry moose. On one evening a large moose stuck his head in our tent and became frightened away.

"As assistant leader it was my responsibility to operate the power plant until the baker had completed his daily duties."

NATURE CARE, PROTECTION AND DEVELOPMENT
They learned how to appreciate their surroundings and care for their natural resource and development.

James M. Newton of St. Louis, Missouri, writes: "I am proud to have been associated with the old CCC's. That is where I met my good wife of almost 45 years now! The things I remember most and appreciate very much, are: 1. The good discipline and morale we had in our camps. In fact I believe it was better than in any army camp I was in later. 2. The way (and being in Exchange and Supply, I had occasion to see this) the CCC's built the character and *physical* body of so many. I can well remember helping issue clothing, etc., to new recruits (mostly from our St. Louis area here) who looked so undernourished or ill fed—their skin did not have a good color at all. Within three to six months, the same young men were 'fattened up', had a good color and looked like healthy individuals. 3. So, I (and I believe many others will agree) feel the CCC's *conditioned* most of us who served in the military in World War II. I regret to say it, but I feel the American youth today is far from being disciplined, body conditioned, etc., for and if another war would break out!!! 4. Just an example of the many things I still see as I ride over the country—The Many Trees We Planted.

"Having been born and raised on the Mississippi River, I know how the CCC helped in the flood of 1937 after I left our company 734. Company 734 can be given credit (I'm sure) of having saved the town of Ellington, Missouri from being burned to the ground late in the 1930's."

David P. Leaptrot wrote: "I enlisted in Perry, Georgia, on July 9, 1934 at the age of 18 upon my graduation from high school. I was sent to a camp outside of Albany, Georgia, where the main project was cutting fire breaks in the many cypress swamps. We lived in tents placed on wooden floors and screened-in sides.

"In the fall of 1934 the camp was moved to Andersonville, Georgia (the infamous Civil War Prison and Cemetery), where we worked on the restoration of the prison grounds, fortifications, trenches and pill boxes. On August 18, 1935, I was discharged and joined the Navy where I remained for 23 years. I served the General Services Administration in Denver as regional communications officer as a specialist, and served the needs of the five states of Colorado, Arizona, Wyoming, Utah and New Mexico until I retired in 1971.

"My short tour in the CCC certainly was responsible for my career having taught me *self reliance* and *discipline*. In my way of thinking, its the one and only government program ever initiated that was 100 percent successful in benefitting thousands of young men and World War II veterans."

Ed Norman of Helmet, California: "My service was in northern Wisconsin in an area that had been logged over several decades before by the big timber interests. Our main purpose was to plant trees in the National Forests, to fight fires and build roads.

"There were days in February that, due to the extreme cold when we were lucky to work out for a few hours. Sometimes we would be restricted to camp for all but nine days in the entire month.

"During the summer months we were busy planting seedlings to get them established before winter time. A surprising number of these plantings survived in spite of the deer and porcupines.

"The fire season followed with great demands upon the CCC boys. Hard long days were put in by the crews. Some special crews would travel from camp to camp using vehicles that had been stripped of engine governors allowing the drivers to go at emergency speeds to us there. The crews were billeted and fed the best with officials knowing they would be called to put in long hours on the fire lines without relief.

"During late fall, the deer hunters would enter the areas of the National Forests and the CCC men would be called upon to maintain check stations to log in the kills. The CCCs had no authority. Most hunters were glad to oblige in giving their experiences. This information was useful to surveys kept by the forestry people. Needless to say, the highway kill of deer during the period kept the mess sergeant with a full locker of venison.

"Filling in these busy days of our work schedule, there were, of course, free days, Sundays and Holidays. Much of our free time was spent on studies and self improvement.

"The men upon discharge went many ways. Few of us would deny that character building was a great part of our inheritance from the C-Cs. This writer went into the Marine Corps and now is entering retirement with a commission as a Warrant Officer-4."

Taylor Brown: "I was in the CCC from October 8, 1936 to March 5, 1937, at Kettle Falls, Washington near Growden. Most of the youths were farm boys who had never been away from home.

"That winter was one of the worst winters they ever had. It went to minus 48°.

"The boys who had been in the camp before us were from the state of New York. They must have been pretty rowdy...got to town on Saturday nights and got drunk. They caused a lot of trouble by throwing toilet paper all over town and so some were put in jail. A lot of us went to church on Sunday where I led the singing."

George T. Nixon: "I was born and reared in Saline Co., Missouri. At 16 years of age I enrolled in the CCC and was sent to Salisbury, Missouri. One crew or section as we were called worked in the 10 acre forest tree nursery weeding, watering, cultivating the small seedlings. As this was a soil erosion camp, our work was to prevent soil erosion in farmers' fields and meadows. Ditches were graded, bottoms and banks rounded and dams constructed of osage orange hedge, as we called it, by driving a double line of posts across and in the banks. The space between, we filled with smaller pieces of hedge, limbs, branches, etc. It was then packed tightly and bound tight to the posts on either side with heavy wire.

"In late autumn we dug up the little locust seedlings, tied them in bundles and dug trenches and heeled them in for protection from freezing during the winter months. During the winter we went to nearby river bottoms where there were thickets of small willows. We cut these from ½ to 1½ in. diameter into approximately two foot lengths, tied them into bundles and stored them for the winter. In the spring we took the willows and the locusts to the ditches where we built the dams and planted the locust along the banks. Then while there was mud in the bottoms we drove or pushed the willow sticks into the bottom hoping they would sprout and grow into trees to halt erosion.

"In January, 1936, a part of us were transported to a camp near Murphy, California. There we worked maintaining and building forest service roads and fire trails. I was discharged in April, 1936, and reenrolled in October, 1937. I was sent to a camp near Nevis, Minnesota, which was a forest service camp. We spent the fall days cleaning up a strip on each side of the highway. We cut up the dead, diseased and dying trees into approximately six foot lengths and stacked them up on end (teepee) fashion and burned them after the winter snow came. In the spring, I was transferred to a soil erosion camp at Caledonia, Minnesota near La Crosse, Wisconsin where the work was mainly building ponds and terracing.

"I recall some interesting happenings. We had a very sudden drop in temperature while in the Minnesota camp. Having a couple of agitators in the crew we rebelled and quit working, so the foreman took us back to camp and told the commander that we were on strike. After a stern warning the commander dismissed us. That same night three or four of us took sandwiches and coffee with us and spent the entire night in a shack on a nearby lake, where we spent the time ice skating and eating and drinking coffee. Since this was Friday night we knew that we would not have to work the next day.

"At another time in California we had a load of coal come in by railroad to a nearby town. We were notified that the coal would have to be unloaded that day, Sunday. We were taken over by truck and found out that it was an ordinary box car filled with coal which we had to scoop out by hand and load it into trucks. It was a filthy job which lasted till late in the night. We were black with coal dust with no place to clean up. The commander took us to an all night cafe and ordered a dinner for us all. After looking at us the waitress asked if we had been fighting fire. One of the boys with a glib tongue told her about the terrible task which he colored up with casulaties and all.

"Tricks were always played on new enrollees at each camp. A spark coil from an abandoned model T Ford was attached to the urinal in the bathhouse. When quite a line arrived at the urinals, the switch was turned on, which caused subsequent whooping that reverberated for some time."

Cleon Cain of Co. 2617, Hayward, Wisconsin: "We found our shoes frequently frozen to the floor in the morning—not to mention the disappearance of any sexy aspirations once our footsies touched those ice cold floors."

Bert Holland notes that his Co. 2521, Pinedale, Wyoming was considered as being the farthest city from a railhead in the U.S. It was 110 miles to Kemmer, Wyoming and everything had to be brought in by truck.

Thomas V. Munson stated, "My CCC duty started on July 4, 1937 at Okmulgee, Oklahoma, Camp SP-14-0, Company 2809. After about six months the camp was closed and the men were transferred to nearby camps. Some of the projects were clearing rocks and brush for picnic areas, fireplaces, trails and roads, small bridges and water fountains. About this time more stress was placed on soil conservation in most of Oklahoma. I was transferred to Co. 2808 at Checotah, Oklahoma. The other camps in which I served were located at the following Oklahoma sites, Nashoba and Pryor."

Mr. Munson was a 1st Lieutenant in the CCC. He entered the Army in 1940 where he served for 29 years until his retirement. Ed.

BIBLIOGRAPHY

Reports of Director of Emergency Conservation Work
   April 5, 1933 to September 30, 1933
   October 31, 1933 to March 31, 1934
   April 5, 1933 through June 30, 1935
   Fiscal Year ending June 30, 1936
   Fiscal Year ending June 30, 1937

Report of Director of the Civilian Conservation Corps
   Fiscal Year ending June 30, 1938
   Fiscal Year ending June 30, 1939

Federal Security Agency—Summary of Certain Phases of CCC Program from
   April 5, 1933 to June 30, 1942.
   Fiscal year ending June 30, 1943.

Secretary Harold L. Ickes report on the CCC Program, March 1933-June 30, 1943

Final Report to Secretary of Interior, June, 1944.

Report of the U.S. Forest Service Programs Resulting from the New England Hurricane of September 21, 1938.   February, 1943, 137 Pp.

Report of the ten regional foresters to the Chief of the U.S. Forest Service, 1942.

Biennial report copies and letter from the State Foresters and State Park Directors of the 50 states—1933-1942.

Over 300 letters from former CCC enrollees, Officers and Work Supervisors telling of their experiences in the CCC program.

Humphrey, Hubert. "In A Sense Experimental: the CCC in Louisiana" Louisiana History. 5:27-52, 1964.

Records of the CCC No. 11 National Archives, 1947.

Doze, William H., 1977, Trees, Prairies and People-Tree Planting in the Plains States. U.S. Forest Service and Texas Women's University, Denton, Texas.

Organization and Development of the Soil Conservation Service, 1935.

U.S. Department of Agriculture Century of Service.

The Author's Experience and Knowledge of operations and direction of the CCC Program and his service as State Forester and Selection Agent in 1933.

PART III

THE VALUE OF THE CIVILIAN CONSERVATION CORPS TO THE STATES

For each state, which is listed in alphabetical order, there is a report of the CCC accomplishments during the period 1933-1942. The name of the incumbent state forester or comparable official is listed under the state name, with the date of the establishment of the department or supervisory board shown to the far right. Some states changed their department administrators often, as may be noted. The CCC supplied two types of camps for state land depending upon the Federal supervisory agency and the major type of field work to be accomplished. Camps with the letter "S" before the camp number were engaged chiefly in forest work on state lands. Those with an "SP" were state park camps, whose enrollees were busied with park work. "P" camps were known as private land camps and were chiefly under the forest service. Their work under Federal law restricted the work chiefly to forest fire prevention and suppression which included the construction of truck trails, lookout towers with cabins and telephone lines.

The list of approved projects accomplished in accordance with the Federal laws, as shown earlier in this book, are described in the following pages.

Each state forester and state park director was requested to furnish a xerox copy of his biennial report for the CCC period. Due to losses from fires and other causes, there was no information furnished by a few states, or it was not complete. Information common to more than one state was not repeated in much detail. In some states, Departments of Forests and Parks were formed or enlarged as a result of the CCC.

ALABAMA

Page S. Bunker 1924-1939   Act passed in 1907
J. Brooks Toler 1939-1942   Commission created 1933

Camps
The average distribution of camps by services in Alabama on June 30, 1937 was as follows: National Forests 5, State Forest 1, Private Forests 3, T.V.A. 3, Soil Conservation Service 11, State Parks 9, T.V.A. Parks 2, Military Reservation 1, Total 37.

Employment
The aggregate number of Alabama men given employment in 1937 was 66,837. This figure included 61,411 junior and veteran enrollees and 5,396 non-enrolled personnel of camp officers and supervisory workers.

Work Accomplishments
Telephone lines, miles 1,846
Truck trails and minor roads, miles 3,151
Check dams, erosion control, number 1,126,700
Gully trees planted, erosion control, number 3,558,446
Trees planted, reforestation, number 60,449
Forest stand improvement, acres 124,514
Fighting forest fires, man-days 135,472
Bridges, all types, number 659

Expenditures
Total obligation in Alabama (Est.) $55,592,358
Allotments to dependents by enrollees (Est.) $16,418,038

Forestry
A 50-man side camp from Camp P-70 was assigned to the state nursery at Autaugaville. The work completed there consisted of the construction of four tree cone sheds, an equipment building, underground mains for a sprinkler system, a 200,000 gallon reservoir and an overhead sprinkler system. A five room office building and a five room dwelling were built. A fence was constructed around the nursery and gravel roads were built within the nursery.

As in other southern states, the major work was forest fire protection with the necessary truck trails, telephone lines, towers and cabins.

State Parks
The work done on state parks, as reported, was as follows:

Cheaha State Park
Facilities constructed by CCC included vacation cabins, roads, picnic areas, lake dam, observation tower, group camp lodge, swimming area and hiking trails.

DeSoto State Park
Vacation cabins, roads, picnic areas, bathhouse and hiking trails.

Gulf State Park
   Vacation cottages, roads, picnic area.

Oak Mountain State Park
   * Vacation cottages, * barracks, trails, lake dam, roads.

Chewacla State Park
   Vacation cottages, residences, picnic areas, lake dam and trails.

Monte Sano State Park
   Vacation cottages, picnic areas, trails, overlooks.

* No longer in use.

ARIZONA

Camps
The number of individual camps in the state at various times equalled about 50.
They were: Bureau of Reclamation 2, National Parks and Monuments 4, County
Park 1, Metropolitan Area 1, Fish and Wildlife 1, Soil Conservation Service 15,
Division of Grazing 4, National Forests 18, State Parks 4.

Employment
The aggregate number of Arizona men given employment was 41,362. This figure
included 17,407 junior and veteran enrollees, 19,520 Indians and 4,435 camp
officers and supervisory workers. The number of individuals who worked in
Arizona regardless of the state of origin was 52,905.

Work Accomplishments
Fences and guard rails, rods. 2,254,245
Telephone lines, miles 3,559
Truck trails and minor roads, miles 5,783
Erosion control, check dams, number. 512,093
Gully erosion, trees planted, number. 1,785,506
Trees planted, reforestation, number. 7,451,179
Tree seedlings collected, number 1,304,179

Expenditures
Total obligation in Arizona (Est.). $58,814,534
Allotments to dependents by enrollees (Est.). . . . . $ 3,710,532

State Parks
The CCC worked on the Phoenix and Tucson and Colossal Caves near Tucson
Hualpai Mountains.

ARKANSAS

Charles S. Gillett 1933-1939   Act passed in 1931
Fred H. Lang 1939-

Camps
The average number of CCC camps operated in the state was 37. At one time, 64 camps with an enrollment of about 13,000 men were in operation in the state.

Employment
The aggregate number of Arkansas men given employment was 75,549. This figure included 69,038 junior and veteran enrollees and 6,511 supervisory workers and those who had charge of operating the camps. The number of individuals who worked in Arkansas regardless of the state of origin was 62,882.

Work Accomplished
Bridges, all types, number 4,956
Telephone lines, miles 6,956
Truck trails or minor roads, miles 5,288
Check dams, erosion control, number 82,190
Trees planted, reforestation, number 19,463,745
Forest stand improvement, acres 496,068
Fighting forest fires, fire prevention and
    presuppression, man-days 493,899

Expenditures
Total obligation in Arkansas (Est.) $64,173,024
Allotments to dependents by enrollees (Est.) $17,466,630

Camps
At the height of the CCC program, 16 camps were assigned in Ouachita National Forest, which number dwindled in 1940-41 to 12. At that time there were four camps left under the direction of the forestry department, working on forest fire control. In 1936, there were 15 SCS camps which number was reduced to three in 1941. There were four camps left on state parks and one each on national parks and U.S. Fish and Wildlife Service lands.

Forestry
In May, 1933, Arkansas became the 41st state to establish a state forestry program. Under the direction of State Forester, Charles S. Gillett, a state forestry program was built from scratch. Most of the forestry work then centered on protecting the forests from fires on private lands. Forest fire protective organizations were established on a cooperative basis and agreements were entered into with the state so such protection could be given to private lands.

After an agreement was signed by a fire protective association, the CCC enrollees were allowed to build roads through private forest areas so fire fighters could rapidly reach a fire at its beginning. In addition to roads, forest fire lookout towers and ranger cabins were constructed. The towers were then connected to forest fire headquarters with telephone lines.

The forestry department gained 80 critically needed forest lookouts. The CCC built four district forestry headquarter buildings and 4,000 miles of telephone lines.

The CCC also built the department's first forest tree nursery at Bluff City. CCC crews were trained to aid the department in a program of mapping forest areas by types of forest and sizes.

State Parks

At the beginning of the CCC program, Arkansas had three state parks which were in need of further development.

Petit Jean, a popular area, was established as a state park on 116 acres in 1923 with eventual expansion to 2,500 acres. The CCC work in the park comprised the construction of a bathhouse with beach, a boat dock, parking lot, sewage and water system and water treatment plant. The buildings and other work were accomplished by Veteran Company #1853.

Mount Nebo State Park was established in the 1920's near Dardanelle. With the aid of a land grant the park was eventually expanded to 3,374 acres. The CCC enrollees cleared underbrush, built roads, cut out foot trails, erected small cottages and recreational facilities, which included an amphitheater, lakes, swimming pools, a lodge and an amusement center with a large dancing pavilion.

Crowley's Ridge State Park was established in 1933 in Greene County, and consisted of 270 acres with a three acre lake as the main attraction. The CCC youths built a three thousand seat amphitheater, four miles of park roads and five miles of foot trails in addition to the development of recreational facilities.

Devil's Den State Park, the pride of Northeast Arkansas, grew out of 1,720 acres of tax forfeited land in 1913 and was increased to over 3,600 acres in 1936. There were two CCC camps in the park, which lay in a tree-laden valley, bisected by the meandering Lee Creek. The CCC built 15 miles of roads together with a dam, swimming area, pavilion, trails and picnic areas.

A new method of constructing barracks was used here. They were designed to house 20 to 25 enrollees so that they could later be converted for tourist use as cabins.

Lake Catherine State Park of 2,500 acres was given to the state by a private citizen. The CCC built picnic areas alongside a fish rearing pool for the Arkansas Game and Fish Commission. A major allurement in the park was the "Fishing Village" made up of boat docks, buildings and other facilities, handy for fishermen. The park, which is near Hot Springs, has eight miles of indented shore line along the shore of Lake Catherine.

Municipal Parks

The CCC built in the Boyle and Fair Parks in Little Rock a large pavilion, trails and facilities for a caretaker. In the 231 acre Fair Park, the CCC enrollees worked on a keeper's lodge, public toilets, picnic area and roads.

Soil Erosion

The farmers grew cotton relentlessly on the upland rolling acres for so many years that by 1930, the soil fertility was gone, crops failed and farms were abandoned. With the erosion of lands there was little left but gullies and waste land.

At once soil conservation districts were formed and a camp was installed in each district. The CCC youths hauled and planted sod, built check dams on small creeks, filled in gullies, crushed and hauled limestone to be spread on these fields and planted trees on many acres.

Wildlife
The White River Migratory Waterfowl Refuge consisted of about 8,000 acres of lake area. Three CCC camps worked on this area planting nutgrass, wild millet and smartweed for food. Eight headquarters buildings were constructed and levees, dams and boat trails built. The refuge was surrounded by 27 miles of "hog-proof" barbed wire fence.

CALIFORNIA

M.B. Pratt 1921-1944   Forest Board created 1885

Camps
On the average, California had 98 CCC camps. In the year 1937, the 101 camps were divided as follows among the several services: National Forests 50, Private Forests 10, Biological Survey 1, Soil Conservation Service 9, National Parks 11, State Parks, 15, Division of Grazing 3, Bureau of Reclamation 1, Military Reservation 1.

Employment
The aggregate number of California men given employment was 135,401. This figure included 120,063 junior and veteran enrollees, 2,438 Indians and 12,900 non-enrolled personnel of camp officers and supervisory workers. The number of individuals who worked in California regardless of the state of origin was 166,832.

Work Accomplishments
The major work accomplishments included the following:
Lookout towers and houses, number................................. 306
Telephone lines, miles 8,704
Truck trails and minor roads, miles............................. 1,161,921
Fire prevention and presuppression, man-days...................... 980,010
Trees planted, reforestation, number........................... 30,776,050
Tree and plant disease control, acres............................ 792,612

Expenditures
Total obligation in California (Est.)........................... $154,545,757
Allotments to dependents by enrollees (Est.).................... $ 25,643,910

Camps
Eighteen months previous to the CCC program, the California State Forestry Division had established state labor camps. The concept of government gathering

otherwise unemployed persons and engaging them in productive public works must have originated in the distant past. Thus it is questionable as to who started the idea of work camps.

In 1932, Franklin Delano Roosevelt, as governor of New York, secured legislation for a tree planting program which would give employment to 10,000 young workers in forest camps. Thus it is not surprising that Franklin Roosevelt sent his message to Congress asking for legislation "to relieve distress, build men and build up the Nation's forest resources."

State Forester, M.B. Pratt reported that during the first period of the CCC, the Division of Forestry had the supervision of 22 CCC camps and during the summer of 1934, the number was increased to 32. During the period of 1937-1938, the number had dropped to seven, one in Tuna Count in Los Angeles County, Whitmore, Northwestern, Pine Grove, Mu Madonna and Maxon Ranch. Four of these were in Los Angeles and one in Ventura County. In 1935, the Division had direct supervision over 14 P-camps, while Los Angeles and Ventura had one. There were many other camps on private lands in the state which were supervised by other agencies. From these seven camps there were 25 spike (side) camps.

As a result of severe forest fires, a master plan was developed cooperatively in 1930 by the regional forester, the California Forest Experiment Station and the State Division of Forestry to protect California's forest from fire and devise plans for forest fire suppression. With the advent of the CCC program an opportunity was presented to carry out forest fire presuppression plans, as well as plans for fighting forest fires.

Earlier, the U.S. Regional Forester, Bevier Show, had made the suggestion of

Looking north at south face and summit of Mt. St. Helena. This was difficult road construction. Note brushed telephone line up to South Peak, along ridge to lookout on North Peak. This was all a CCC project.

constructing a forest firebreak at the lower level of pine timber along the Sierra front which was given the name of the Ponderosa Way Firebreak. The original concept of the fireway would have extended a total of 687.5 miles from the Pitt to the Kern River. To compliment the protection a roadway was built as a rule below the firebreak. Twenty-four camps were established to work on this firebreak. The highway was finally taken over by the County Highway System, which road was finally extended to the Shasta lookout. Many fires were prevented from spreading beyond the firebreak.*

In California, the U.S. Forest Service built several forest research stations, such as the Placerville Forest Generic and Tree Breeding Station. Here millions of genetically improved and hybred trees for out-planting were raised each year. The other station at San Dimas in southern California, did research on the watershed problems, which were and still are so critical in California. In southern California there were several unique projects: (1) water spreading grounds on the mountain foothills to replenish the underground reservoirs, (2) brush and rock cabins to protect miles of stream banks, (3) construction of hundreds of miles of firebreaks (50 to 100 feet in width) in the chaparral covered watershed mountains, and (4) wattles to check erosion on exposed slopes.

Mr. Dewitt Nelson was involved in the CCC program from the start in 1933 at Sims in the Sacramento River Canyon, as deputy supervisor of the Shasta National Forest. He had about a dozen CCC camps on his forest at a time. Like in most forests, road access was the first project which was needed for fire fighting access and the management of the forest resource.

State Parks
California had on an average 15 CCC camps which worked on state parks. Work was performed on a large number of the 70 state parks. Among the parks upon which the CCC enrollees worked were: Griffith Park in Los Angeles, Brand Park in Glendale and Steckel Park in Ventura County.

* *California Government and Forestry II* by C. Raymond Clar and published by California Division of Forestry, F.H. Raymond, state forester.

DISTRICT OF COLUMBIA

Camps
There were two camps in the District of Columbia.

Employment
The aggregate number of District of Columbia men given employment was 11,470. This figure included 10,605 junior and veteran enrollees and 865 non-enrolled personnel of camp officers and supervisory workers.

Work Accomplishments
The construction of roads and trails, landscaping and the development of recreational facilities in Rock Creek Park and at the National Arboretum. From 400 to 600 enrollees were at work in the District. Many of the young men selected in the District worked in Maryland and Virginia and some in the western states.

At the National Arboretum, the enrollees constructed roads and trails, ponds, cleared and graded land for shrub and tree planting, looked after nursery stock and eradicated undesirable species.

A partial record of the work performed was as follows:

Bridges, all types, number 20
Camp stoves and fire places, number. 47
Table and bench combinations, number 94
Pipe and tile lines and conduits (flood control), lin. ft. 76,972
Moving and planting trees and shrubs, number 59,943
Lake and pond development, wildlife, man-days. 19,080

Expenditures
Total obligation in District of Columbia (Est.) $4,396,458
Allotments to dependents by enrollees (Est.) $1,982,864

COLORADO

Russell E. Ford, part time 1938-1945

Camps
The CCC camps in Colorado as of June, 1937 was 38, which were divided among the services as follows: National Forests 10, Soil Conservation Service 10, National Parks 6, State Parks 5, Division of Grazing 4, Reclamation Bureau 3. The average number of camps which operated in this state was 34.

Employment
The aggregate number of Colorado men given employment was 35,495. This figure included 29,695 junior and veteran enrolles, 497 Indians and 5,303 camp officers and supervisory workers. The number of individuals who worked in Colorado regardless of the state of origin was 57,944.

Work Accomplishments
Protection to 13,551,000 acres of national forests and 1,159,000 acres of state forests was given to these lands by the construction of fire lookout towers, truck trails and telephone lines. Irrigation facilities were cleaned and improved. Grazing control operations restored grass and water to vast stretches for cattle and sheep grazing. The major work is classified as:

Impounding and large diversion dams, number 577
Truck trails and minor roads, miles 2,000
Check dams, erosion control, number 108,614
Trees planted, reforestation, number. 21,848,085
Fighting forest fires, man-days 201,904
Rodent and predatory animal control, acres 2,676,965
Insect pest control, acres. 3,274,155
Range vegetation, acres 84,528

Expenditures
Total obligation in Colorado (Est.) $63,737,001
Allotments to dependents by enrollees (Est.) .... $ 6,917,708

State Parks
The state of Colorado was one of the last states in the Union to establish a state park system. The Civilian Conservation Corps preceded a state park agency in Colorado.

CONNECTICUT

Austin F. Hawes 1921-1944   Act passed 1901

Camps
The average number of camps was 13. As of June 30, 1937 there were the following camps listed by operating services: State Forests 13, Private Forests 3, State Parks 1.

Employment
The aggregate number of Connecticut men given employment was 30,670. This figure included 28,447 junior and veteran enrollees and 2,223 non-enrolled personnel of camp officers and supervisory workers. The number of individuals who worked in Connecticut regardless of the state of origin was 22,114.

Dust Storm—Colorado. U.S. Forest Service.

Work Accomplishments

Bridges, all types, number. 123
Lookout towers, number 9
Fences and guard rails, rods 29,419
Trees planted, reforestation, number. 5,563,000
Fire prevention and presuppression, man-days. 50,685
Tree and plant disease control, acres 1,606,730
Public camp and picnic ground development, acres. 1,102

Expenditures

Total obligation in Connecticut (Est.) $20,728,446
Allotments to dependents by enrollees (Est.). $ 6,294,182

Three small nurseries were maintained on the Peoples, Natchaug and Nye-Robinson State Forests. From these nurseries about five million seedlings were used to reforest Connecticut idle lands. The species planted included the following: red, white and Scotch pine, Norway and white spruce, Douglas fir and European larch.

Many man-days were expanded in the control of white pine blister rust and the gypsy moth. The Dutch elm disease was first detected in Connecticut in 1933. Over 100,000 dead and diseased trees were cut and destroyed by the enrollees working out from the Danbury camp.

All dead and dying material along the highways was removed and burned 100 feet on either side of the highway. The greensprouts along the sites served as a firebreak. Thousands of waterholes were dug throughout the state, so as to have an available water supply for fire fighting.

State Parks

During this period, Mr. Arthur Parker was the superintendent of state parks. Three state forest camps were located on state parks. At Haystack Mountain a well graded road was constructed to the summit. Road work was carried out at the following state parks: Mohawk, Devil's Hopyard, Rocky Neck, Macedonia Brook, Black Rock, Mt. Tom, Hammonasett, Kent Falls and Squantz Pond.

Recreational development was made on state forests to supplement that which had been done on state parks, so as to accommodate those people who like to get into a wilder setting and away from the crowds. These picnic areas have only a few picnic tables, fireplaces and sanitary facilities. Drinking water was provided by dug wells. Ponds were built by digging or damming streams at the following state forests: Tunxis, Mohawk, Paugnut and Salmon River. Winter sports were encouraged by the development of a system of ski trails. Bathhouses were built at Peoples Forest along the Farmington River, Meshomusic, Nipmuck and Pagnut Forests.

Fishing and Hunting

Fishing and hunting was improved by planting shrubs and trees which bear fruit, nuts and seeds for the wildlife. Many streams were improved as described in other states by riprapping, bank planting, etc.

On Wednesday, March 18, 1936, the dam above Hartford washed out due to heavy rains that flooded one-fifth of the city. Immediate help by CCC enrollees cleaned out 2,950 buildings and over 800 other structures.

Camp Names
Each camp received the name of some prominent person either national, such as President Roosevelt and Robert Fechner or, Connecticut personages such as professors at Yale or leaders in state government.

Forestry
State Forester, Austin Hawes, was more imaginative and far-seeing than other state foresters. One of such projects was the revival of the charcoal industry which once flourished in New England.

Three large brick kilns were built in the Mehomasic, Pauchaug and the Cockaponset State Forests. These kilns had a capacity of about 45 cords. By improving the method of spacing wood in kilns, the production was raised from 44⅔ bushels per cord to 54. The object of this project was to make use of the thinnings and waste wood production by the CCC and to lower the cost of production of charcoal.

Truck Trails
Since the E.C.W. law did not provide for the building of roads, the U.S. Forest Service invented the term "truck trails". The construction of roads and trails in a forest was necessary for the management of the forest and its protection from fire. There were over 150 miles of roads cut and about 400 miles of old log roads cleared.

Administrative Buildings
Forest ranger cabins were constructed and old farm houses in and adjacent to the state forests were repaired for state use. In the Peoples Forest, a nature museum was built using field stone and finished inside with chestnut, a tree which had been killed by the chestnut blight disease.

Sawmills and Shingle Mills
On each of a number of the state forests a building was constructed with a cement foundation to support a portable sawmill, which could be moved to a location where small or large quantities of logs could be sawn. A shed was attached to the building to store sawdust. In other forests, sheds were built for the storage of lumber and shingles.

Insects and Diseases
About 18% of all CCC labor in this state was used in the control of forest insects and disease. (See other New England reports).

About 30 man-days per acre were spent on the management of forest stands, which had not had treatment since they were first cut-over, burned-over or damaged by storms. This work required about five man-days per acre.

DELAWARE

William S. Taber 1927-   Board created 1909
                                                          No funds till 1927

Camps
The maximum number of camps operated in Delaware at any one time was eight. One camp was a State Camp S 53 and the others were soil conservation and mosquito control camps.

Employment
The average number of Delaware men given employment was 5,382. This figure included 4,400 junior and veteran enrollees and 982 non-enrolled personnel of camp officers and supervisory workers. The number of individuals who worked in Delaware regardless of the state of origin was 6,718.

Work Accomplishments
Clearing and cleaning channels, flood control, sq. yds. 12,682,775
Trees planted, number. 274,000
Forest stand improvement, acres. 692
Moving and planting trees and shrubs, number. 31,462
Mosquito control, acres. 52,874
Tree preservation, man-days. 5,841

Expenditures
Total obligation in Delaware (Est.) $8,340,533
Allotments to dependents of enrollees (Est.). . . . . $ 963,831

Camps
Until the purchase by the State Forestry Commission of 1,133 acres of the Redden State Forest, Delaware was the only state in the United States without a CCC camp. In October, 1933, a company of veterans was moved from the Winooski River Flood Control Project in Vermont to a site on the State Forest. This camp was S 53 and the company was #2233V, which was later replaced by a junior company #1293 from New Jersey.

State Forests
The state forests and acres upon which the enrollees worked during the period were as follows:

Redden tract	2,332
Owens tract	179
Ellendale tract	483
Red Lion Demonstration	5
Appenzeller tract	41
	3,030

The type of work accomplished on these areas included: survey and marking of boundaries, truck trail construction, salvage dead and down timber, reforestation, forest stand improvement, fire hazard reduction, foot and horse trails, collection of tree seed and recreational developments.

A forest fire lookout tower on the boundary with Connecticut was jointly operated. The CCC added a 20 foot extension to its base bringing its height to 120 feet.

Recreation
On the Ellendale State Forest, a roadside picnic area with sanitary facilities, log benches and walks were built. On the Redden State Forest, the banks of the Nanticoke River were cribbed. Here, a picnic shelter and facilities were constructed.

Gift
The Red Lion Tract was given to the state in 1930 by Mrs. T. Coleman DuPont. It was reforested with loblolly pine, shortleaf pine and Scotch pine, but up to the inception of the CCC, no work had been done there.

FLORIDA

Harry Lee Baker 1928-1940
Henry J. Malsberger 1940-1945

Camps
The average number of camps operated in Florida was 21. The average distribution by services as of June 30, 1937 was as follows: National Forests 7, Private Forests 9, Animal Industry 1, Biological Survey 1, State Parks 5.

Employment
The aggregate number of Florida men given employment was 49,014. This figure included 45,887 junior and veteran enrollees, 101 Indians and 3,026 non-enrolled personnel of camp officers and supervisory workers.

Work Accomplishments
Bridges, all types, number 2,736
Telephone lines, miles 2,259
Truck trails and minor roads, miles 3,620
Trees planted, reforestation, number 18,924,000
Forest stand improvement, acres 341,121
Fighting forest fires, man-days 97,993
Tree and plant disease & insect control, acres 29,957

Expenditures
Total obligation in Florida (Est.) $34,246,312
Allotments to dependents by enrollees (Est.) $11,037,142

Camps
During the period June 1, 1933 to June 30, 1934, an average of 14 CCC camps worked under the jurisdiction of the Florida Forest Service on 23 locations.

"During the beginning of the Florida Forest Service, forestry progress was an uphill struggle. Open range conditions permitted livestock to graze on anyone's land. The range cattle were usually poor, scrawny animals. The range cattle's main food was a wire grass, good for eight to ten weeks in the spring after the old tough grass of the previous year had been burned. The fire made it easier for the cattle to get the tender green spears for a few weeks. This widespread burning to give cattle new grazing areas resulted in a tremendous number of wild fires for on the average of five months from December to May.

"The advent of the CCC gave the Service man power, trucks, truck trails and bridges which gave quick access to areas not formerly approachable.

"The Service established three types of fire control cooperation:

1. *Individual demonstration*, The landowner fought his own fires with his help. The state provided towers, telephones and hand tools for fighting. The landowner paid the state three cents per acre protected.

2. *Group Unit*, The landowner paid five to ten cents per acre to the state. The state provided detection service, telephone lines, firefighters and fire fighting equipment. The landowner gave some help.

3. *County Wide Protection*, The county paid the state three cents per acre of forest land protected and the state did the entire job.

"A forest tree nursery was established at Olustee along the Jacksonville highway. The buildings constructed included a packing shed, a heeling-in shed, seed extraction plant and residences for the nurseryman and his assistant. Telephone lines were constructed as needed. The CCC personnel assisted in the maintenance of the nursery, the collection of pine cones, seed extraction, and reforestation.

"In addition to the construction of many forest fire towers, cabins and telephone lines, the CCC built truck trails and bridges and did other forestry work. They also built a maintenance and repair shop at Percy.

"A forest survey of approximately five million acres was made.

"A veterans' camp on the Floriday Keys, which was assigned the task of

Towerman's Subsistence Homestead.

eradicating wild cotton plants, was hit by a tornado. The camp was wiped out, killing and injuring many veterans. The railroad was severely torn up." *

State Parks
The act establishing the Florida Forest Service was enacted in 1927. In 1934-1935, the legislature provided for the creation and management of a system of state parks. This new function was delegated to the Florida Board of Forestry. The result was the establishment in the service of the branch of State Forests and Parks. Eventually the name of the department was changed to the Florida Forest and Park Service.

From 1934 to 1942, 12 state parks had been developed wholly or partially by the CCC. At the termination of the CCC program, there were 12 state parks with a combined area of 24,810 acres, The Myakka State Park, serving Manatee and Sarasota counties, was the largest with 12,233 acres.

The development and facilities in these parks are, as a rule, similar to those in many other states. The regular development included picnic and camping area with water and sanitary facilities, picnic and camping layouts, cabins, beach developments with bathhouses. Some of the parks are historical areas which have been developed to bring out those features. Other areas bring out old plantation life, protection of rare forest and plant growth and bird life.

The developed state parks by counties are as follows: Highlands Hammock in Highlands, Hugh Tyler Birch in Broward, Hillsborough River in Hillsborough, Gold Head Branch in Clay, Fort Clinch in Nassau, Myakka River in Manatee and Sarasota, Torreya in Liberty, Florida Caverns in Hamilton and Swannee, Tomoka in Volusia, Pan American in Broward and O'Leno Recreation Area in Columbia and Alachua.

* Reported by C.H. Coulter, ex-State Forester.

GEORGIA

B.M. Lufburrow 1925-1936   1925
Elmer E. Dyal 1936-1937
Frank Hayward 1937-1939
W.C. Hammerle 1939-1942

Camps
The average number of camps operated in Georgia was 35. As of June 30, 1937, the camps under the direction of the various services were as follows: National Forests 9, Private Forests 10, Soil Conservation Service 9, National Park Service 2, State Parks 6, Military Reservation 1.

Employment
The aggregate number of Georgia men given employment was 78,630. This figure included 72,379 junior and veteran enrollees and 6,251 non-enrolled personnel of camp officers and supervisory workers.

Work Accomplishments
Telephone lines, miles 3,638
Check dams, erosion control, number 425,829
Erosion control, planting, seeding or sodding, acres 25,082
Gully-trees planted, number. 1,672,905
Trees planted, reforestation, number. 22,915,095
Fighting forest fires, prevention and presuppression, man-days 153,022

Expenditures
Total obligation in Georgia (Est.). $69,515,199
Allotments to dependents by enrollees (Est.). $19,840,065

Forestry
In 1921, the legislature appointed a board to investigate forestry. In 1925, the first State Forester, B.M. Lufburrow, was appointed by the board. In 1934, the Division of Forestry was placed within the Forestry and Geological Department.

The Timber Protective Organization, which originated in Georgia, made it possible to get CCC camps to work on private forest land in fire protection and suppression. The reduction of fire hazards on thousands of acres were reduced. Lookout towers and houses were built and connected with miles of telephone lines. Truck trails with bridges were built to reach fires sooner. Over 4,250,000 acres were placed under 29 TPO's.

Two forest tree nurseries, one at Albany and the other at Blairsville, were established in 1932.

The Division of Forestry was included in the Department of Natural Resources under a bill passed on March 5, 1937.

Fire Protection. On the Baxley Demonstration forest, the CCC built a residence, office building and machine shop. At headquarters of the TPO units during 1938, 500 watt radio transmitters were erected at two sites for the purpose of contacting fire trucks and towers. The CCC built telephone lines at other locations. District headquarter buildings for five TPO Associations were built.

View of CCC Camp, located at Homerville, Ga.

State Parks
The creation of the Division of State Parks, within the Department of Natural Resources, was legally authorized on March 5, 1937 with Charles N. Elliott as director. Previously, the State Parks were administered by the State Forest Service. Except for Indian Springs, the state park movement was increased with the CCC furnishing man power and funds.

A system of state parks, located within easy reach of the citizens of Georgia, was attained in 1938 with the establishment of eight state parks. They were as follows:

Indian Springs-Butts County. Ceded by Creek Indians to state in 1825.
Vogel-Union County. In 1926 given to state by Fed and August Vogel.
Alexander H. Stephens-Taliaferro County.
Fort Mounlton-Murray County.
Pine Mountain-Harris County.
Cheaw-Lee-Dougherty County.
Little Ocmulgee-Telfair-Wheeler.
Santo Domingo-Glynn, a state monument.

The developments at the state parks included cabins, inns, bathhouses, boat houses, historic and recreational areas with picnic tables and fireplaces.

IDAHO

A.W. Middleton 1933-1935   Established 1925
Franklin Gerard 1937-1944

Camps
The average number of camps operated in Idaho was 51. The average distribution of camps by services was as follows: National Forests 33, State Forests 5, Private Forest 1, Soil Conservation Service 5, State Park 1, Total 51. These figures were for September 30, 1937.

Employment
The aggregate number of Idaho men given employment was 28,074. This figure included 20,292 junior and veteran enrollees, 1,038 Indians and 6,744 non-enrolled personnel of camp officers and supervisory workers. The number of individuals who worked in Idaho regardless of the state of origin was 86,775.

Work Accomplishments
Lookout houses and towers, number..................................236
Impounding and large diversion dams, number.........................91
Telephone lines, miles..3,034
Trees planted, reforestation, number........................28,614,000
Fighting forest fires, man-days...............................484,149
Tree and plant disease and insect pest control, acres.........641,464
Rodent and predatory animal control, acres.................4,049,971

Expenditures

Total obligation in Idaho (Est.) $82,145,878

Allotments to dependents by enrollees (Est.).................... $ 4,134,899

White Pine Blister Rust Control

One of the problems inherent in the West, was the destruction of the western white pine by the fungus disease known as white pine blister rust. Since this disease likewise affects eastern white pine, refer to the New York State report for a description of the disease.

The host plant of the disease, in addition to the white pine, is the currant and gooseberry bush which has the Latin name, *Ribes* sp. The CCC enrollees pulled *Ribes* from several hundred thousand acres. The cost and time spent per acre varied from .27 to 6.45 man-days per acre depending upon the topography and profusion or scarcity per acre. One problem with the control of this disease and forest fire control was the intermingling of Federal and privately owned lands.

State Parks

The only state park in Idaho during the CCC period was located at Heyburn State Park in northern Idaho. This park, which was on an Indian reservation, was sold to the state of Idaho in 1908.

Many state agencies have administered this park since that time - Fish and Game, Public Works, Highways, Lands, and finally in 1965, the Idaho Parks and Recreation Department.

The CCC enrollees moved into the area in October, 1934, and started a park improvement program. The work included the improvement of the park road system, foot trails and bridle paths to various viewpoints, clearing dead and down timber and sanding beaches. The work was carried out under the direction of the San Francisco office of the National Park Service. A shake-roofed bathhouse and caretaker's dwelling was constructed of natural stone. Group picnic shelters were also built. The restrooms and the lodge at Rocky Point are still in use. (Courtesy of Ruth V. Kassens)

ILLINOIS

R.B. Miller 1926-1934   Conservation Department
Stan S. Locke 1935-1936   Established 1917
A.J. Tomasek 1936-1947

Camps

The average number of camps operating in Illinois was 54. The average distribution of camps by services for the period ending September 30, 1937 was as follows: National Forests 8, Private Forest 1, Agricultural Engineering 5, Soil Conservation Service 4, State Parks 27, Military Reservation 1.

Employment

The aggregate number of Illinois men given employment was 165,347. This figure included 155,045 junior and veteran enrollees and 10,302 non-enrolled personnel of camp officers and supervisory workers. The number of individuals who worked in Illinois regardless of the state of origin was 92,094.

Work Accomplishments
Bridges, all types, number. 394
Truck, foot and horse trails, miles 1,192
Check dams, erosion control, number 223,880
Gully erosion, trees planted, number. 28,001,387
Water control structures, flood control, number 4,742
Trees planted, reforestation, number. 32,938,000

Expenditures
Total obligation in Illinois (Est.). $103,669,230
Allotments to dependents by enrollees (Est.). . . . . $ 36,233,793

INDIANA

Ralph F. Wilson 1928-1936   State Board of
H.A. Woods 1936-1941   Forestry 1901-1909
                                      State Forester 1919

Camps
The average number of camps which operated in Indiana was 30. The average distribution of camps by services for the period ending September 30, 1937 was as follows: National Forests 3, State Forests 12, Agricultural Engineering 8, Soil Conservation Service 10, State Parks 7, Military Reservation 1.

Caretakers Quarters—Public, Loggia and Restrooms.

Employment
The aggregate number of Indiana men given employment was 63,742. This figure included 58,673 junior and veteran enrollees and 5,069 non-enrolled personnel of camp officers and supervisory workers. No figures given on out-of-state employees.

Work Accomplishments
Bridges, all types, number...596
Erosion control, check dams, number.............................416,814
Erosion control, planting, acres 81,128
Gully erosion, trees planted, number.......................... 15,767,840
Trees planted, reforestation, acres.............................. 23,676,000
Moving and planting trees and shrubs, landscaping, number.......... 2,063,082
Wildlife shelters, number 580

Expenditures
Total obligation in Indiana (Est.).............................. $55,300,723
Allotments to dependents by enrollees (Est.).................... $13,686,184

State Parks
The work by the CCC on the development of the state parks was carried on under the Indiana Department of Conservation on the following state parks: Brown County, Clifty Falls, Indiana Dunes, Lincoln, McCormick Creek, Pokagon, Shakamak, Spring Mill, Tippecanoe River, Turkey Run, Versilles.

The construction work on both state forests and state parks through 1938, may be summarized as follows: service buildings 11, custodian cottages 7, barns 11, shelter houses 23, lodge 1, mill building 1, ranger cabins 9, forestry buildings Clark County 6, museum buildings Jackson County 1, nursery service buildings 3, lakes and dams 16.

Much work was accomplished for the Fish and Game Department which included: beaver houses 2, incubator houses 2, animal shelter sheds 4, animal feed sheds 8, raccoon feeding sheds 20, quail brooder houses 66, animal corrals 12, fish rearing ponds 40.

State Forests
CCC projects were accomplished on the following state forests: Clark County, Morgan-Monroe, Brown County, Harrison County, Jackson County, Jasper-Pulaski, Dubois County, Warrick County, Pike County, Wells County and Orange County.

IOWA

G.B. McDonald 1933-1957   Conservation Commission 1933

Camps
The average number of camps operated in Iowa was 29. The average distribution of the camps by services for the year ending in June, 1937 was as follows: State Forest 1, Biological Survey 1, Soil Conservation Service 20, Agricultural Engineering 5, State Parks 8.

Employment
The aggregate number of Iowa men given employment was 45,846. This figure included 41,190 junior and veteran enrollees, 60 Indians and 4,596 non-enrolled personnel of camp officers and supervisory workers. The number of individuals who worked in Iowa regardless of the state of origin was 49,266.

Work Accomplishments
Fences and guard rails, rods. 737,129
Erosion control, check dams, number 75,077
Trees planted, reforestation, number. 6,420,000
Tree seed collected, hardwoods, pounds. 877,086
Tree and plant disease control, acres 1,866,391
Insect pest control, acres 69,298

Expenditures
Total obligation in Iowa (Est.). $48,443,339
Allotments to dependents by enrollees (Est.). $10,690,285

Just prior to the authorization of the CCC camps by President Franklin D. Roosevelt, Lieutenant Governor Nels G. Krashcel and State Forester G.B. McDonald, took a proposal for Iowa camps to Washington. A detailed plan for 16 proposed camps outlined the location, supervisory force, equipment, and the approximate cost for the operation of such camps for six months of operation. The CCC Director, after a brief review of the proposal remarked, "That is just what the President is looking for." Within the next few days a wire from the CCC Director's office authorized the establishment of the camps.

The original CCC camps, which at the start were largely used for soil erosion control, soon were authorized for many phases of work on private, state and national forests and parks. For the first several years, the state forester served as director of the program. From year to year the number of camps varied from 16 to 45.

In 1935, the General Assembly appropriated one million dollars for the CCC work. The state funds made possible the acquisition of about 12,000 acres of state forests in southern and northeastern Iowa and the addition of a number of new state parks as well as increasing the area of many existing parks. Among the forest-park acquisitions was the purchase of the largest remaining white pine stand in the state - some 600 acres, which were added to the existing forest reserve in Delaware County.

Largely through state financing a nursery of 100 acres in Ames was purchased and equipped. A second tree nursery in southeastern Iowa was also developed on Federal land.

State Parks
Backbone State Park, near Lamont, was developed by camp SP - No. 17. The developments included a concrete dam which impounded a 102 acre lake, along which a beach and stone bathhouse were constructed. Other construction included a stone custodian's residence, 12 overnight cabins, two picnic shelters with the usual water and sanitary facilities. The needed park roads and parking areas, together with foot and nature trails, completed the project.

Bixby State Park
The construction here consisted of a log and stone shelter, picnic areas, park roads, parking areas and foot trails.

Brush Creek Canyon
There was constructed here a stone shelter with water and sanitary facilities, park roads and trails and landscaping.

Echo Valley State Park and *White Pine Hollow State Park* had some construction work completed.

KANSAS

No State Forester until 1961
No State Park Agency until 1955

Camps
Average number of camps operated in Kansas was 15.

The average number of camps operated in Kansas was 15. The average distribution by services as of June 30, 1937 was as follows: State Forest 1, Soil Conservation Service 16, State Park 1, Military Reservations 2. About 10,000 junior CCC Kansans worked in western states.

Employment
The aggregate number of Kansas men given employment was 38,163. This figure included 35,306 junior and veteran enrollees, 145 Indians and 2,712 non-enrolled personnel of camp officers and supervisory workers.

Work Accomplishments
Impounding and large diversion dams, number 169
Fences and guard rails, rods. 278,432
Check dams, erosion control, number 38,879
Gully erosion, trees planted, number 2,968,098

Diversion ditches, linear feet.................................... 1,939,801
Sheet erosion planting, acres....................................... 73,432
Contour plowing and ridges, miles   943
Trees planted, reforestation, acres............................... 6,040,000

Expenditures
Total obligation in Kansas (Est.).............................. $32,692,668
Allotments to dependents by enrollees (Est.)..................... $ 9,249,352

State Parks
Kansas had no state parks until 1955.

KENTUCKY

K.G. McConnell 1934-1944   1920

Camps
The average distribution of camps by services in June, 1937 was as follows:
National Forests 8, State Forest 1, Private Forests 8, Agricultural Engineering 2,
Soil Conservation Service 14, National Parks 4, State Parks 6, Military
Reservation 1, Total 44.

Employment
The aggregate number of Kentucky men given employment was 89,511.
This figure included 83,474 junior and veteran enrollees and veterans and
6,037 non-enrolled camp officers and supervisor workers.

Work Accomplishments
Telephone lines, miles.. 1,193
Check dams, erosion control, number............................. 120,601
Gully erosion, trees planted, number........................... 17,847,887
Trees planted, reforestation, number........................... 8,703,345
Moving and planting trees and shrubs, number................... 1,864,943
Nurseries, man-days... 115,245
Fire prevention and presuppression, man-days..................... 187,971

Expenditures
Total obligation in Kentucky (Est.)........................... $62,281,315
Allotments to dependents by enrollees (Est.).................. $19,113,130

State Forests
Kentenia State Forest in Harlan County consists of seven tracts measuring
3,624 acres. The CCC constructed on the forest an administration building
at Putney which furnished an office and living quarters for the district
forester, a 3-car garage and an equipment storehouse. An old house on the
property was reconstructed for seed extraction and cone drying use. The
area was given to the state in 1919 by the Kentucky Catron Corporation.

Kentucky Ridge State Forest of 12,000 acres in Bell County, on the waters of Clear Creek, was one of the areas acquired by the Resettlement Administration and leased to the state for 50 years. Most of the area was best suited for timber production, but a part of the area was utilized for recreation by the Division of State Parks. The CCC completed vacation cabins, a lodge, picnic area and hiking trails in this area.

To protect the forest, two lookout towers, telephone lines and truck trails were built.

Private Forests
The Kentucky Forest Service supervised the work of 11 camps which worked on private lands. The work on the private lands was in the field of forest fire control and the type of projects carried out were similar to those in other southern states.

Soil Conservation
There were 14 CCC camps in western and mid-western parts of the state, which worked on the control of gully erosion. The gully erosion was controlled here first by building check dams out of logs, earth and rocks followed by the planting of trees and clover seed.

State Parks
A thousand acres of the Kentucky Ridge State Forest was managed by the Division of State Parks in connection with the Pine Mountain State Park.

LOUISIANA

V.H. Sonderegger 1929-1940   First Appropriation
V.M.E. Brashers 1940-1942   1918

Camps
The average number of camps operated in Louisiana was 30. The average distribution of camps by services in June, 1937 was as follows: National Forests 7, State Forest 1, Private Forests 9, Agricultural Engineering 5, Soil Conservation Service 15, State Park 1, Military Reservation 1.

Employment
The aggregate number of Louisiana men given employment was 51,820. This figure included 46,597 junior and veteran enrollees and 5,223 non-enrolled personnel of camp officers and supervisory workers. The number of individuals who worked in Louisiana regardless of the state of origin was 51,225.

Work Accomplishments
Bridges, all types, number 3,717
Fences, rods 980,986
Clearing and cleaning channels, sq. rds. 35,365,001

Trees planted, reforestation, number.......................... 165,792,000
Fighting forest fires, man-days.................................... 100,461
Firebreaks, miles.. 4,374
Moving and planting trees and shrubs, number.................... 1,510,147

Expenditures
Total obligation in Louisiana (Est.)........................... $55,892,601
Allotments to dependents by enrollees (Est.).................... $13,147,929

Forestry
The state was alloted 20 camps, 19 of which were located on private land, one, S 63, was situated on the Nott tract at Mandeville. The CCC built two nurseries, one at Valde Rouge and the other at Breaux. The enrollees worked in the nursery pulling weeds, lifting plants and on reforestation of the Nott tract. An attractive log administration building was constructed (in use today, 1979). The Alexander State Forest was acquired during the period of 1923 and 1938 and comprised 7,961 acres.

Three residences were constructed on the forest for the forest supervisor, automotive shop supervisor and the towerman respectively. Woodworth Tower, with a height of 175 feet, is the tallest one in the state. Near the nursery site of Valde Rouge, the CCC constructed an air strip and a hangar.

Construction work at Woodworth included a complete automotive repair shop, a carpenter shop, a cold storage plant for seed storage. The work from the camps on private land was similar to that which was performed by all southern states as described therein.

State Parks*
Louisiana, along with other states, had no National Parks, only National Monuments. The state did not own any park land nor any organization to cooperate with the CCC park program. There was an undeveloped tract of land, which had been given to the state by the former Chief Justice, Joseph A. Breaux, lying in the historic town of Martinsville along the banks of Bayou Teche. By legislative act in 1930, the area was designated as a state park.

Under an agreement with the Louisiana Conservation Department, a CCC camp was moved onto the site on October 20, 1933. For some unknown reason, the camp was closed in late October. The citizens became infuriated and caused the legislature to create legislation which established the Louisiana State Parks Commission in 1934. In 1936, the Commission received a donation of a large tract by the Crossett Lumber Company together with some other areas.

The development of a 500 acre park was begun here in January, 1936, by a second CCC camp, which operated until 1938. Many improvements were made to the grounds and six brick and wooden cottages, a brick clubhouse and a large pump house were constructed.

As a result of a 1937 recreation survey, the state purchased two outstanding areas and two CCC camps were assigned to them. These camps were at

*Louisiana History, Vol. VI, No. 1, 1965, pp. 27-52.

Telefuncte (later named Fontainbleau) State Park near Mandeville which was acquired in 1937 and Chicot State Park near Ville Platte acquired in 1938.

At Fontainbleau, a camp was established in 1938 on which area a large lagoon was dredged to provide a quiet fishing area. Other work there had to be completed by the state, which included a bathhouse, picnic shelter and group vacation cottages for family use.

Chicot State Park had a great variety of work accomplished by the CCC enrollees. The work here included service roads and bridges, clearing and dredging of the 2,000 acre lake bottom of heavy timber growth and the construction of a mile long levee, four feet high, with a concrete spillway.

MAINE

Neil Violette 1933-1935   Forestry Act 1891
Waldo Seavey 1935-1939
Ray Randall 1940-1942

Camps
The average distribution of camps by services for the period ending June 30, 1937 was as follows: National Forest 1, State Forest 1, Private Forests 8, National Parks 2, State Parks 2, Military Reservation 1.

Employment
The aggregate number of Maine men given employment was 18,298. This figure included 16,686 junior and veteran enrollees and 1,612 non-enrolled personnel of camp officers and supervisory workers. The number of individuals who worked in Maine regardless of the state of origin was 20,434.

Work Accomplishments
Bridges, all types, number. 468
Truck trails, miles. 389
Foot and horse trails, miles. 818
Fighting forest fires, man-days 38,521
Tree and plant disease control, acres. 421,151
Emergency work, man-days 42,108
Timber estimated, acres. 822,612

Expenditures
Total obligation in Maine (Est.). $18,583,694
Allotments to dependents by enrollees (Est.). $ 4,002,633

Camps
The state of Maine is known as the Pine Tree State from the abundance of white pine trees along the Atlantic Coast and in the southern part of the state. The state has two distinguishable districts, the southern and the northern part of the state. The northern part is a wilderness area covered with the spruce and balsam fir. Both of these regions have an intermixture of

hardwoods. It can be readily seen why the first camps installed and maintained in the state had forest protection as their main project.

During the first CCC period the work in Maine had the following camps:

Location	Camp Number	Personnel	Natives of
Rangeley	P 55	Youth, Jrs.	Rhode Island
Flagstaff	P 56	Youth, Jrs.	Connecticut
Greenville	P 57	Youth, Jrs.	Maine
+ Seboomook	P 58	Veterans	U.S.A.
Millinocket	P 61	Youths	Maine
Patten	P 60	Youths	Maine
Beddington	P 54	Veterans	U.S.A.
Princeton	S 5	Youths	Maine
+ + Alfred	P 52	Youths	Massachusetts
Lewiston	P 59	Youths	Massachusetts
Jefferson	P 51	Veterans	U.S.A.

+ Moved to Grant Farm, P 62, in October, 1933, camp discontinued April, 1934.
+ + Moved to west side Mt. Katahdin (Baxter Park) SP 2 on June 1, 1934 and returned to Alfred on October 15, 1934.

Forestry

Maine used many side camps since the work extended for a considerable distance, especially in the northern wilderness areas. The main projects there were road and bridge construction, telephone lines and tourist camp sites for parties travelling the roads, trails for fishing, hunting or simply trying to get away into the great out-of-doors. The developments varied from a single

Luncheon shelter built of local materials, with split roof and fireplace: at Seboeis Stream, Maine.

fireplace near a spring, to one equipped with a sleeping and lunching structure for overnight use. In some places, lean-to shelters covered with split cedar on the roofs were built in out-of-way places.

In the southern part of the state, the organized towns, the work was chiefly insect and disease control. The gypsy moth, which defoliates the trees, was the project for the camps located at Alfred, Jefferson, Bridgton and Lewiston during the period of October through April. During the rest of the year, the work was the control of the white pine blister rust.

Gypsy moth control work encompassed the creosoting of the egg masses in the cocoons and some spraying, while the control of the white pine blister rust was accomplished by the pulling of the currant and gooseberry bushes as described in the New York report.

The European spruce sawfly had gained a foothold in practically every spruce stand in the state. The aid of the CCC enrollees in the camps at Wesley, Princeton, Bar Harbor and Jefferson was restricted to scouting and making reports to the Forest Service of the locations and degree of infestation.

Forest fires were fought by all the camps. The 1938 hurricane did considerable damage in the state and is described in the Vermont section. A large amount of manpower from several camps was used to open up roads and trails and remove blowndown timber from around buildings to protect them from fire.

The Princeton camp is situated in Indian Township, which is a state forest subject to treaty rights of the Passamaquoddy Indians. The work here was the usual forestry work and truck trail construction.

State Parks
Sleeping shelters were built along the Appalachian Trail. Trails were constructed on the Mt. Katahdin Park. Other construction included boat houses and wharves at some areas, which had both recreational use and a means of getting to accessible forest areas.

MARYLAND

F.W. Besley 1907-1942   1906

Camps
The average number of camps operating in Maryland was 21. The average distribution of camps by services was as follows: State Forests 13, Mosquito Control 2, Animal Industry 3, Agricultural Engineering 3, Soil Conservation Service 3, State Parks 2, Military Reservations 3, Naval Reservation 1.

Employment
The aggregate number of Maryland men given employment was 32,859. This figure included 28,454 junior and veteran enrollees and 4,405 non-enrolled personnel including camp officers and supervisory workers. The number of individuals who worked in Maryland regardless of the state of origin was 35,830.

Work Accomplishments
Bridges, all types, number. 274
Check dams, erosion control, number 3,431
Trees planted, reforestation, number. 4,378,000
Forest stand improvement, acres. 60,326
Fire hazard reduction, acres. 23,281
Moving and planting trees and shrubs, number 969,255

Expenditures
Total obligation in Maryland (Est.). $39,784,090
Allotments to dependents by enrollees (Est.). $ 6,328,525

Departments Established
In 1906 the brothers, John and Robert Garrett of Baltimore (and the Baltimore and Ohio Railroad), gave 1,917 acres of land in Garrett County to the state with the proviso that a forester would be hired to manage this land. On April 5, 1906, the General Assembly created the Board of Forestry to manage the Garrett gift, to provide for the protection of the woodlands and to advance forestry in Maryland. The area was called the Swallow State Forest Reserve. The land was later divided between the Garrett State Forest and the Swallow Falls State Park. The state continued to acquire land after this gift from the Garretts.

In 1907, Fred W. Besley became one of the first state foresters of the nation and held the position for 35 years. In 1923, the Board of Forestry was superceded by the Department of Forestry under the direction of the University of Maryland. Then in 1941, this department was replaced by an independent agency, the Department of Forests and Parks. By 1930, some of the state forests were set aside and designated as state parks.

The Department of Natural Resources was created by the General Assembly in 1969 to combine all conservation and environmentally related agencies in a single unit under a secretary. The Maryland Park Service was established in 1972 as a separate unit of the Department of Natural Resources, which also included the Department of Forests.

State Parks
The following state parks were benefited by major development during the CCC period 1933-1942: Harrington Manor, Swallow Falls, New Germany, Cambrill, Cunningham Falls, Elk Neck, Big Run, Fort Frederick, Washington Monument, Cedarville, Patapasco Valley and Milburn Landing.

Elk Neck State Park, of 368 acres, was given to the state by William Abbott in his will of 1933. The CCC developed roads, trails, cabins and picnic facilities on this area. Fort Frederick, which was built by the Colony of Maryland in 1756, was acquired by the state in 1923. The CCC restored the fort walls and the foundations of the long-gone barracks. A picnic area, a museum and other support buildings were built. The CCC built roads, trails and shelters on the Cambrill State Park, which was given to the state by the City of Frederick in 1934.

State Forests
The Savage River State Forest, which was established in 1929 in Garrett

County, had two areas developed as recreation areas, which included cabins and a lake at New Germany. In 1964, the legislature carved two parks, Big Run State Park and New Germany State Park, out of the forest.

Cedarville State Forest, which was first acquired in 1930, was developed with recreational facilities during the 1930's. In 1974, part of the area was designated as a state park. In 1974, the entire tract was designated as a National Resources Management Area with the park service responsible for its administration. The Swallow Falls State Forest was increased by the acquisition of 656 acres in 1917. The CCC developed the area for recreation with the construction of roads, trails, cabins, a lake and picnic facilities. In 1964, there were 365 acres of this area, which was designated as Herrington Manor State Park. In 1931, the state acquired two tracts, Milburn Landing and Shad Landing, located on the Pocomoke River in Worcester County for the state forest reserve. Milburn was improved by the CCC as a forest recreation area in the 1930's. The two areas became state parks in the 1960's.

MASSACHUSETTS

Samuel A. York 1933-1935
Ernest J. Dean 1936-1940
Raymond J. Kenney 1940-

Forest Act passed 1904

Camps
The average number of camps in Massachusetts was 28. The average distribution of the camps by services was as follows: State Forests 17, Private Forests 4, State Parks 16, Military Reservation 1.

Employment
The aggregate number of Massachusetts men given employment was 99,517. This figure included 95,063 junior and veteran enrollees and 4,454 camp officers and work supervisors.

Work Accomplishments
Bridges, all types 473
Trees planted, reforestation, number 12,112,000
Fighting forest fires, man-days 36,123
Fire presuppression, man-days 64,961
Tree and plant disease control, acres 95,687
Tree insect control, man-days, acres 972,617
Emergency work, man-days 161,703

Expenditures
Total obligation in Massachusetts (Est.) $45,146,456
Allotments to dependents by enrollees (Est.) $20,189,427

Camps
Due to the economic conditions in many of the forests, it was realized by the end of 1933, that the purchase of additional acreage was a necessity

in order for the enrollees to remain in Massachusetts and serve the state in a beneficial manner. Therefore, acquisition of suitable lands for the Division of Forests and Parks was accelerated during 1933 and continued through 1939, as long as the camps remained alive. During this period, approximately 50,585 acres of state lands were purchased.

During the period of the program, the state had 32 SP (state park) camps, 31 S (state forest) camps and 2 P (private) camps on private land. The camps were located in all counties of the state with the majority in Berkshire (12), Franklin (11), and Worcester (10).

Forest Projects

In the early CCC days, much of the work was by manual labor for two reasons—tools and equipment had not been delivered, and the object was to give employment to as many enrollees as possible.

The forestry projects included: the collection of cones and extraction of the seed which the CCC sowed and planted on the idle acres; the management of the forests through thinning, pruning, cutting and harvesting; fire control by hazard reduction, firebreaks, truck trails, water hole construction, fire towers and telephone lines; insect and disease control of the gypsy moth, white pine weevil, span worm, white pine blister rust.

Fish and Game Management

Fish and game management included fish raising, stocking, stream improvement, raising and care of game birds, planting food trees and bushes, and providing shelter and nesting areas.

Recreation

Construction of picnic and camping areas with the necessary appertances such as water and sanitary facilities, roads, trails, parking, cabins, lodges, ski areas and lodges, bathing beaches with bathhouses, pavilions and fishing piers.

MICHIGAN

Marcus Schaaf 1910-1949   Forestry Act 1899

Camps

The average number of camps operated in Michigan was 57. The average distribution of camps by services on June 30, 1939 was as follows: National Forests 43, State Forests 20, Private Forests 2, Biological Survey 1, State Parks 9.

Employment

The aggregate number of Michigan men given employment was 102,814. This figure included 94,548 junior and veteran enrollees and 8,266 non-enrolled personnel of camp officers and supervisory workers. The number of individuals who worked in Michigan regardless of the state of origin was 97,132.

Work Accomplishments
Lookout houses and towers, number.................................... 1
Telephone lines, miles.. 2,065
Truck trails and minor roads, miles 6,989
Trees planted, reforestation, number......................... 484,981,000
Forest stand improvement, acres................................. 204,460
Fish stocked, number...................................... 156,660,922

Expenditures
Total obligation in Michigan (Est.) $94,659,455
Allotments to dependents by enrollees (Est.)..................... $20,970,043

Camps
During the first enrollment period, 42 state forestry camps were established. Twelve of these camps were located on state forests. Three camps were established on state game refuges and the remaining 27 were established on unadministered state and private land areas of extremely inaccessible nature or upon areas with a high fire hazard.

Forestry
As in most other states, forest fire presuppression and forest fire suppression were the main projects. The protection of Michigan forests comprised the construction of new forest fire towers and miles of woods roads and truck trails to reach fires rapidly, especially in formerly inaccessible locations. Cabins for the forest fire watchmen and district headquarters houses were also important. District fire supervisors' residences, the Roscommon Forest Fire Experiment Station, storage sheds and repair shops were also built.

A large dining room and kitchen unit was constructed at the Higgins Lake Conservation School. Several thousand bushels of hardwood seeds and pine and spruce cones were collected by the CCC for planting at the Higgins Lake and Hardwood State Forest Tree Nurseries. From these seeds, millions of trees were raised for the reforestation of Michigan's idle acres. The CCC enrollees

Michigan CCCs constructed towerman's cabin.

spent thousands of man-days in seed collection and the raising and outplanting of the forest tree seedlings.

In the construction of buildings there were many thousands of board feet of timber, which was cut by the CCC in the Michigan State Forests. At the nurseries, combination packing sheds, offices and laboratory buildings, together with underground cold storage buildings for tree seed were built.

Michigan, during the CCC, may have led the nation in planting 485,000,000 trees. For game purposes they raised planting stock of red osier (dogwood), sumac, black and choke cherry, box elder, wild plum, honey locust, maple and others.

Fish and Game

Michigan probably spent as many, if not more, CCC man-days improving the habitat for fish and game and planting fish than any other state. For the fish and game divisions some of the work accomplishments were: the construction of attractively landscaped fish rearing pools, log cabins for the caretakers were built at these rearing stations, many miles of streams have been improved for fish rearing by the construction of dams, spawning bed shelters and others.

Near the end of the CCC program, 12 CCC camps had completed over 700 projects, varying in size from Muskegon River Dam flooding 2,500 acres for water fowl breeding grounds to the comparatively minor service of clearing fish ponds at state hatcheries.

State Parks

A large majority of the 170 acres of public campgrounds were built on the state forests. Some of the most popular ones were located at Garnet Lake, Muskellonge Lake, the Lake Michigan and Twin Lakes campgrounds. The CCC built concrete stoves, permanent wells with concrete pits, adequate latrines, picnic tables and benches and harmonious landscaping. Since October 1, 1936, the following projects were completed by the CCC enrollees previous to the end of the program: at all the parks - water and sanitation facilities, bathhouses.

Tables and benches, roads and trails, parking areas, boundary fences, etc., were usually built at: Lake City State Park, Higgins Lake State Park, Indian Lake State Park, Onaway State Park, Wilson State Park, Youngs State Park, Marquette State Park, Fletcher State Park, Burt Lake State Park, Hoeft State Park and others.

MINNESOTA

G.M. Conzet 1924-1937   Forest Service
E.A. Foster 1937-1939   Established 1911
H.G. Weber 1940-1948

Camps

The average number of camps operated in Minnesota was 51. The average distribution of camps by services in June, 1937 was as follows: National Forests 27, State Forests 14, Biological Survey 1, Soil Conservation Service 12, State Parks 10.

Employment
The aggregate number of Minnesota men given employment was 84,411. This figure included 74,688 junior and veteran enrollees, 2,536 Indians and 7,187 non-enrolled personnel of camp officers and supervisory workers. The number of individuals who worked in Minnesota regardless of the state of origin was 86,777.

Work Accomplishments
Impounding and large diversion dams, number 218
Truck trails and minor roads, miles 3,754
Trees planted, reforestation, number 123,607,000
Fighting forest fires, man-days 285,172
Fire hazard reduction, acres 165,045
Fish stocked, number 245,097,051

Expenditures
Total obligation in Minnesota (Est.) $84,901,851
Allotments to dependents by enrollees (Est.) $17,525,553

State Forests
The Itaska State Park was created by the legislature in 1891. In 1892, Congress granted to Minnesota all lands within the Park amounting to 6,956 acres. In 1907, the Itaska State Park was made a state forest reserve by legislative enactment.

In 1933, a law was passed to acquire state forests to expedite the work of the CCC. The forests acquired included the following: Beltrami Island, Cloquet Valley, Finland, Fond Du Lac, Foot Hills, Grand Portage, Kabetogama, Land O'Lakes, Pine Island, Savanna, Third River, White Earth, and lands in Becker and Mahnoman Counties.

In 1935, additional state forests were acquired which were: Bay Lake, Buena Vista, Crow Wing, Mille Lacs, Mississippi Headwaters, Nemadji, Rum River, Smoky Hills, Waskish and Black Duck.

The Badoura Nursery, started in 1931, was enlarged in the CCC days and a second nursery, Willow River in Pine County, was started in 1939. The CCC enrollees completed a U-shaped building here which was started by the WPA.

The forestry work on both state and private land was comparable to the types accomplished by the CCC enrollees in other states.

State Parks
The division of state parks was created in 1935 by the legislature, when all the powers and duties regarding to state parks were turned over to the director of state parks from the director of forestry. The director of forestry still retained jurisdiction over the timber in Itaska State Park.

There were 22 state parks upon which developments were made by the CCC. A very interesting publication of the Division of State Parks, Box 39, Centennial Building, St. Paul, Minn. 55155, lists the developments made by the CCC enrollees on state parks. The state parks are: Baptism River, Blue Mountain, Buffalo River, Camden, Cascade River, Charles A. Lindberg, Flandau, Fort Ridgely, Gooseberry Falls, Interstate, Itaska, Jay Cooke, Lac Du Parle, Lake

Bemidge, Monson Lake, St. Croix, Scenic, Sibley, Split Rock Creek, Temperance River and White Water.

MISSISSIPPI

Fred B. Merrill 1929-1941   1926

Camps
The average number of camps operated in Mississippi was 33. The average distribution among the services in June, 1937 was as follows: National Forests 16, Private Forests 3, Soil Conservation Service 15, National Parks 3, State Parks 9.

Employment
The aggregate number of Mississippi men given employment was 57,960. This figure included 52,678 junior and veteran enrollees, 129 Indians and 5,173 non-enrolled personnel of camp officers and supervisory workers. The number of individuals who worked in Mississippi regardless of the state of origin was 56,264.

Work Accomplishments
Lookout houses and towers, number.................................. 118
Telephone lines, miles.. 2,689
Truck trails and minor roads, miles................................ 23,346
Trees planted, gully erosion, number........................... 17,406,752
Trees planted, reforestation, number........................... 147,091,000
Fighting forest fires, man-days.................................. 130, 721

Expenditures
Total obligation in Mississippi (Est.) $60,969,271
Allotments to dependents by enrollees (Est.)..................... $15,328,790

Camps
The camps for fire protection in the state were located as follows: P 51 in Stone County, P 52 in Hardwick, P 63 in Jackson, P 64 in Calhoun, P 73 in Hunphreys, P 70 in Simpson and P 76 in Lauderdale.

Forestry
The main work of the CCC program was forest fire presuppression and suppression, which consisted of the building of roads, fire towers and fire houses and the reduction of fire hazards along trails and roads. Most of this work was carried out on private forest lands with the few acres of public lands getting the same protection. In southern Mississippi, there were two camps which worked on the University State Forest and the five million acres of private forest.

In particular places, the roads were built with a crushed rock surface.

Reforestation
In 1935, the CCC enrollees planted black locust, long leaf pine and slash pine from the State Tree Nursery at Perkinston on the University State Forest. From the University Nursery over one-half million slash pine seedlings were planted.

From a tract of cypress the CCC cut enough logs to make shingles at Granada to supply the needs for all tower houses (lookout houses). In addition, over ten thousand telephone poles were cut and installed to construct telephone lines from fire towers to headquarters.

Erosion

Ten camps in northern Mississippi worked on the Tallahassee watershed for the purpose of controlling erosion and streamflow. The methods were the same as used in other states.

State Parks

Mississippi had no state parks previous to the advent of E.C.W. The Forestry Commission of the state did not really become involved in the vastness of the E.C.W. program until approached by a representative of the National Park Service in early 1934. The Mississippi legislature was in session at the time that a meeting between the state forester and officials of the National Park Service occurred. Since there was neither legislation nor funds to acquire state parks, a bill Number 446 was introduced into the House and supported by many interested citizens. The bill provided for the use of state land for state parks and for counties to purchase land to be deeded to the state for this purpose.

As a result of public interest in many parts of the state, three areas were given approval for CCC camps—namely, LeRoy Percy at Hollandale, Tombigbee at Tupelo and Clarkco at Quitman. By June 23, 1934, construction of camps had started on these three sites. With increased interest in park areas, development of new park areas on the Legion Lake State Park began on October 12, 1934; Tishomingo State Park on June 19, 1935 and Holmes County State Park, located near Durant, on July 10, 1935. Other parks with their dates and

Mississippi Erosion. U.S. Forest Service.

locations were Roosevelt State Park near Morton on August 1, 1935, Spring Lake State Park near Holly Springs and Percy Quinn near McComb were occupied on June 23 and July 15, 1935 respectively.

As a result of the Forestry Commission's request that two or three persons with interest in and knowledge of state park development be appointed to the State Forestry Commission, the Governor, Martin S. Conner, complied. He appointed Mrs. Paul Gambill of Greenville and Mr. M.B. Miller of Meridan to fill commission vacancies and later Mr. D.R. Johnson of Batesville was appointed.

In 1936, House Bill No. 858 establishing a State Park Agency was passed but with no funds with which to operate. Under the bill, the three members known as the Board of Park Supervisors were appointed as part of the Forestry Commission. The development of the state parks continued with the aid of E.C.W. funds. As long as such funds were available the state seemed reluctant to appropriate funds for operation. From April, 1934 to June, 1941 the Federal government's share in the development of Mississippi's ten state parks amounted to $4,465,000.

By 1950, the legislature gave substantial support to the park program by appropriating $300,000 for operational expenses and $575,000 for development programs.

MISSOURI

George O. White 1938-1959   State Board 1925
No forestry funds 1934-1937

Camps
The average number of camps operating in Missouri was 41. The average distribution of camps by services in June, 1937 was as follows: National Forests 12, State Forests 3, Agricultural Engineering 6, Soil Conservation Service 22, State Parks 9.

Employment
The aggregate number of Missouri men given employment was 102,200. This figure included 93,445 junior and veteran enrollees and 8,646 non-enrolled personnel of camp officers and supervisory workers.

Work Accomplishments
Lookout houses and towers, number................................... 126
Erosion control, check dams, number 47,118
Trees planted, gully erosion control, number 11,833,585
Clearing and cleaning channels, sq. yds......................... 98,696,059
Trees planted, reforestation, number........................... 36,127,000
Wildlife shelters, number.. 1,877

Expenditures
Total obligation in Missouri (Est.)............................. $71,127,000
Allotments to dependents by enrollees (Est.).................... $24,174,443

State Parks

In June, 1933, the CCC enrollees started work in three state parks, Sam A. Baker, Meramec and Roaring River. At the termination of the CCC in 1941, developments had been made on ten state parks, and three Federal recreation areas, which were eventually transferred over to the state. These areas include the following parks: Babler, Baker, Alley Spring, Arrow Rock, Bennett Spring, Big Lake, Big Spring, Cuivre River, Lake Ozark, Lewis and Clark, Meramec, Montauk, Montserrat (Knob Noster), Mark Twain, Roaring River, Round Spring, Van Meter and Washington.

The facilities developed here were those which were common to all state parks. The primary needs included roads and parking area, water and sanitary systems. To make the areas useful to the public, recreation buildings, dining lodges, concession buildings and bathhouses were built.

Some of the special developments included the restoration of the old mill at Montauk, a dining lodge at Big Springs, cabins at Meramec, construction of a dam and lake at Roaring River, picnic and trailside shelters at Sam A. Baker, a store and concession building at Bennett Spring, a park superintendent's residence at Washington and a stable at Babler.

Lake Ozark was developed to provide underpriviledged persons and groups, sponsored by charitable organizations, an opportunity to enjoy the out-of-doors. The Cuivre River and Montserrat Parks were provided by the CCC with facilities primarily for vacation purposes.

The first two state parks in Northwest Missouri, Big Lake in Holt County and Wallace in Clinton County, were acquired in 1932. In 1932, increased interest in Indian heritage resulted in the acquisition of Van Meter Park in Saline County which was once the home of prehistoric Indian tribes, and Washington State Park in Washington County which contains ancient rock carvings of prehistoric Indian ceremonials and culture. Lewis State Park in Buchanon County was added in 1934 in memory of the two well known explorers of the west.

Mess Hall of the 3735th Co. CCC Camp Centerville, F-22, Centerville, Missouri.

Conservation Commission

A conservation commission was established under a constitutional amendment passed on November 3, 1936. The commission was given control, management, and regulation of the bird, fish, game, forestry and all the wildlife resources of the state. On July 1, 1937, the Missouri State Park Board was created by the legislature.

MONTANA

Rutledge Parker 1924-1953   1909

Camps

The average number of camps operated in Montana was 24. The average distribution of camps by services as of June 30, 1937 was as follows: National Forests 13, State Forest 1, Biological Survey 1, Soil Conservation Service 1, National Parks 4, State Parks 2, Bureau of Reclamation 2.

Employment

The aggregate number of Montana men given employment was 25,690. This figure included 17,687 junior and veteran enrollees, 5,068 Indians, and 2,935 non-enrolled camp officers and supervisory workers. The number of individuals who worked in Montana regardless of the state of origin was 40,868.

Work Accomplishments

Bridges, all types, number. 776
Impounding and large diversion dams, number 458
Trees planted, number 5,495,000
Fighting forest fires, man-days 241,330
Fish stocked, number 2,494,560
Rodent and predatory animal control, acres 2,339,683

Expenditures

Total obligation in Montana (Est.). $42,330,918
Allotments to dependents by enrollees (Est.). . . . . $ 3,990,893

State Parks

At the Morrison Cave State Park, the CCC made the following developments:
• A tunnel of 538 feet in length was constructed through limestone rock. The tunnel makes an exit from the lowest cavern without retracing the way;

A Montana CCC Camp.

• The Headhouse was constructed of stone, wood, steel and cement and comprised a main lobby with fireplace and space for a concession, an office room, lavatories, storage quarters and a large open porch which gave a splendid view of the surrounding country;

• The installation of a 200 volt lighting system, comprising a heavy insulated cable, extends for 1,200 feet throughout the cave with numerous outlets for lighting. A large parking space for 200 cars was built near the headhouse. Not far from the headhouse a picnic area with all the necessary facilities was built;

• A winding scenic mountain road, of standard width and grade built by the CCC, leads from Highway #10 for a distance of about three miles to the headhouse on the hill;

• Two mountain trails, each 3,300 feet long, one leading from the headhouse to the entrance of the cave on a 10% grade, and the other a level trail from the headhouse to the exit of the cave.

State Forests

Montana state forests, all of which were originally granted to the state by the Federal government and allocated to the various state institutions (educational and otherwise), contained about 519,000 acres. It was estimated in 1937, that the remaining virgin timber contained within this area was one-half billion board feet. At the time, the state forester estimated that the lands could produce on a sustained yield basis of 25 million board feet annually. In 1934 and 1936, there were serious fires in two western Montana State Forests, Coal Creek and Swan River. Under the exchange law, scattered timber lands were exchanged for over 4,000 acres which were added to the Sula State Forest. In a similar transaction of equal acreage, 2,232 acres were added to the Thompson State Forest.

During the summer periods, CCC camps were operated on the Stillwater and Swan River State Forests. The work here consisted of fire protection improvements, truck trails, bridges, horse trails, telephone lines, lookout houses, equipment and supply buildings, hazard reduction, public recreation camps and other minor improvements.

National Parks

There are two well known National Parks in Montana—Yellowstone and Glacier National Park, which were a considerable distance from many of the citizens. So the CCC created interest in the development of state parks and the formation of a separate park service.

National Forests

There were, in 1942, over 15 million acres of National Forest units in Montana, located largely in the western part of the state. With so much land in public ownership, it was not until the 30's that the citizens became interested in the ownership of land over which they had some control of its use and development.

In the Stillwater State Forest, two picnic and campgrounds with a capacity of 200 people were developed by the CCC. Good swimming was available at these sites. In the Swan River State Forest one picnic area and camping area was constructed with a capacity of 50 people.

NEBRASKA

Clayton Watkins 1926-1935
1937-1940
Earl G. Maxwell 1935-1936
1940-1952

Camps
The average number of camps which operated in Nebraska was 16. The average distribution of camps by services in June, 1937 was as follows: National Park 1, Biological Survey 1, National Forest 1, State Parks 2, Bureau of Reclamation 2, Soil Conservation Service 16.

Employment
The aggregate number of Nebraska men given employment was 30,739. This figure included 27,159 junior and veteran enrollees, 70 Indians and 2,873 non-enrolled personnel comprising army personnel and supervisors.

Work Accomplished
Impoundments and large diversion dams, number 92
Erosion control, check dams, number 52,091
Trees planted, gully erosion control, number 19,229,194
Trees planted, reforestation, number 12,498,000
Moving and planting trees and shrubs, number 7,498,100
Rodent and predatory animal control, acres 281,831

Expenditures
Total obligation in Nebraska (Est.) $34,280,100
Allotments to dependents by enrollees (Est.) . . . . $ 7,849,091

CCC Shelter belt planting—Nebraska. U.S. Forest Service.

NEW HAMPSHIRE

John Foster 1919-1951   Forest Commission 1893

Camps
The average distribution of camps by services in New Hampshire was as follows: National Forests 10, State Forests 4, Private Forest 1, State Parks 3, Naval Reservation 1, Total 19.

Employment
The aggregate number of New Hampshire men given employment was 10,618. This figure included 8,791 junior and veteran enrollees and 1,827 non-enrolled personnel of camp officers and supervisory workers. The number of individuals who worked in New Hampshire regardless of the state of origin was 22,114.

Work Accomplishments
Bridges, all types, number..287
Trees planted, reforestation, number............................6,499,000
Forest stand improvement, acres....................................58,694
Forest fire fighting, prevention, presuppression, man-days..............88,787
Tree and plant disease and insect pest control, acres.................156,947
Fish stocked, number..2,653,543

Expenditures
Total obligation in New Hampshire (Est.)......................$32,779,807
Allotments to dependents by enrollees (Est.)...................$ 2,026,649

Bridge over Smith River, Hill-Alexandria town line, built by the Danbury CCC camp after great flood of March, 1936. New Hampshire. Photo by Forestry Department.

Camps

New Hampshire had 11 camps of which seven were state forests (S), three were state parks (SP), and one was located on private land (P).

Camp Name	Number	Occupied	Company No.	Location
Pillsbury	S 51	6/5/33	122	Goshen
Pawtucket	S 52	6/12/33	123	Deerfield
Hemenway	S 53	6/5/33	117	Tamworth
Cardigan	S 54	6/16/33	126	Danbury
Monadnock	S 55	6/5/33	118	Rindge
Warner	S 56	9/14/35	1,147	Warner
Claremont	S 57	9/3/35	1,185	Unity
Connecticut Lake		9/4/35	1,146	Pittsburg
Moose Brook	SP 1	5/14/34	392 V	Gorham
		8/8/35	1,129	
Bear Brook	SP 2	10/16/35	1,123	Allenton
Bellamy Park	SP 3	6/29/35		Strafford County
		11/1/35	transfer to	Deerfield

Side Camps

Where there was considerable distance to travel from the main camp or where a camp had left with unfinished projects, a side camp was established. Such camps usually had no more than 25 enrollees. Side camps were established as follows: from S 54 at Wellington Beach, Brunswick, Vermont on a timber survey in northern Vermont and New Hampshire in cooperation with the U.S.F.S. Others at Endicott, Rock Park, Danbury, Laconia, Goshen, Wiley House, White Lake in Tamworth, Lafayette Clearing, Franconia Notch, Woodstock and Haverhill were used.

Forestry

Forestry work in New Hampshire was similar to what was accomplished in other New England states. Camp S 57 was established at Unity chiefly to combat the gypsy moth.

At other locations, the enrollees worked on white pine blister rust control and other insect and tree diseases.

After the 1938 New England hurricane, camps at Rindge and Danbury were reactivated to work on clean-up and fire hazard reduction. Other camps which were busied in this work were those at Warner, North Woodstock and Swanzey Lake. The work following the hurricane included the cleaning up of timber around buildings, villages and strips 50 to 100 feet wide along roadways, trails and wood roads. Reduction of inflammable material around lumber yards and log collection centers was another project.

State Parks

Recreational projects were developed from both forest and state park camps. Some of the many recreation developments were foot trails and ski trails on Bald Mt. for slalom run and also on Piper and Belknap Mountains. At Cannon Mountain, the work centered around the aerial tramway, which included trails, parking areas, ski trails and observation platform. Other work performed is listed herewith:

Bear Brook - Bathhouse, day outing area and public campground.
White Lake - A cottage for the lifeguard.
Wellington Beach - Enlarged the parking area.
Endicott Rock (The Weirs) - Bathhouse and beach.
Peterborough - Pool and bathhouse.
Moose Brook - Bathhouse and recreation area.
Monadnock Campground - New buildings constructed.
Franconia Notch - New campground.
White Lake in Tamworth - Bathhouse and recreational facilities.

NEW JERSEY

C.P. Wilber 1922-1953   1906

Camps
The average distribution of camps by services as of June 30, 1937 was as follows: State Forests 12, Private Forests 3, Mosquito Control, Soil Conservation Service 3, National Park 1, State Parks 8, Military Reservations 2, Total 36.

Employment
The aggregate number of New Jersey men given employment was 91,593. This figure included 87,106 junior and veteran enrollees and 4,577 non-enrolled personnel of camp officers and supervisory workers.

Work Accomplishments
Bridges, number 199
Impounding and large diversion dams, number 47
Fences and guard rails, rods 57,102
Field planting, trees, number 21,745,080
Forest stand improvement, acres 52,641
Tree and plant disease control, acres 152,032

Expenditures
Total obligation in New Jersey (Est.) $46,798,499
Allotments to dependents by enrollees (Est.) $18,508,794

State Forests
Many of the old CCC records were destroyed in a fire. There were three camps (P 65 Morris County, P 66 Passaic County and P 57) which worked on Dutch elm disease control. Camp S 61 was located on the Greenbank State Forest. The work here consisted chiefly in the construction of truck trails and forest stand improvement. Camp S 58 was located on the Jenny Jump State

Forest where the enrollees worked on timber stand improvement and truck trails. Three camps, S 52, S 59 and S 69 were located on the Lebanon State Forest, which is now a park area. On the Penn State Forest, camp S 60 enrollees worked on the development of a picnic area and campgrounds. They built a bathhouse, a forest fire tower and a dam on Lake Onega. Other work included the construction of truck trails and forest stand improvement. The camps S 51, S 57 and S 71 on the Stokes State Forest, accomplished the construction of a bathhouse, 11 overnight cabins and office building, equipment building, five shelters, campground and picnic development and earth dams. They built water and sanitary facilities, truck trails, lake side clearing and did reforestation and forest stand improvement.

The following S camps, with location, were on state forests: 51, 57 and 71 on Stokes, 52, 69 and 59 on Lebanon, S 60 on Penn, S 61 on Greenbank, 53 and 80 on Belleplain, 55 on Bass River and 58 on Jenny Jump. State park camps were located as follows: SP 1 at High Point, SP 4 at Parvin and SP 5 at Voorhees.

Many of the forestry records were destroyed in a fire.

There were 12 CCC camps at various times on, what then were called state forests and three on state parks. The following camps were developed on land, then classified as state forests: S 51 Stokes, S 52 Lebanon, S 53 Belleplain, S 55 Bass River, S 57 Stokes, S 58 Jenny Jump, S 59 Lebanon, S 60 Penn, S 61 Greenbank, S 69 Lebanon, S 71 Stokes and S 80 Belleplain. The three state park camps were as follows: SP 1 High Point, SP 4 Parvin, SP 5 Voorhees.

The work done by the enrollees on the Stokes State Forest included the following projects: reforestation, forest stand improvement, truck and foot trails, overnight cabins, bathhouse, dam, office building, shelters, camp and picnic ground facilities.

On the Penn State Forest, the work consisted of the development of camp and picnic grounds, a dam on Onega Lake, a bathhouse, a fire tower, truck trails and forest stand improvement.

On the Jenny Jump State Forest, the enrollees worked on timber stand improvement, truck trails and flood control.

The following state forest areas were transferred after development to the state park system: Lebanon State Forest, Bass River State Forest and Belleplain State Forest.

There were three camps on private land which worked on Dutch elm disease control, namely: P 65 Morris County, P 66 Passaic County and P 57 on the Stokes Forest.

The forestry work was quite similar to that carried on by all the northeastern states. The work included the reforestation of open fields and denuded lands, the collection of forest tree seed, the work of raising seedlings in the state nursery, the protection of New Jersey forests by the construction of forest fire lookout towers, the clean-up of trails and roadsides and the construction of firebreaks and many man-days checking the spread of the Dutch elm disease.

NEVADA

General

The extensive grazing lands of Nevada provided the scene of most of the CCC operations in the state. More than a thousand miles of fences were built to control stock movements on the ranges. Numerous springs and water holes were cleaned and made available to livestock, while check dams and water control and impounding structures were built to conserve the water supply and to prevent erosion. The Corps was active in ridding the range country of rodents and predatory animals, as well as insect pests and poisonous plants. Revegetation of the ranges and their protection against the dangers of fire and excessive grazing were important contributions of the Corps to conservation of Nevada's natural resources.

Camps

The average number of camps operated in Nevada was 18.

Employment

The aggregate number of Nevada men given employment was 7,079. This figure included 3,761 junior and veteran enrollees, 970 Indians and 2,328 camp officers and work supervisors. The number of individuals who worked in Nevada regardless of the state of origin was 30,791.

Work Accomplishments

Bridges, all types, number. 146
Fences, rods 445,166
Telephone lines, miles. 587
Erosion control, check dams, number 18,441
Range revegetation, acres 46,600
Rodent and predatory animal control, acres. 988,398

Expenditures

Total obligation in Nevada (Est.) $31,930,656
Allotments to dependents by enrollees (Est.) . . . . $ 724,270

State Parks

Fort Churchill Historical State Monument, near Silver Springs, was an active Civil War fort constructed of adobe, which had deteriorated badly by 1930. The CCC camp, located at the camp site of the fort, rebuilt the walls as a restoration project.

Lahontan State Recreation Area, near Fallon, had several retaining walls near the dam constructed by the CCC in 1938. Throughout the Fallon area, many of the irrigation canals and control gates were constructed by the CCC. The valley of the Fire State Park near Overton, and the Lost City Museum in Overton, received much construction from the CCC. Here the CCC built picnic and camping shelters.

NEW MEXICO

Land commissioners changed, as a rule, about every two years from 1933 on. The first state forester, Ray L. Bell, was appointed in 1958. The cooperative program with the U.S. Forest Service was authorized in 1921.

Camps

The average number of camps operated in New Mexico was 32. In 1937, the distribution of camps numbering 38 was as follows: National Forests 8, Soil Conservation Service 15, National Park 1, State Parks 3, Division of Grazing 7, Reclamation Service 4.

Employment

The aggregate number of New Mexico men given employment was 32,385. This figure included 22,316 junior and veteran enrollees, 4,470 Indians and 5,599 non-enrolled personnel of camp officers and supervisory workers. The number of individuals who worked in New Mexico regardless of the state of origin was 54,585.

Work Accomplishments

Bridges, all types, number. 795
Lookout houses and towers, number. 472
Impounding and large reservoir dams, number. 658
Fences, rods. 2,318,455
Trees planted, gully erosion control, number 4,151,749
Rodent and predatory animal control, acres 10,312,104
Trees planted, reforestation, number. 2,119,000

Expenditures

Total obligation in New Mexico (Est.). $63,375,368
Allotments to dependents by enrollees (Est.). $ 5,794,226

State Parks

The only records available seem to point that five state parks were at least partially developed by the CCC. On the Hyde State Park, 7½ miles northeast of Santa Fe on the Hyde Park Road, there remains an old lodge building and four rock shelters with fireplaces.

On the Elephant Butte State Park, seven miles northeast of Truth or Consequences, a number of buildings remain.

On the Conchas Lake State Park, 34 miles northwest of Tucumcari, the central portion of South Conchas Lodge remains.

On the Bottomless Lakes State Park, 16 miles southeast of Roswell, there is a rock building and shade structures which are now used primarily as a concession building.

At the Santa Fe River Park, in downtown Santa Fe, both sides of the stream bed were lined with rock.

NEW YORK

William G. Howard 1927-1948   State Forest Commission
                                                        created 1895

Camps
The average number of camps in New York state was 68. The average distribution of camps by services on June 30, 1937 was as follows: State Forests 39, Private Forests 9, Soil Conservation Service 8, State Parks 28, Corps of Engineers 13, Military Reservations 5.

Employment
The aggregate number of New York men given employment was 220,752. This figure included 209,775 junior and veteran enrollees, 240 Indians and 10,737 non-enrolled personnel of camp officers and supervisory workers.

Work Accomplishments
Camp stoves and fireplaces, number.................................2,773
Trees planted, reforestation, number..........................221,589,000
Fighting forest fires, man-days....................................78,134
Tree and plant disease control, acres............................1,124,575
Tree pest control, acres...3,781,347
Public camps and picnic ground development, acres...................1,448

Expenditures
Total obligation in New York (Est.)...........................$134,562,779
Allotments to dependents by enrollees (Est.)..................$ 41,211,953

Detailed Work Projects
The state of New York is treated in considerable detail, since it represents what was accomplished in many states east of the Mississippi.

Recreational Developments
Recreational developments included truck trails, horse and foot trails, camping and picnic facilities, caretakers quarters and shelters, barns, boat houses, lean-tos, ski trails, landscaping, planting trees and shrubs, dams and bridges.

Ranger headquarters were built at the Lake George Battleground, Lake Durant, Margaretville, Lower Saranac Lake and at other recreational areas and administrative locations. Probably the most outstanding work was accomplished at Glen Island ranger headquarters.

Upon the lands of the three college sites, Cornell, Wanakena and Hamilton County, similar developments were made.

Fish and Game Improvements
The work carried out under this classification included the development of the Randolph Hatchery and work at the Pharsalia and Littlejohn refuges. Stream improvement was carried out only where the state had obtained the fishing rights from the riparian owners. The types of work included: the erection of bank piers to hold the stream in place, deflectors, small dams to form deeper pools, rock pools, fish barriers to prevent fish from coming up-

stream, riffles, and the planting of willows and shrubs to prevent erosion and to give shade.

The dams varied in size from a small one to hold a pool, to the large Marcy dam. Some were built for swimming, while others had wildlife value as a breeding area for ducks.

Forestry

Fire Control

The tasks upon which the enrollees worked were to make forest fire control more effective. They included: the construction of truck trails to allow the passage of forest fire fighting equipment with power pumps and tanks of water, foot trails, small dams and water holes. Every CCC camp was furnished with a sufficient number of five gallon hand fire pumps, fire rakes and other tools.

Lookout towers, some steel, some wood, were erected at such prominent points as Petersburg, Mt. Georgetown Hill, Irish Hill, Paddoc Hill, Sugar Hill and many other points. Cabins at the summits were built for the use of the watchmen. Telephone lines connected to commercial lines were constructed to the towers. Many forest tool boxes were built and placed at strategic sites.

During the fire season, many CCC crews were used on forest fire suppression. September, 1941, was a very dry period and many fires got started. All the enrollees, from five camps, were used to suppress fires on reforestation areas in St. Lawrence County and at Keeseville in Clinton County.

Truck Trails

Truck trails were banned by law in the Adirondack Preserve and could be used only for fire protection purposes. They were closed to all other traffic. The following figures represent the number of miles of truck trails built under the several categories: forest preserve 76, camp sites 30, college forests 48, fish and game areas 40, reforestation areas 191, and others 6, making a total of 391 miles. During the CCC period, a total of 73 vehicle bridges were built. The type of bridge built in the Adirondack Preserve, as also in other places, was: multiple arch, 11 feet; reinforced concrete, 15 feet; multiple plate arch, 10 feet; and reinforced concrete, 28 feet.

Insects and Diseases

Control included the following forest pests: white pine blister rust, Dutch elm disease, gypsy moth, brown moth, European shoot moth, European spruce sawfly and the white pine weevil.

White pine blister rust is a fungous disease which was imported from Germany in the early 1900's on some white pine seedlings. To live and spread, the disease needs two hosts, white pine trees and currant or gooseberry bushes (both wild and cultivated bushes known as Ribes). The disease is borne by the wind blowing minute spores or seeds from Ribes fruiting bodies to a white pine needle. There it germinates and eventually spreads to a limb and then to the trunk of the pine tree. When the disease has progressed around the circumference of the tree, it kills the tree. The fruiting bodies on the pine send forth small seeds which germinate and grow on Ribes leaves, completing the cycle. The disease needs both hosts to complete its life. It cannot be carried from pine to pine. Thus the disease is controlled by the removal of currant and gooseberry bushes within a determined distance (up to 900 feet) from white pine trees.

The camps, which were located in the gypsy moth barrier zone, were used from spring to fall on white pine blister rust control, and during the rest of the year on gypsy moth. The number of camps used in New York varied from six in 1933, to 38 later on. During the CCC camp period, 1,071,000 acres were eradicated of Ribes bushes.

A barrier zone was established from the Hudson River easterly to the New England boundary to control the westward spread of the gypsy and brown tail moths. The first task of the enrollees was to make a location survey of the insect damage. Control work then was carried out by spraying the infested trees, creosoting or picking off the cocoons. Also, traps containing an artificially prepared attractant for male moths were attached to trees in the infested areas. Then a three foot band of tanglefoot paper was attached around the tree, catching many fluttering moths. In a year, crews from five camps covered about 300,000 acres of forest and about the same amount of open land.

The white pine weevil was controlled by cutting off the terminal shoot with the insect in it. Spruce sawfly work consisted of locating it.

NORTH CAROLINA

J.S. Holmes 1913-1945   1905

Camps
The average number of camps operated in North Carolina was 45. The average distribution of camps by services was as follows: National Forests 17, State Forest 1, Private Forests 6, T.V.A. 2, Biological Survey 2, Soil Conservation Service 20, National Parks 4, State Parks 4, Military Reservations 3.

Employment
The aggregate number of North Carolina men given employment was 75,843. This figure included 68,600 junior and veteran enrollees, 431 Indians and 6,812 non-enrolled personnel of camp officers and supervisory workers. The number of individuals who worked in North Carolina regardless of the state of origin was 76,698.

Work Accomplishments
Bridges, all types, number 1,502
Trees planted, gully erosion control, number 4,307,037
Trees planted, reforestation, number 25,839,000
Forest stand improvement, acres 174,286
Erosion control, check dams, number 127,286

Expenditures

Total obligation in North Carolina (Est.)......................... $82,385,406

Allotments to dependents by enrollees (Est.)..................... $16,431,098

Camps

The number of camps in the state varied from one to three working on state forests, three to nine on state parks and from five to 13 on Forest Fire Protective Association land.

Forestry

There were 52 towers purchased and erected by the enrollees in 19 CCC camps. Hundreds of miles of telephone lines and trails were constructed to service communication with these towers. It was conservatively estimated by state officials, that the construction of these elements has advanced the forest fire control program in North Carolina by 20 to 30 years.

The Clayton Nursery which was acquired in 1928, produced a small number of trees until 1933, when a side camp was constructed on the site. After that date, millions of trees were grown and planted on burned, cut-over and eroded lands.

The North Carolina Erosion Control Project was first started on October 11, 1934, when a CCC camp, P 63, was established in Manteo, Dare County, under the supervision of the North Carolina Division of Forestry. This camp entered into a field of work upon which very little had been done on coastal United States, when it undertook the fixation of the sand dunes along the "Banks" from Oregon Inlet north to Duck.

Since the inception of the project, the main work consisted of an attempt to control shifting sands by the construction of fences and the planting of native grasses, shrubs and trees. Due to the limitation of such supplies, two nurseries were established, one at Buxton and the other at Manteo. One of the main features of the work was the construction and maintenance of a line of fence from Hatteras Inlet to the Virginia state line, a distance of about 125 miles. Various types of fences were tried, namely: brush, slab, burlap and brush blanket. The first mentioned, proved to be the most effective. As the beach built up around the fences, grasses, shrubs and tree seedlings were planted to hold further shifting. The plants used included beach grass, Bermuda grass, sea oats and spartina. The following shrubs were then planted: wax myrtle, silverling, water bush, American beauty bush and yaupon. When the shrubs had gained a foothold the following forest seedlings were planted: loblolly pine, longleaf pine, hop hornbeam, bald cypress, black locust and others.

On April 15, 1936, the camp and the project were turned over to the U.S. Biological Survey. It was to continue the task.

The CCC became an efficient and trained group of fire fighters, which aided in the suppression of many forest and wild fires before they got much of a start. Millions of values to the forest, forest wildlife, and forest recreational uses were saved by the CCC.

Hoffman State Forest*

"The work on this forest included the construction of a fire tower, fire lanes, cutting trails, road construction, drainage, fencing for cattle and tree planting.

*By George E. Jackson.

During 1935-1936, we planted 400 acres to loblolly and slash pines, some cypress and juniper.

Hill Forest
"The CCC crew worked on road construction, drainage, fire lanes, tree planting, stand improvement and water supply.

One of the largest projects was the construction of a large hotel or headquarters for the university students in Durham. This two story building was built from Virginia pine logs cut on the forest, peeled, notched and put in place. A caretakers home was also built. Between the two buildings a lake was constructed.

"A part of the Hoffman Forest was known for a long time as the 'White-oak Pocosin'. A pocosin is a high elevated area which is so flat on top that the rain water will not drain off and in the wet seasons it is knee deep in water and in dry times the water either sinks in or evaporates or runs off. There are no streams which run through a pocosin."

State Parks
The Crabtree Creek Recreational Demonstration Project of 6,000 acres was situated about ten miles northwest of Raleigh, on U.S. Highway 70 A. About 80 per cent of the area was forested. The developments on the area included two lakes with bathing facilities, five organized campgrounds for whites and two for blacks and separate day use areas for the two races.

NORTH DAKOTA

F.E. Cobb 1925-1935   1925
R.W. McLees 1935-1937
A.F. Arnason 1938-1943

Camps
The average number of camps operated in North Dakota was eight. In 1937, the services maintaining camps were: Biological Survey 5, Soil Conservation Service 2, State Parks 5.

Employment
The aggregate number of North Dakota men given employment was 32,764. This figure included 27,673 junior and veteran enrollees, 2,606 Indians and 1,489 non-enrolled personnel chiefly camp officers and supervisory workers.

Work Accomplishments
Fences, rods 431,555
Trees planted, reforestation, number 1,773,000
Wildlife shelters 362
Insect pest control, acres 307,645
Rodent and predatory animal control, acres 902,322

Expenditures

Total obligation in North Dakota (Est.)........................$16,241,189
Allotments to dependents by enrollees (Est.).....................$ 7,525,923

State Parks

As early as 1904, in cooperation with the Old Settlers Associations in North Dakota, historic sites were acquired. They formed the nucleus of the present park system. The sites were military posts, fur trading posts, battlefields and archeological areas. These areas were maintained for public visitation through the cooperation of local park boards in the vicinity of each site. It is truly said that the development of North Dakota State Parks and historic sites began with the establishment of the CCC Park program.

In February 1934, as a result of an application by the superintendent of the North Dakota Historical Society, Russell Reid, the first CCC park camp was established. The first camps were assigned to the Badlands south of Watford City and to the International Peace Gardens north of Dunseith. During the same year, additional camps were established at Mandan for Fort Lincoln State Park, Larimore for Turtle River State Park, Medora for the south unit of Theodore Roosevelt Park, and metropolitan parks for Fargo, Jamestown and Bismarck.

Fort A. Lincoln and Turtle River are presently state parks and are under the management of the North Dakota and Recreation Department. The International Peace Garden is operated by the International Peace Garden Board with half of the members from Canada and half from North Dakota and the U.S. Government. The north and south units of the Theodore Roosevelt National Park are Federal entities.

Earth Lodges of Mandan Indians, North Dakota. U.S. Forest Service.

Fort Abraham Lincoln State Park—4½ miles south of Mandan—A historic park. The CCC workers were mainly veterans of WW.I. They reconstructed three blockhouses and a stockade at the Infantry Post of Fort McKeen and five earthlodges and a palisade at the site of the Slant Indian Village. Descriptive markers were placed at all of the buildings at the sites of Fort McKeen and Fort A. Lincoln Cavalry Post. A museum, caretaker's residence, two stall garages and concession stands were constructed of cut native granite. Three picnic areas were established with shelters built of stone and related facilities. Roads were built for erosion control, as well as a vast amount of retaining walls and rock work. The maintenance area complex constructed by the Veterans which included garages, blacksmith shop, sawmill, dry rooms for lumber, an ice house, kitchen and office were retained for park maintenance use.

Turtle River State Park—five miles east of Larimore—A recreational park. The CCC provided roads, parking areas, picnic shelters and related facilities. On a cool, clear creek running through the park, the CCC constructed a dam developing a pool and built a large bathhouse of logs and rocks. A recreational lodge with kitchen facilities for large, organized groups was constructed. Residences were built for the caretaker and his assistant, as well as maintenance buildings. Foot trails were established to allow the park visitor to observe the sanctuary for flora and fauna in the park. All of this work was by the CCC.

International Peace Garden—13 miles north of Dunseith—a boundary park for the two countries. The development of picnic areas, overnight cabins, a large lodge for meeting and community gatherings for residents of the two countries, an amphitheater, a caretakers and gardeners residence, as well as many roads, were all developed in North Dakota. Elaborate plans for a formal garden were begun with some rock construction in walkways and sunken pools on both sides of the border. In 1980, 46 years later, the planned formal garden area is beginning to show completion.

Theodore National Park—a recreational park—is located 16 miles south of Watford City. The major work accomplished here was roads through the beautiful terrain and exceptional geological features of the area. Picnic shelters, hiking and horse riding trails were also a part of the CCC project.

Furnished by Gwen White, Administrative Assistant, Mandan.

OHIO

Edmond Secrest 1906-1937   1906 Department of Forestry
O.A. Alderman 1937-1952

Camps
The average distribution of camps by services as of June, 1937 was as follows: National Forests 4, State Forests 10, State Parks 9, Soil Conservation Service 17, Agricultural Engineering 9, Military Reservation 1, Total 50.

Employment
The aggregate number of Ohio men given employment was 139,448. This figure included 133,551 junior and veteran enrollees and 5,897 non-enrolled personnel of camp officers and supervisory workers.

Work Accomplishments
Fences, rods 626,731
Erosion control, check dams, number 108,939
Trees planted, gully erosion, number 4,656,771
Trees planted, reforestation, number 42,374,000
Fighting forest fires, man-days 45,648

Expenditures
Total obligation in Ohio (Est.) $61,995,265
Allotments to dependents by enrollees (Est.) $28,500,882

Camps
At the outset of the CCC, 18 camps were assigned to Ohio and placed under the direction of the state forester. These camps were located as follows: seven on state forests, one on a state park and ten soil conservation camps on private land. The numbers were increased later to 27, with 13 on state forests and parks and 14 on soil conservation and flood control projects, which were placed under the direction of the Soil Conservation Service.

Forestry
The six state forests - Hocking County, Sciotio Trail, Dean, Shawnee, Mohican and Zaleski - were increased during CCC days by gift and purchase of four more -

Truck trail on Ohio State Forest constructed by E.C.W. for administration and fire protection uses.

Waterloo, Findley, Hocking and Pike. The work performed by the CCC on these areas was similar in most respects to what was done in other states.

Areas for emergency landing fields on the Zaleski and Sciotio State Forests were leveled. Garages and work shops were built. Fences were constructed around the forests and roads, though the forests were the major projects. Timber stand improvements included the cutting of dead trees and the harvesting of over mature ones. From the cutting operations, logs of chestnut, oak, pine, yellow poplar, gum, maple and other species in sizes ranging from poles to fine sawlogs were cut. The better poles were saved and the poorer ones were used for sign posts and firewood. The logs were taken to the mill, sawn, piled, seasoned and used in the construction of facilities on the state forests.

The CCC enrollees were used in the production of tree seedlings at both the Marietta State Nursery and at a special 35 acre E.C.W. Nursery at Zanesville, from which trees were shipped to Minnesota and Wisconsin for erosion control.

Several hundred acres on the state forests were planted to white, red, white and Scotch pines. Other work included boundary surveys and marking, topographic surveying and the thinning of trees in immature stands.

Forest Fire Control
Twelve new steel forest fire towers were erected and 65 miles of telephone lines were built to these areas. About 90% of the forest fire suppression was accomplished by the CCC.

State Parks
Public use areas, both large and small (where the public could picnic, hike, have shelter, water and sanitary systems) were built in state forests and parks. The construction of impounding reservoirs with concrete spillways, served recreational needs as well as fire protection purposes.

A swimming pool and bathhouse were built at Bryan Park. A road was constructed from here to the Edward Orton Park, a gift of Hugh Taylor Birch. The state forest parks, Rock House, Old Man's Cave and Ash Cave were improved. Other parks included Nelson Ledges, Cantwell Cliffs, Cedar Falls and Cook's Hollow.

OKLAHOMA

George R. Phillips 1926-1936   1925
Glen R. Durrell 1936-1946

Camps
The average distribution of camps by services as of June 30, 1937 was as follows: National Forest 1, Private Forests 2, Biological Survey 2, Soil Conservation Service 23, National Park 1, State Parks 12, Military Reservation 1, Total 50.

Employment

The aggregate number of Oklahoma men given employment was 107,676. This figure included 80,718 junior and veteran enrollees, 21,354 Indians and 5,604 non-enrolled personnel of camp officers and supervisory workers.

Work Accomplishments

Fences, rods. 1,005,595
Truck trails and minor roads, miles 2,400
Erosion control, check dams, number. 655,113
Trees planted, gully erosion control, number 5,264,516
Trees planted, reforestation, number. 15,863,000
Moving and planting trees and shrubs, number. 4,604,481
Insect pest control, acres 370,726

Expenditures

Total obligation in Oklahoma (Est.) $63,875,344
Allotments to dependents by enrollees (Est.). $20,421,955

State Parks

"There were seven original state parks built with the help of the Civilian Conservation Corps (CCC) and sometimes the help of the National Park Service. A brief synopsis of the origins of the state parks and the work done by the CCC follows:

Beavers Bend—The park began as a CCC project in 1935 and was opened in 1937 with a bathhouse, small bridge and park drive with some cabins.

Lake Murray State Park, Oklahoma.

Boiling Springs—The area for this park was purchased by the city of Woodward in 1935. A CCC camp was established and the major part of the facilities were built before the camp closed in 1940. A large community building for meetings was constructed, as well as a foot trail, swimming pool, bathhouse, foot bridge and picnic tables.

Greenleaf—Though Greenleaf did not become a state park until 1953, the lake dam and six cabins were constructed by the CCC.

Lake Murray—Construction of the dam began in 1933 and was completed in 1937, with the assistance of the National Park Service and later by CCC. The other construction by the CCC included a stone vehicle bridge, Tucker Tower (now a geological museum), cabins, picnic area and administration building.

Osage Hills—Citizens of Bartlesville and Pawhuska gave the state 500 acres of land in 1935. This gift, plus 300 acres purchased by the state, made up the original park. The CCC built the following: the park, drive, picnic shelter, water pump house, foot bridge, camp stoves and water hydrants.

Quartz Mountain—The city of Altus built a dam across the North Fork of the Red River in 1927, to provide water for the city. This area became a state park in 1935. Development and landscaping built by the CCC included: a low-water bridge across the river, a foot trail, carved stone steps on the foot trail, picnic shelter and a picnic area.

Robbers Cave—Robbers Cave is an outgrowth of a Boy Scout camp established there in 1926. The area was established as a state park in 1935 and the development was under the direction of the National Park Service and the CCC. The CCC built the dam for Lake Carlton, the bathhouse and some of the cabins and a group camp area.

Roman Nose—This park was leased from the city of Watonga and developed by the National Park Service with the facilities constructed by the CCC. Here the CCC constructed the entrance drive to the park, the bathhouse and swimming pool. In addition, they laid out much rock work and stone paths leading to two large springs that feed creeks that flow through the park.''

Information furnished by Glen V. McIntyre,
Planner, Division of Planning and Development

OREGON

L.F. Cronemiller 1930-1935	Board of Forestry
Nelson Rogers 1940-1949	created 1907
J.W. Fergueson 1935-1940	

Camps

The average distribution of camps by services in Oregon in 1937 was as follows: National Forests 18, State Forests 2, Private Forests 7, Biological Survey 3,

Soil Conservation Service 9, National Park 1, State Parks 4, Division of Grazing 3, Reclamation Service 5, Total 49.

Employment
The aggregate number of Oregon men given employment was 34,609. This figure included 25,022 junior and veteran enrollees, 2,767 Indians and 6,820 non-enrollees of Army officers and supervisory workers. The number of individuals who worked in Oregon regardless of the state of origin was 86,775.

Work Accomplishments
Bridges, all types, number 1,317
Lookout houses and towers, number 276
Trees planted, reforestation, number 49,351,000
Fighting forest fires, man-days 681,048
Tree insect pest control, acres 1,100,655
Rodent and predatory animal control, acres 1,657,815

Expenditures
Total obligation in Oregon (Est.) $87,734,444
Allotments to dependents by enrollees (Est.) . . . . $ 6,356,036

Camps
The State Forestry Department was allocated eight camps during the first period. The number was later reduced to six, from which point there was a gradual increase to 14.

Forestry
One of the main problems facing the CCC in Oregon was the fighting of forest fires, the likes of which those from the east had never seen. Also the eastern enrollees had never been back in the forests such a distance. They learned new terms such as snags, high-topping and cat skinners.

Three CCC youths lost their lives in a fire, and 14 others were injured going to a fire in Coos County when their truck went over a 50 foot

Nehalem CCC Camp.

embankment. During another fire, a Rhode Island youth lost his life when a snag fell and hit him while he was fighting a fire.

Oregon takes the nation's prize in building construction with a nice headquarters building at Salem, Oregon. The interior is finished in native woods, each room of which displays a separate wood: Douglas fir, spruce, hemlock, white fir, ponderosa pine, juniper, myrtle, maple and many others.

The building consists of 14 rooms on the first floor (exclusive of restrooms) and a vault and five rooms on the second floor. There is a full basement with a boiler room, vault for storage of records and eight other rooms, all bright and spacious.

Additional buildings on the area, also built by the CCC, include machine storage measuring 50 x 30 feet, a warehouse of similar size, a garage and machine shop.

For the Coos County Association, the CCCs built the following buildings: a residence, office, warehouse, and a combined water and lookout tower. Other headquarters buildings include those at Roseburg, the West Lane Fire Patrol Association at Veneta, and the Northeast Oregon Patrol unit at La Grande. The headquarters buildings at the Black Butte Association at Sisters were improved.

Due to the distance of much work located away from the main camp, side camps were established at the following locations: Reehers, Boyington, Fairdale, Dry Lake Side, Marshfield, Long Tom, Camp Wilark, Wimer, Valsety, Silverton spike camps, and others. Spike camp is the term used in the west for side camp. During the summer of 1938, Oregon and Washington enrollees were sent to a camp on Mt. McKinley in Alaska. Many enrollees were sent to Oregon from Kansas, Nebraska and Missouri. Enrollees were also sent to Annette Island, Alaska, to build runways. Some 15 camps, which were to go west, were canceled due to eastern Governors' protests of sending their youths west.

Work Projects

As a result of the Tillamook and Wolf Creek fires, which burned over 300,000 acres, several hundred enrollees with intensive training were held ready for fire suppression.

As a result of the danger of forest fires, truck trails were built deep into the forests to reach fires quickly. The construction of truck trails eased the task of carting the materials necessary to build the forest fire towers, lookout watchmen's cabins, telephone lines and many other items.

With the labor of the enrollees from Camp Arboretum, it was possible to perform all the work in raising millions of forest seedlings.

Many man-days of labor were expended by the CCC in felling snags— dead and dying trees.

State Parks

The Oregon State Park system had 17 CCC camps. At the Silver Falls State Park, the CCC developments included: road construction, parking areas, trails, foot bridges, stove shelters, benches and tables, camp area buildings, and water and sanitary systems to meet the demand for recreational facilities.

At the Jessie M. Honeyman Memorial State Park, on the Oregon Coast and Woahink Lake, there was constructed a foreman's cottage, a large stone bathhouse, roads and trails, a waterlevel control dam among other projects. The CCC developed 22 state parks for camping, namely: Blue Mounds, Buffalo River, Cascade River, Charles A. Lindbergh, Flandrau, Fort Ridgely, Gooseberry Falls, Interstate, Itasca, Jay Cooke, Lac Que Parle, Lake Bemidji, Lake Shetek, Monson Lake, St. Croix, Scenic, Sibley, Split Rock Creek, Temperance River, and White Water.

Park Information by Elizabeth Potter

PENNSYLVANIA

L.E. Staley 1931-1935   Division of Forestry
T.C. Buchanan 1935   Established 1895
R. Lynn Emerick 1936-1946

Camps
The average distribution of camps by services, in Pennsylvania, as of June 30, 1937 was as follows: National Forests 7, State Forests 63, Private Forests 2, Soil Conservation Service 9, National Park Service 2, State Parks 11, Military Reservations 2, Total 95.

Employment
The aggregate number of Pennsylvania men given employment was 194,572. This figure included 184,916 junior and veteran enrollees, and 9,656 non-enrolled personnel of camp officers and supervisory workers.

Work Accomplishments
Impounding and large diversion dams, number 102
Truck trails and minor roads, miles 3,273
Trees planted, reforestation, number 59,806,000
Forest stand improvement, acres 201,468
Tree and plant disease control, acres 406,059
Fish rearing ponds, number 1,698

Expenditures
Total obligation in Pennsylvania (Est.) $126,435,051
Allotments to dependents by enrollees (Est.) . . . . $ 39,536,770

Recollections of the CCC in Pennsylvania
by Ralph Wible, State Forester, 1953 -

By 1933 (when the CCC came into being), Pennsylvania had more than 30 years of state forestry programs. Shortly after the turn of the century, the early efforts in the field of forest land acquisition and forest fire control occupied the attention of the early foresters. The problems of fire prevention and control were great, while the combating forces were small, although willing, strong and undiscouraged.

The years leading to the CCC program, were years of slow but determined progress in which stronger and better trained fire control programs were developed. State forests of almost two million acres were being developed and protected. Roads and trails were built and areas were reforested where needed. Small forest parks and picnic areas were developed.

With the establishment in Pennsylvania of more than 50 CCC camps on state forests, state game lands, and national parks, there was a promise that many dreams of rapid development and protection of the national resources would come true.

Some 50 thousand young men from all parts of the state, found a new and happy life in hastily erected barracks in the forests of our state. The Department of Forests and Waters (now the Department of Environmental Resources) was well equipped to plan and supervise the work of the camps. Very fortunately, the state forestry department had field districts throughout the state, supervised by one or more qualified foresters, and this formed the core of program planning and organization for these new camps. The accomplishments of the CCC during 1933-1942 were as follows:

Forestry

Inventory of state forest timber—A system of tree inventory was in progress when the camps were closed. A new and more modern method emerged later which enabled the work to be completed and management plans prepared for each state forest district.

Reforestation—The existing four state forest tree nurseries were increased in production during the CCC years. Almost all camps engaged in reforestation. Many acres of idle state forest and state park lands were reforested. Many areas of sparse growth were reinforced with forest seedlings.

TSI and Timber Salvage—Because of the past lumbering methods, as well as the effects of forest fires, many areas of state forest lands were in need of TSI measures. Under trained foresters, this work was undertaken and completed on thousands of areas. Some areas required salvage treatment. The resultant wood was used as fuel in the camps or state parks.

Fire Control—New and improved telephone lines were constructed, many miles of fire prevention trails were constructed, several new fire towers were built.

A voluntary forest fire warden system was in existence at the opening of the CCC program and is still in successful use. There were numerous times, however, that the CCC enrollees were used to advantage to supplement the local voluntary crews. The CCC was only called upon during unusual or hazardous times.

Tree Disease—A statewide program on white pine blister rust control was initiated in many camps and kept in full operation during the life of the camps.

Truck Trails and Foot Trails—Under the old department program, probably 15 hundred miles of truck trails and one thousand miles of trails had been built during a period of 25 years.

In less than six years, this mileage was not only doubled but many of the existing truck trails were rebuilt to a higher standard. Likewise, the foot trails were doubled also.

Recreation
Numerous existing state forest parks and picnic areas were completely revamped and expanded. New parks were planned, designed, and built. Prior to CCC, the parks were mainly in the forested areas of the state and not necessarily near centers of population. Five new large recreational areas were constructed closer to larger cities.

Miscellaneous Programs
Camps assisted in marking state forest boundaries. They assisted the Pennsylvania Fish Commission in numerous developments on streams to improve fishing conditions. They helped in propagating fish.

The flood of 1936, in the Susquehanna water shed, was disastrous to property and some lives were lost. The enrollees of at least eight camps helped in disaster areas to restore order and in the general clean up.

Summary
It is estimated that the total work accomplished by the camps advanced conservation and development on the state forests and state parks by 20 years.

It would be impossible to measure the social, economic, and physical benefits to enrollees, businesses, and families. We'll really never know the full story of the good this program accomplished. The stories and incidents exist everywhere in every corner of the state. The relating of them would fill a book.

RHODE ISLAND

Eric G. Jacobson Chief Forester   1939-1952   1939

Camps
The average number of camps in Rhode Island was four, divided as follows: State Forests 1, Private Forests 3, State Parks 2.

Employment
Average number of Rhode Island men employed was 15,915. This number included 15,088 junior and veteran enrollees and the rest (827) who were camp officers and supervisory personnel.

Work Accomplishments
Trees planted, reforestation, number 912,000
Fire hazard reduction, acres 7,921
Tree and plant disease control, acres. 649,244
Tree insect pest control, acres 639,000
Emergency work, man days. 32,181

Expenditures
Total obligations in Rhode Island (Est.) $8,883,704
Allotments to dependents of enrollees (Est.) $3,460,705

State Forests
If Rhode Island was to receive its proportionate share of CCC funds, it was felt that it was necessary to acquire state forest lands. Consequently, from 1934 the acquisition of state forests progressed as rapidly as funds were made available. However, from an initial purchase of 35 acres in 1928 there was no increase in such holdings until 1934, when 1133 acres of forest land, known as the Redden Tract, was purchased. On October 6, 1934, a veteran's camp moved on to the Appenzeller tract. A forest demonstration and experimental area was developed by enrollees from the Redden camp. The Ellendale Tract was also a part of the Redden camp work area. The other area known as the Owens Tract of 170 acres was purchased with funds contributed by the State Federation of Women's Clubs.
Work projects, On October 6, 1934, a veterans CCC camp was established on the Redden State Forest. The men from this camp worked on all the state forest tracts previously mentioned. The work executed by camp S 53 was similar to that which was carried out in other New England States.

The work projects included reforestation, timber stand improvement, truck trail construction, fighting forest fires and the erection of a 123 foot fire tower. A severe ice storm in January, 1935, caused serious damage to both state and private forests. The CCC aided in clean-up on state land. Logs from the blow-downs were saved to build shelters and other facilities.

The CCC enrollees were also used for the production of forest tree seedlings at the state tree nursery.

Parks
The Burlingame Reservation was increased in 1936 by the condemnation of about 89 acres. This reservation surrounds Watchaug Pond of 500 acres, where picnic and camping facilities were constructed.

The George Washington Memorial Reservation was donated to the state by a group of public spirited women's clubs and patriotic organizations as a state memorial to George Washington.

The 1186th company of camp SP1 worked hard on the development of the Dawley Memorial Park in the town of Richmond. This area was given by Mrs. Mary Dawley as a memorial to her husband. The land was cleared and new growth planted to beautify the area through which foot trails were built. A large shelter was built in the picnic area.

Wickaboxed Falls area, one of the most picturesque areas in the state, was developed into a picnic and wildlife preserve. The picnic area is located around Step Stone Falls, and the land along Wood River is preserved for wild game. A shelter was constructed there.

Beach Pond, a popular bathing area, was developed with the addition of a bathhouse and bathing facilities. The Hendrick's lot was cleared and served as an entrance area to Beach Pond, where a large shelter was built.

Other completed park work included trails to and in Goddard Park, the Indian Burial Ground, Fort Neck, Queens Fort, Diamond Hill Forest Reservation, Peter Randall Reservation, Breakheart Brook Area, Olney Pond area and Lincoln Woods.

SOUTH CAROLINA

H.A. Smith 1931-1941   1927

Camps

The average number of CCC camps operated in South Carolina was 29. The average distribution of camps by services in June, 1937 was as follows: National Forests 8, State Forests 2, Private Forests 5, Soil Conservation Service 13, Biological Survey 1, National Park 1, State Park 1, State Parks 3, Bureau of Reclamation 1.

Employment

The aggregate number of South Carolina men given employment was 48,171. This figure included 42,395 junior and veteran enrollees and 5,776 non-enrolled personnel of camp officers and supervisory workers. The number of individuals who worked in South Carolina regardless of the state of origin was 49,266.

Work Accomplishments

Bridges, all types, number. 895
Lookout houses and towers, number. 129
Check dams, erosion control, number 218,047
Gully tree planting, number. 1,478,696
Trees planted, reforestation, number. 56,788,000
Fighting forest fires, man-days 113,846

Expenditures

Total obligation in South Carolina (Est.). $57,146,020
Allotments to dependents by enrollees (Est.). $12,458,000

Without Federal approval to work on private land when there were no fire protective organizations, and without any land in state ownership, South Carolina could not take advantage of the CCC program. The 1933-1934 legislature placed the administration of the state parks under the administration of the State Forest Commission. Finally, the Federal government approved work on timber protective organized lands.

Camps

The first camps in the state were located at Walhalla, Cleveland, Parr, Summerville, Moncks Corner, Fort Moultrie, Sumter, Parris Island and Selma. Later there were 12 camps located in District I at Georgetown, Montmorenci, Waterboro, Florence, Kinstree, Blaney, Nichols, Witherbee and Luray. The final three were at the Second Corps Area Camps, summer locations in Idaho and Montana. During the first few months of 1935, the June enrollment was doubled and 17 camps were ordered to be constructed because the state had acquired more land to work on. When a camp was closed, a side camp was established to complete work projects.

Forestry

The usual work projects carried on in the southern states were in operation in South Carolina. These projects included: lookout towers, cabins, telephone lines, firebreaks, roadside clearings, and truck and foot trails—all of which aided in the reduction and cost of forest fire control in this state. An unusual project was developed here in South Carolina. A building housed machinery that CCC enrollees used to construct pipe of concrete for road drainage.

At the beginning of the fiscal year 1934, there had been established 12 forest protective associations. By 1942, county-wide forest fire protection had been extended to 24 of the 46 counties.

An interesting development in this state was the acquisition of ten acres around each proposed tower site so the towerman could get partial subsistence from tilling the land—especially on the off-fire season.

The state forest tree nurseries at Camden, Georgetown, Ceasar's Head and Bennetsville produced, with CCC help, millions of forest seedlings for planting idle and eroded lands. The CCC aided in the collection of tree cones, extraction of seed, nursery work and reforestation.

Much work was accomplished which aided the development of fish and game resources.

Dining and recreation hall for summer camping of groups at Parris Mountain State Park near Greenville. Built by CCC.

In 1939, two state forests aggregating 121,000 acres in Chesterfield and Sumter Counties were leased by the Federal government to the Forestry Commission for a period of 95 years. In addition to the Aiken State Forest, which was started in 1934, work on three additional state forests was commenced. These state forests were located in the following counties: Oconee, Greenville, and Lee. Many recreational projects were developed in all of these forests, in addition to the development of fire protection and timber management. Other work of the state forests included timber type mapping and timber cruising.

State Parks

South Carolina had no state parks previous to 1933. Soon thereafter, an area of 704 acres near Cheraw was donated to the state, having been purchased by donations of Chesterfield County citizens and business firms. Other counties were prompt to follow this example and, among the first additional areas to be deeded to the state for this purpose, were those of Givans Ferry in Dorchester County, Poinsett in Sumter County, Myrtle Beach in Pickens County, Edisto Beach in Charleston County and Chester County.

In June, 1940, two Federally owned recreational demonstration areas (Cheraw and Kings Mountain) were leased to the State Commission on Forestry and included in the state park system. By April, 1941, the state system was composed of 16 state parks with a total area of 34,753 acres.

The state parks developed by the CCC comprised the following: Aiken, Barnwell, Cheraw, Chester, Edisto Beach, Givans Ferry, Greenwood, Hunting Island, Kings Mountain, Lee, Myrtle Beach, Parris Mountain, Poinsett, Oconee, Sesqui-Centennial, and Table Rock.

Recreational development was carried on from both the forest and the park camps. The recreational developments in South Carolina were quite similar to what was executed in other states. In addition to the usual picnic and camping developments, mention should be made of group camping areas, scenic roads, trailer camps, beach developments with bathhouses, swimming pools, dams with lake areas and landscaping.

SOUTH DAKOTA

J.D. Snow 1934-1939   Division of Forestry 1945
Ed Gray 1940-1943

Camps

The average distribution of camps by services in 1937 was as follows: National Forests 10, State Forest 1, Biological Survey 1, Soil Conservation Service 4, National Park 1, State Parks 3, Bureau of Reclamation 1, Total 21.

Employment

The aggregate number of South Dakota men given employment was 31,097. This figure included 23,709 junior and veteran enrollees, 4,554 Indians, 2,834 non-enrolled personnel of camp officers and supervisory workers. The number of individuals who worked in South Dakota regardless of the state of origin was 32,471.

Work Accomplishments

Bridges, all types, number..498
Impounding and large diversion dams, number........................ 468
Telephone lines, miles.. 1,381
Truck trails and minor roads...................................... 1,528
Trees planted, number... 22,238,000
Fighting forest fires, number, man-days............................ 77,091
Fish stocked, number.. 4,119,316
Rodent and predatory animal control, acres...................... 2,735,878

Expenditures

Total obligation in South Dakota (Est.)........................ $ 6,214,850
Allotments to dependents by enrollees (Est.)................... $30,497,394

State Parks

The CCC camp on Farm Island, in the Missouri River below Pierre, was established in the summer of 1933. The first work on Farm Island consisted of the removal of all dead timber. Underbrush was selectively cut to keep the impression of nature undisturbed. A beautiful picnic area was built. A small bridge spanned a small pond.

A causeway was built from the island and constructed with brush and dirt amounting to about 9,140 cubic feet. The dike was protected on the upstream side by driving 24 foot cottonwood piling down into the river bed. It was then backfilled with willow brush to prevent erosion until the gap was closed. The segment from the main land was made of rock fill.

The causeway and road to the park was completed on or about October 1, 1934, when Mayor Whipple of Pierre dedicated the causeway. After the road was surfaced, Company 796 left the island for Hayes Center, Nebraska on November 1 and 2, 1934.

Work of Other Camps

The National Forest Camps were engaged in work on the Black Hills, Harney and Custer National Forests. Much of their work was in the field of forest fire protection, timber stand improvement, reforestation and recreational development.

The Bureau of Biological Survey camps were engaged in carrying out wildlife conservation measures on the Sand Lake Refuge and the LaCreek Teal Refuge.

A state park camp continued the development of American Island Metropolitan Park and two others. They worked on the Custer State Park, an area of 102,734 acres located in the rugged and scenic part of the Black Hills. This area was stocked with elk, deer, buffalo and Rocky Mountain sheep and goats. The work here consisted of the development of boating, fishing, bathing and camping facilities. The National Park Service had a camp at Wind Cave, a wildlife refuge. There, improvements were made to the trails within the cave and facilities were developed within the park.

TENNESSEE

James O. Hazard 1930-1951   1921

Camps
The average distribution of camps by services in Tennessee on June 30, 1937 was as follows: National Forests 10, State Forests 6, T.V.A. 16, Soil Conservation Service 6, National Parks 8, State Parks 5, T.V.A. Parks 3, Total 54.

Employment
The aggregate number of Tennessee men given employment was 72,655. This figure included 66,303 junior and veteran enrollees, and 6,352 non-enrolled personnel of camp officers and supervisory workers. The number of individuals who worked in Tennessee regardless of the state of origin was 76,698.

Work Accomplishments
Bridges, all types, number. 772
Check dams, erosion control, number 502,797
Gully trees planted, erosion control, number. 45,024,715
Trees planted, reforestation, number. 36,437,000
Fighting forest fires, man-days. 155,984
Fire presuppression and prevention, man-days. 169,137
Fish stocked, number. 1,887,669

Expenditures
Total obligation in Tennessee (Est.). $71,940,568
Allotments to dependents by enrollees (Est.). $16,844,548

State Parks
The development of state parks in this state was under the direction of the Tennessee Valley Authority. The Department of Conservation with a Division of State Parks was formed by the state legislature in 1937. The Departments of Agriculture and Interior, through their divisions, were the operation agencies in The Tennessee Valley Authority.

The Tennessee Valley Authority continued its policy of developing parks, which by 1938 numbered five. Parks were administered on the shores of Pickwick Lake, Cove Lake, two on Norris Lake and one on Harrison Island in Chickamauga Lake. With the exception of Pickwick Park, these developments were turned over to the State of Tennessee as Cove Lake State Park, Big Ridge State Park, Harrison Bay State Park and Norris Dam State Park. From 1938 to 1951, these parks were leased to the state of Tennessee.

These parks were developed as multiple recreation areas with facilities for swimming, boating, fishing, camping, hiking and picnicing. A special project was the Norris Parkway, constructed along the approach to Norris Dam and Park by the CCC. By 1938, the Tennessee Park department acquired a 92 acre tract of land adjoining TVA property from the citizens of Caryville.

With the aid of the CCC, the Resettlement Administration and the National Park Service, Montgomery Bell, Fall Creek Falls, Shelby Forest and Steele Creek recreational areas were acquired and reforested. The idea was to turn these areas over to local government following development and legislation. In some areas, artificial lakes were built for swimming, boating, fishing, and other water sports. Some areas were developed for day use, consisting of picnic areas, day visitor and group camping, while other areas were for limited use such as foot and bridal trails and nature study. In 1943 and 1944, these four developments were deeded to the state to be used as state parks. Steele Creek, renamed Watauga State Park, proved to be unsuitable as a state park and was deeded to the city of Bristol to be used as a municipal park.

The Department of Agriculture, under its authority by the New Deal Act, developed five areas which became state parks. CCC labor was used in these developments. The areas included Cedars of Lebanon, Natches Trace, Chickasaw, Standing Stone and Cumberland Homesteads Park. These areas were acquired by the state in 1939 under a 50-year lease. The administration of the areas as parks or forests was a bit confusing.

State Parks

After 1925, the state took no action on state parks development until the days of the New Deal. The State Park and Forestry Commission acquired lands for the National Government between 1927 and 1931. The legislature appropriated one and one-half million dollars in 1927 for the purchase of lands for the Great Smoky National Park Service, and saw this project through to completion.

CCC camps finished considerable work at Cumberland Head and Booker T. Washington State Parks. The Tennessee Valley Authority developed the Pickwick Dam Park.

TEXAS

E.O. Siecke 1918-1942   1915

Camps

The average distribution of camps by services in Texas as of June 30, 1937 was as follows: National Forests 9, State Forest 1, Private Forests 7, Soil Conservation Service 31, State Parks 22, Bureau of Reclamation 1, Military Reservations 4, Total 75.

Employment

The aggregate number of Texas men given employment was 156,404. This figure included 146,966 junior and veteran enrollees and 9,438 non-enrolled personnel of camp officers and supervisory workers.

Work Accomplishments

Bridges, all types, number 7,793
Fences, rods. 3,672,060
Telephone lines, miles 3,359
Truck trails and minor roads, miles 6,085

Erosion control, check dams, number 61,634
Sheet erosion, planting, acres 50,638
Contour furrows, ridges, miles 51,955
Trees planted, reforestation, acres 72,784,000

Expenditures
Total obligation in Texas (Est.) $110,610,267
Allotments to dependents by enrollees (Est.) . . . . $ 37,612,408

Establishment of Camps
The first four camps were established on May 27, and 28, 1933, at Lufkin,
Trinity, Livingston and on the state forest at Kirbyville. By June 18,
eight additional camps were established at the following locations: Center,
Pineland, Maydelle, Honey Island, Woodville, Weches, Oakhurst and Conroe.
During October and November, 1933, additional camps were erected at Woden,
Groveton, Jasper, Cleveland and Huntsville.

Construction, Building
A new office building to house the Division of Forest Protection at Lufkin,
together with a warehouse, was constructed with funds made available by
the state legislature in 1934. Another warehouse was also constructed at
Lufkin with CCC funds. Ten of the 14 rooms of the office building were
finished in different wood paneling, donated by operating lumber companies
of East Texas. The citizens of Lufkin, through the Chamber of Commerce,
provided a building site for the office and the two warehouses.

Truck Trails
Numerous truck trails were constructed in remote forest areas. These roads,
together with the extensive communications system and numerous lookout

Texas Dust Storm, 1935. U.S. Forest Service.

towers constructed by the enrollees, made it possible to provide much more efficient forest fire protection.

Forestry

About 110 miles of fire breaks were built. Large areas of idle land were reforested and acres of timber mapping carried out. During this period, Texas had four state forests upon which stand improvement work was conducted. Over 60,000 cypress shingles were obtained from the state forests. Over 2,700 cords of wood were cut from the four state forests and used at the CCC camps and the surplus was sold. About 100,000 board feet of timber cut from the road right-of-way on the state forests and a large number of telephone poles, together with many fence posts, were cut for state use.

During the CCC period, the following recreational facilities were added on the state forests: a large log recreational and meeting hall on State Forest #1; with a residence and necessary outbuildings; similar buildings for the technical forester were constructed in State Forest #3; a cottage for the lookout watchman and caretaker was constructed in State Forest #4. Fire towers were erected on State Forests #3 and #4. State Forest #5 was acquired as a gift from the citizens of Houston County, supplemented by some state funds. This state forest of 117 acres embraces the location of the old Mission San Francisco de los Tejas, which was founded in 1690 and later destroyed.

On the tract, the enrollees constructed an observation tower from which a view is available into three counties. An attractive picnic site was built on the site. Native pines, slash pines and flowering plants such as dogwood were planted.

State Parks

Texas parklands hardly deserved the term "park system" when the CCC was organized in 1933.

The Bastrop State Park, in 1933, consisted of 4,000 acres of cut-over pines, oak and black sand hills. The CCC built a large refectory building, which has been used as a site of family reunions, club meetings and a general activity center. On a hill overlooking the park, a native stone overlook was constructed. A dozen cabins, shelters, picnic units and other structures were built at this park. In addition, the corpsmen fabricated much of the furniture, metal work and other equipment eventually used in the park.

At the Lockhart State Park, a swimming pool was built alongside scenic Plum Creek.

Similar park work was accomplished at other Texas state parks: Longhorn Cavern State Park, Palmetto State Park, Balmorhea State Park, Tyler State Park, Lake Corpus Christi State Park, Goose Island State Park, Palo Duro Canyon State Park, Cleburne State Park, Mathis State Park.

The state parks developed or improved by the CCC were as follows: Abilene, Balmorhea, Bastrop, Big Spring, Blanco, Buescher, Caddo Lake, Daingerfield, Davis Mountain, Fort Parker, Garner, Goliad, Huntsville, Kerrville, Lake Bromwood, Lake Corpus Christi, Lockhart, Longhorn Cavern, Meridian, Mission Tejas, Old Fort Parker, Palmetto, Palo Duro Canyon and Tyler.

UTAH

Paul Dunn 1941-1942   Bd. Fire Control Created 1937

Camps

The aggregate number of camps in Utah was 27. The average distribution of camps by services in June, 1937 was as follows: National Forests 12, Agricultural Engineering 1, Soil Conservation Service 4, State Park 1, Bureau or Reclamation 10, General Land Office 2.

Employment

The aggregate number of Utah men given employment was 22,074. This figure included 16,872 junior and veteran enrollees, 746 Indians and 4,456 non-enrolled personnel of camp officers and supervisory workers.

Work Accomplishments

Impounding and large diversion dams, number 423
Fences and guard rails, number...................................... 662,054
Truck trails and minor roads, miles 4,246
Trees planted, reforestation, number............................. 3,255,000
Ranges, revegetation, acres.. 214,290
Rodent and predatory animal control, acres...................... 1,654,256

Expenditures

Total obligation in Utah (Est.)................................. $52,756,183
Allotments to dependents by enrollees (Est.).................... $ 4,166,084

VERMONT

Perry H. Merrill 1929-1966   Forest Commissioner 1904
                                                     State Forester 1908

Camps

The average distribution of camps by services in Vermont as of June 30, 1937 was as follows: National Forests 4, State Forests 7, Private Forests 4, State Parks 4, Corps of Engineers 10, Military Reservation 1, Total 30.

Employment

The aggregate number of Vermont men given employment was 11,243. This figure included 6,567 junior and veteran enrollees and 4,676 non-enrolled camp officers and supervisory workers. The number of individuals who worked in Vermont regardless of the state of origin was 40,868.

Work Accomplishments

Bridges, all types, number.. 197
Camp stoves and fireplaces, number 531
Excavation, channels, canals, ditches (flood control), cu. yds........... 94,144
Clearing and cleaning, channels, levies, cu. yds..................... 329,072

Trees planted, reforestation, number............................ 1,122,000
Tree insect pest control, acres................................ 1,030,624
Emergency work, man-days 58,969

Expenditures
Total obligation in Vermont (Est.)............................ $40,548,385
Allotments to dependents by enrollees (Est.)................... $ 1,793,780

Supervisory Force
The first responsibility of the state forester, Perry H. Merrill, was the selection of camp superintendents, foremen and other employees for the operation of the Civilian Conservation Corps program. This was accomplished, in many cases, by personal interviews with about 200 people. Many foresters, engineers, landscape architects and other needed personnel were without employment, so it was not difficult to obtain high grade, efficiently and technically trained personnel for each position. There were eight to ten men with practical experience who were selected for each camp. These local experienced men (LEM) served as crew leaders to teach and direct the unexperienced enrollees how to accomplish their tasks.

Fortunately, most of Vermont's supervisory force was employed before Congress awoke to the fact that they might be losing a lot of political patronage. However, directives were received from Director Fechner that certain employees would be selected from a list by a Congressman or by the Democratic National Committeeman (Vermont's Hon. Frank Duffy of Rutland). Mr. Duffy was very cooperative and never suggested anyone for employment who was not qualified for one of the few openings.

When the CCC program started, the state forester had only one assistant,

Start of CCC Truck Trail, Vermont.

Charles R. Lockard. Three district foresters in the field were E. Huntley Palmer, Wilbur E. Bradder and P.H. Teachout. The rest of the field force included two forest engineers, Francis Smalley and Horace Squire. The office force included Alba P. DeColaines, secretary, and Norma Ralph, clerk.

It was evident that the amount of clerical and fiscal work to be handled needed more help, so Director Fechner's office agreed to the employment of the necessary help to take care of the numerous forms, and to see that the thousands of bills were checked and sent to the Federal fiscal office for payment. Experienced people were selected for these positions.

Reasonable and timely inspections were made of the fiscal and work progress in Vermont and other states by the district and regional offices of Director Fechner, the U.S. Forest Service and the National Park Service.

Forestry

One of the main CCC projects in Vermont was the improvement and management of the state and municipal forests. Trees of minor value for saw timber, such as crooked or diseased ones, were cut out in the thinning process and used as camp firewood. In other cases, trees of undesirable species and those suppressed were removed to allow for increased growth of the more valuable trees. Overspreading "wolf" trees were also cut. Many plantations were pruned to produce higher grade lumber.

Other tasks were forest fire presuppression and fighting of forest fires. New steel forest fire lookout towers were built on the following mountains: Belleview Hill, Gore, Cushman, Gilson, Stratton, Townshend and West Pond. Some of these towers were replacements of old wooden ones which were built 30 years previously. New wooden towers were erected at Mt. Alice, Burke Mountain and Spruce Knob. New lookout cabins were built at Gilson, Gore, Mount Olga, Mt. Alice, Pico, Spruce Knob, Stratton and West Pond. Telephone lines were built or rebuilt at these and other tower sites to the nearest commercial telephone line, and to cabins.

For the CCC, many dozens of fire rakes, Indian back pumps, hazel hoes, power pumps and hose were acquired, as were bull dozers and jack hammers.

At the 900 acre Essex Municipal Forest, fire roads were constructed within and around the perimeter of the forest.

Insect and disease control was the major task of some of the camps. Two of the principal defoliators of the sugar maple and other valuable tree species were the gypsy and brown tail moths. The control of these moths is described in the New York State Report.

Reforestation

Some of the enrollees from the Waterbury Camp #191 were used at the Essex tree nursery to seed, transplant, dig, bale and ship nursery stock of pines and spruces for the reforestation of private and state forest land. The enrollees from several camps were used in the reforestation of state forest lands.

Roads and Truck Trails

The CCC from a number of the camps built over 105 miles of roads and truck trails, chiefly on state land. The longest stretch of ten miles which connected U.S. #2 at Marshfield with U.S. #302 at Groton was built through the

Groton State forest. At the Marshfield end, three miles of road were improved, including the relocation of over a quarter of a mile of town road. The state took over the ten mile stretch and made it a part of the state highway system because it was so well built with drainage and grade.

Roads of recreational as well as other values were constructed up to or near mountain summits. Such roads included the McCullough Road. It was built to the summit of the Green Mountains. Later, it was extended down the other side of the mountain by the State Highway Department to make a short cut to some communities. Two miles of recreational road were built up Burke Mountain in the Darling State Park. This park area was given to the state by L.A. and Henry Darling. At Ascutney Mountain State Park, a road was constructed to near the summit. Other roads for recreational use and needed parking areas were built in all the state parks. These roads were graveled, crowned and well drained. They varied from ten to 20 feet in width depending upon the use. Roads and picnic areas were built in Hubbard Park, Montpelier.

Fish and Game
The forest, the natural home for wild animals, serves as their shelter and their source for food. The enrollees in the CCC carried on much work to make the environment better for our fish and wild animals. Cuttings in the forest, correctly made, opened up the forest so that food plants would furnish berries and other food for small game. During the deep winter snows, deer would grow and thrive on the sprouting growth. The habitat for fish in the streams was improved by providing riffle logs to make deeper pools. Shrubs which produce berries were planted in open places.

The CCC made Vermont The Ski Capital of the East.
A CCC camp at Waterbury furnished 25 men in a side camp at Stowe, Vermont. They built the first ski trails on the mountain in Mt. Mansfield State Forest. The trail design and layout was under foreman, Charles D. Lord, recognized by the skiing fraternity as a trail design master in the skiing world. He designed trails at Mt. Mansfield and at the other CCC developments as well. Later he was an adviser to private developments. To expedite the recreational development, a full CCC camp was built at Moscow in the town of Stowe.

The first trail constructed on Mt. Mansfield was the Bruce, named after an old lumberman in the Ranch Valley, a valley in which the trail was extended to the mountain toll road. Soon, another trail was built from the Ranch Valley to another site on the Mountain Toll Road. Other early trails built by the CCC enrollees included; the Ski Meister, the Overland, the Perry Merrill, the (Charley) Lord, the S-53 and the important Nose Dive. As a result of the construction of some of these trails, popular opinion demanded that the Notch Road be plowed to a point opposite the base of the Nose Dive and the State Ski Shelter. Here, a large parking area was built by the CCC enrollees. and enlarged several times to hold several hundred cars. It was in 1940 that state officials signed a lease with the Mt. Mansfield Company to build a ski lift up Mt. Mansfield. This development was the forerunner of many ski areas being built in Vermont and the northeast. Ski developments were made on several other tracts of state land.

Camp William James, Sharon, Vt.

After the CCC Camp at Sharon was closed, a group of Dartmouth and Harvard youths, who had previously served in the CCC on the Downer State Forest, were instrumental in getting the camp reopened. Their first task was to obtain the approval of Director McIntee. President Roosevelt gave his approval for the reopening of the camp.

A detachment from the Bellows Falls CCC camp was sent to Sharon to reactivate the camp buildings. Mrs. Eleanor Roosevelt, the President's wife, a strong promoter, believed that young Americans should be encouraged to serve their country in the spirit expressed in the famous treatise of William James, "The Moral Equivalent of War". Other well known people who gave their support to the establishment of Camp William James included the authors, Dorothy Thompson of Woodstock and Dorothy Canfield Fisher of Arlington, Senator Ralph Flanders of Springfield and Senator George D. Aiken of Putney.

Eugene Rosenstock Huessey, a social philosophy professor at Dartmouth College, gave the spark and intellectual leadership to the camp. The youths at the camp were engaged in such projects as the resettlement of abandoned farms, improvement of roads to them and soil erosion. Help was given for improving and maintaining rural school buildings and for labor as needed on the farms.

A non-profit educational corporation was formed to guide the camp. Paul V. McNutt, administrator of the Federal Security Agency at the time, stated that the students at Dartmouth and Harvard were eligible to enter the camp under Federal regulations. Out of an enrollment of about 50, only about 12 were college students or graduates.

The camp was opened in 1940, with appropriate remarks by Congressman Engel. Due to the approach of WW II, everybody's interest, including the President's, turned from the camp to the war situation. So, after a short operation during a part of 1940, the camp was terminated in 1941.

Poultney S.C.S. Camp

The only S.C.S. camp in Vermont was located on the James Brayton farm in Poultney. The Poultney-Mettowee Conservation District, the first one organized in Vermont, was the cooperating agency with the U.S. Soil Conservation Service. The work consisted of tree planting, soil conservation and stream bank protection. The protection of the banks of the Mettowee, Wells, and Poultney Rivers was accomplished by planting willows and rip-rapping the river banks with native slate which was hand-placed.

VIRGINIA

F.C. Pederson 1934-1944   1914

Camps

The average distribution of camps in Virginia by services on June 30, 1937 was as follows: National Forests 14, Private Forests 24, T.V.A. 4, National Parks 16, State Parks 11, Military Reservations 3, Naval Reservation 1, Total 83.

Employment
The aggregate number of Virginia men given employment was 75,197. This figure included 64,762 junior and veteran enrollees and 10,435 non-enrolled camp officers and supervisory workers. The number of individuals who worked in Virginia regardless of the state of origin was 107,210.

Work Accomplishments
Bridges, all types, number..986
Fences and guard rails, rods...................................865,866
Erosion control, check dams, number............................202,522
Gully trees planted, erosion control, number.................4,616,306
Trees planted, reforestation, number........................10,644,000
Fire hazard reduction, acres...................................152,000

Expenditures
Total obligation in Virginia (Est.)........................$108,914,121
Allotments to dependents by enrollees (Est.)...............$ 15,207,626

Camps
On June 4, 1933, the first of eight CCC camp enrollees arrived by railroad near to the camp location. These were in the counties of Tazewell, Bland, Craig, Roanoke, Albemarle, Chesterfield, King and Queen and Charles City. The enrollees at Camp King and Queen were colored WWI veterans, and those at Charles City were white veterans. Both groups were a part of the Bonus Marchers, which have been mentioned elsewhere.

Politics
In the early days the district forester was unhampered by politics. However, later the so-called "Friant" master list, maintained in Washington from information submitted by local politicians, made it impossible for a person to get a technical or foreman's job without political approval. To combat this situation, the district foresters turned to their county chief wardens for camp personnel.

Work Projects
Work projects consisted of the standard CCC approved ones, which were the construction of truck trails, erecting fire towers, bridges and telephone lines to towers and headquarters, fire fighting and timber management on the state forests.

Forest fires—In 1933, there were only 58% of the 100 Virginia counties that supported a forest fire protection organization. At the termination of the CCC there were 92 such counties. The CCC impact on fire suppression was considerable, both in the size of the average size of fire of 84.5 acres in the period 1929-1933 to 24.1 acres for the period of 1937-1941, inclusive. For the same periods, the average annual percent of the protected area burned, dropped from 1.44 to 0.48.

It was during the later years of the CCC that the General Assembly enacted the so-called "4 o'clock no burn law", which prohibited the burning of brush and debris within 300 feet of forest land during the months of March, April and May 1-15. During the late 40's and early 1950's when the General Assembly enacted several far reaching pieces of legislation, many of us recognized that the favorable forestry climate was in no small measure due to the favorable impact of the CCC.

During the late 40's, with the approach of war, there developed less enthusiasm for the CCC. The enrollees were younger and less responsive to work regulations. The so-called "educational phase" became more and more dominant to the point that it was difficult to accomplish much in satisfactory work projects.

The Army officers were, as a whole, less responsive to work accomplishment. In one camp, enrollees refused to obey an order to fight a forest fire because it was a Sunday.

In 1934, the President requested each of the governors on which CCC work was done on private land, to establish a policy which would ensure maintenance of projects constructed. In Virginia, Governor John Garland Pollard included $29,000 annually in the 1934 budget for maintenance, of which amount grew to $220,000 in 1974 due to inflation.

In 1933 or 1934, a severe hurricane came up the Atlantic coast. The high tides and wind in the Chesapeake Bay area caused numerous boats of varying sizes to be washed ashore. After the storm, many boats were in the middle of stands of young pine trees. The Westpoint King and Queen camps assisted in moving boats from dry land back into the water in several of the counties—especially in Matthews, Gloucester, York, Lancaster, and Northumberland. It was gratifying to see these veterans devising cradles, dolly trucks and other devices to move the landlocked vessels into the water.

Concurrently, with the CCC program was the Resettlement Program headed by Rexford Tugwell. This program resulted in the Federal acquisition of some 45,000 acres of "Marginal" land in the south central Piedmont counties of Buckingham, Cumberland, Appottox and Prince Edward. These areas were designated as state forests under the lease and later title deeds were given to the state. Considerable CCC work was accomplished on these lands which included timber inventory, development of recreational areas, lakes, roads, reforestation and timber management.

The CCC movement met with public approval in several manners. In eastern Virginia, several of the camps held young negro men and boys. In several nearby communities, where there was a considerable black population, the grapevine indicated that quite often fires were attributed to some of the local girls who enjoyed seeing the CCC boys come out and spend a while in their neighborhood.

The CCC was a real "boom" to forest conservation in Virginia. It is impossible to calculate the favorable impact on public recognition of the need for fire prevention and control, reforestation and better management of the timberlands.

by George W. Dean, State Forester, 1944-1973.

WASHINGTON

T.S. Goodyear 1933-1949   State Forest Board
                                                          created 1923

Camps
The average distribution of camps in Washington by services was as follows: National Forests 19, State Forest 1, Private Forests 7, Soil Conservation Service 7, National Parks 2, State Parks 6, Reclamation Service 2, Military Reservations 5, Naval Reservation 1, Total 50.

Employment
The aggregate number of Washington men given employment was 51,313. This figure included 40,309 junior and veteran enrollees, 3,830 Indians and 7,174 non-enrolled camp officers and supervisory workers. The number of individuals who worked in Washington regardless of the state of origin was 73,339.

Work Accomplishments
Lookout houses and towers, number.................................... 260
Telephone lines, miles.. 4,023
Truck trails and minor roads, miles 4,960
Trees planted, reforestation, number......................... 50,682,000
Fire hazard reduction, acres...................................... 95,495
Fighting forest fires, man-days 437,490

Expenditures
Total obligation in Washington (Est.)......................... $76,655,597
Allotments to dependents by enrollees (Est.)................... $10,296,970

Forests
A letter from Don Lee Fraser, Environmental Consultant furnished the following information:

In June, 1933, the Forestry Division had 12 CCC camps working on state and private land. This number varied from 16 in the first winter when four camps came down out of the national forests, to seven to eight later on. The program had a drastic impact in providing protection from forest fires on more than 12 million acres of state and private forest lands. This was accomplished by

1. Building new access roads (including conversion of abandoned logging Railroad grades) totaling 1,450 miles, including 360 bridges.
   This action provided the needed access into the areas of high forest fire hazard for rapid fire detection and suppression.
2. Built over 200 miles of access trails.
3. Erected 25 fire lookout towers.
4. Built over 200 miles of telephone lines to fire lookouts and guard stations.
5. Effected fire hazard reduction on more than 30,000 acres, including the felling of several hundred thousand highly inflammable snags.
6. The CCC crews spent 152,000 man-days (not 8-hour days) fighting forest fires, and they demonstrated the effectiveness of the type of trained fire fighting crew needed to cope with the fire problems, so

they were replaced (though in smaller numbers) when the CCC program terminted.

7. There are usually many factors that contribute to the total acreage lost to fire each year, but it is interesting to note that on the state and private forest land in the state of Washington, the average acreage burned over each year during the CCC program was 65,000 acres or just half the annual acreage loss during the preceding ten year period. (I should note that the average loss now is under 5,000 acres but the CCC's made a big contribution.)

8. CCC crews built the Department's first set of district headquarters buildings (23 of them) statewide, and also constructed a central shop and complete warehouse in Olympia that is still in use.

9. The CCC labor supplied the help to build and operate the first state forest tree nursery. They also provided more than 25,000 man-days to this project, and before they were through, the nursery, cleared of stumps, had a complete set of buildings for seed extraction, storage, etc., and seed beds with a capacity of producing 6 million seedlings annually.

10. CCC crews planted ten million trees on 14,500 acres of state-owned forest land and conducted timber stand improvement work on 4,000 acres.

WEST VIRGINIA

J.W.K. Holliday 1931-1933   Department of Forestry 1929
D.B. Griffin 1934-1941
Robert O. Bowen 1941-1943

Camps
The average distribution of camps by services in West Virginia on June 30, 1937 was as follows: National Forests 13, State Forests 5, Private Forests 8, Soil Conservation Service 7, Corps of Engineers 1, Other 7, Total 41.

Employment
The aggregate number of West Virginia men given employment was 55,056. This figure included 50,391 junior and veteran enrollees and 4,665 non-enrolled personnel of camp officers and supervisory workers.

Work Accomplishments
Cabins, overnight, number...112
Pipe or tile line..228,829
Fish stocked, number..4,454,669
Trees planted, number......................................26,874,000
Table and bench combinations, number.............................1,000

Expenditures
Total obligation in West Virginia (Est.).......................$50,202,959
Allotments to dependents by enrollees (Est.)...................$11,669,993

Camps
During the first CCC period, the State Division of Forestry was alloted seven camps which number was increased to 20 in the fifth period. Fifteen of these

camps were placed on private lands where forest fire protection, including truck trails, were the chief projects. The other five camps were placed on state-owned forest lands, where the major types of work were boundary survey, timber stand improvement, lake and dam construction, stream improvement, game survey, game protection, vermin control, landscaping and planting forest trees. In 1937, the number of camps on private land was reduced to seven, with further reduction to three in 1938 to two in 1939. When the CCC was terminated in July, 1942, there remained only one camp on private land and three on state land.

A camp was built at Tomlinson River site in 1941 and was never occupied.

Forests

At the beginning of the CCC program, there were no state parks and only two state forests. One of the state forests was commandeered to start the state park system. Six state forests were acquired and largely developed during the CCC program. They ranged in size from 5,000 to 10,000 acres each. From then up to 1979, only two more state forests had been added.

The Seneca State Forest of 10,847 acres of mountainous land was acquired in 1924. The entire forest was set aside as a game refuge with no hunting allowed.

The Kumbrabow State Forest was purchased in December, 1934. This forest of 8,932 acres was operated along the same lines as the Seneca.

The Cabwaylingo State Forest was purchased in 1935 and contains 7,000 acres of mixed hardwoods in Wayne County.

The Cooper's Rock State Forest contains 12,913 acres. During the fiscal year 1938, two new state forests, Greenbrier and Kanawha were purchased. The original purchases were financed by 10% of the fishing and hunting funds as authorized by law. Greenbrier and Kanawha were acquired during the fiscal year 1938.

On the Seneca State Forest, a good system of roads and an artificial lake with eight cabins on the shore was built. On the Cabwaylingo State Forest, the CCC work consisted of timber stand improvement (T.S.I.), construction of a forest fire tower with telephone line, log cabins, ranger stations and truck trails. On the Kanawha State Forest, a fire tower was erected. On the Greenbrier, a skyline drive was built with a 12 mile loop from White Sulphur Springs over the top of Kates Mountain at an elevation of 37,000 feet and thence down to U.S. Route 60. Cabins and picnic areas were constructed in this forest. On the Kumbrabow State Forest, a fish rearing station was built. A stone based road was built through the length of the forest. The Cooper's Rock State Forest embraces two popular picnic areas with attractive buildings, large shelters, amphitheater and other usually found facilities. The large amount of fish and game work is, of course, due to the use of fishing and hunting funds.

Forest Protection

One of the more important projects was forest fire protection. Not only was there need to protect the timber, but also the habitat for wildlife and recreation. It was accomplished in the same manner as in other states.

WISExISCONSIN

Ralph M. Immell 1933-1934   Forestry Board
H.W. McKenzie 1934-1942   Established 1905

Camps
The average number of camps operated in Wisconsin was 54. The average
distribution of the camps by operating service in June, 1937 was as follows:
National Forests 26, State Forests 19, Soil Conservation Service 17, State
Parks 14,

Employment
The aggregate number of Wisconsin men given employment was 75,242.
This figure included 63,965 junior and veteran enrollees, 2,190 Indians and
9,087 non-enrolled personnel of camp officers and supervisory workers. The
number of individuals who worked in Wisconsin regardless of the state of
origin was 92,094.

Work Accomplishments
Bridges, all types, number. 483
Telephone lines, miles 4,040
Truck trails and minor roads, miles 4,390
Trees planted, reforestation, number. 265,631,000
Fighting forest fires, man-days 269,447
Fish stocked, number 517,792,648

Expenditures
Total obligation in Wisconsin (Est.). $96,549,503
Allotments to dependents by enrollees (Est.). $16,465,146

The work done by the CCC enrollees was as diverse as the unit of the
government to which a camp was assigned. Wisconsin got an assignment of
better than a dozen camps under the sponsorship of the old Conservation
Department for work on its vast areas of county-owned forests which are
jointly managed by the state.

The work of the camps in the northern part of Wisconsin, both Federal
and state, was mostly concerned with the many phases of forestry. A
prime use of the men was for fire suppression and fire hazard education.
For the first time, adequate trained crews served to finally gain control
of the historically bad fire areas which followed logging.

The men in the forestry camps, other than their famous fire fighters,
became known for doing a good job in general forest practices. Tree planting
perhaps was the most obvious one. In nurseries built and staffed by the CCC's,
millions of tree seedlings were grown from seed that were collected and
out planted.

At the peak of the CCC program, the Nicolet Forest had 22 camps. Later, a
veteran's camp was established on this forest. The Nicolet National Forest's
Trees for Tomorrow Center offers year round seminars and programs on
such subjects as winter ecology, outdoor sports, safety, environmental education
and survivial skills. The center was constructed by the CCC crews.

From the inception of the CCC program, the state camps did work in almost every phase of forestry and conservation in accordance with plans laid out by the conservation department. These phases were mainly fire pre-suppression, actual fire suppression, erection of structures, construction of forest protection facilities, transportation, improvements, hazard reduction, nursery development and maintenance, forest planting and seeding, forest stand improvement, disease and insect pest control, landscaping, recreational development, wildlife and other related activities.

Devil's Lake State Park located in the southern part of Wisconsin, is the largest state park in the state.

Many roadside and state parks were developed and enlarged by the CCC. The facilities installed included buildings, water systems and sewage disposal systems. The grounds were landscaped and timber stands in adjacent areas were cleaned up. There was development of roads and trails, nature trails, springs and ponds cleaned out.

Camps
On January 1, 1938, the number of operating state CCC camps was reduced from 25 to 12. Phelps Camp on the Nicolet Forest was comprised of veterans.

Forestry
From the inception of the CCC program, the state CCC camps were engaged in almost every phase of forestry and conservation. These phases of work were mainly forest fire pre-suppression, forest fire fighting, erection of structures, construction of forest protection facilities, transportation, improvements, hazard reduction, nursery development and maintenance, forest planting and seeding, forest stand improvement, disease and insect control, landscaping, recreational development, wildlife and other related activities.

Fish and Game
The CCC boys got out at 3 a.m. and backed their fish truck up to hasten their trip to a lake or stream where the fish were planted. When these boys heard about newspaper reports of boondoggling, they knew that the editors were not up in the woods on frosty mornings to watch the CCC boys plant fish.

State Parks
Devil's Lake State Park, in the southern part of Wisconsin and the largest park in the state, received complete park development with the aid of the CCC enrollees. Several of the original camp buildings have been retained and improved for the use of such agencies as the Boy Scouts, Girl Scouts and similar organizations.

Nicolet National Forest
At one time there were 22 camps on this National Forest. Among the developments there were the Anvil Lake Camp Ground and the Franklin Lake Campground.

The Trees For Tomorrow Environmental Center, near the town of Eagle River, was constructed by the CCC. The Center is used today on a year round basis with such programs as winter ecology, outdoor sports, safety, environmental education, and teaching orienteering and surviving skills.

WYOMING

No state forester at the time

Camps

The average number of camps operated in Wyoming was 21. The average distribution of camps by services was, as of September 30, 1937, as follows: National Forests 9, Plant Industry 1, National Parks 5, State Parks 3, Division of Grazing 2, General Land Office 1.

Employment

The aggregate number of Wyoming men given employment was 12,866. This figure included 9,260 junior and veteran enrollees, 1,039 Indians and 2,567 non-enrolled personnel of camp officers and supervisory workers.

Work Accomplishments

Fences and guard rails, rods. 311,088
Fighting coal fires, man-days. 147,568
Trees planted, reforestation, number. 7,386,000
Fighting forest fires, man-days 110,043
Fish stocked, number 6,503,781

Expenditures

Total obligation in Wyoming (Est.). $38,508,920
Allotments to dependents by enrollees (Est.). $ 1,973,898

Forestry

All the forestry work at this time was carried on through the regional forester. A large proportion of the state is in public ownership.

State Parks

Guernsey State Park is located in southwest Wyoming about 40 miles west of the Wyoming-Nebraska boundary line. The Guernsey Dam, completed in 1927, is located in a steep rock-walled canyon called the "Narrows". The dam is a composite structure of sluiced clay, sand and gravel, covered, on the upstream side, with a three foot layer of rock riprap and, on the down hill slope, with rock fill. Two structures, built by the Bureau of Reclamation and CCC camps Br 9 and BR 10, were a garage and repair shop now used for the storage of park materials.

A museum built by the CCC is an L-shaped one story structure 59 by 100 feet, constructed of buff-colored sandstone rock. The gable roof is framed with heavy hand hewn timbers covered with two inch plank, which in turn, are covered by split cedar shakes. Roads were built on either side of the reservoir. On the west side of the reservoir, at what is known as Brimmer Point, there was built an eight by ten foot lookout enclosed by a low wall, which gives a comprehensive panorama of the park.

Along Lake Shore Drive there are three picnic areas, two built mainly of stone and the other of logs and stone. At the northern terminus of the Sky Line Drive on a high bluff overlooking the reservoir, is the largest and most complete picnic shelter, known as the Castle. Its approximate dimensions are 50 feet by 34 feet by 13 feet high. In the shelter there is a stone fireplace. The picnic area contains a number of fireplaces.

From U.S. #26, about six miles of gravel road were constructed to the parking area. The road was built by a veterans' company in 1939.

Gurnsey Park, Wyoming.

GREEN MOUNTAIN NATIONAL FOREST

Camps

The Vermont legislature of 1935 approved, by legislation, a purchase area in 30 Vermont townships for the Green Mountain National Forest to be acquired by the Federal Government. Under the Act, each purchase first needed the approval of the town selectmen and then the State Board on National Forests. As of July 1, 1979, the area purchased amounted to 270,809 acres. The purchase area lies on both sides of the Green Mountain range and extends from Warren to the Massachusetts line. The office of the forest supervisor is in Rutland, Vermont.

Camp Danby, F.1, Company #1148 was located in Mt. Tabor. The camp was first occupied as a tent camp on June 18, 1933 and was occupied by Vermont and Massachusetts enrollees. The camp was evacuated that fall and reoccupied on May 19, 1935. In May, 1939, the enrollees were transferred to the West River Camp.

Camp Peru, F.2, Company #166, located in the town of Peru, was first occupied May 19, 1933, as a tent camp for a short while until barracks could be constructed. Most of the enrollees were from Vermont.

Camp West River, F.3, Company #133, located in the town of Weston, was activated on June 24, 1933. Before wooden barracks were built, military tents were used until the middle of the winter. The enrollees were chiefly from Massachusetts. This camp was discontinued in November, 1940.

Camp Rochester, F.4, Company #1143, located in the village of Rochester, was established on June 18, 1935. These enrollees also were chiefly from Massachusetts, with a sprinkling of Vermont and Rhode Island youths. Most of the Massachusetts youths were from the Boston area and surrounding areas of Lynn, Lowell, Lawrence and New Beford.

The camp in Ripton was constructed late in the program but was never used by the enrollees.

Recreation

The usual recreational facilities were constructed at Hapgood Pond (man-made), Greendale area and Texas Falls. The developments included the building of dams to impound water, the construction of picnic and camping grounds containing the necessary supply of pure spring water or driven wells. Foot trails were constructed so as to have accesses to the Green Mountain Long Trail which extends the length of the state from Massachusetts to Canada. Scenic trails were also made which gave a view of the White Rock slides and the Danby white mountain quarries. Along portions of the Long Trail several peeled log shelters were constructed and several miles of the trail were rebuilt and maintained. The interests of the sportsmen were not overlooked. Small log weirs were erected in the streams so as to form deep pools to provide fish survival.

Previous to the expensive development of the area by private interests, three miles of ski trails and runs were built on Federal land on Bromley Mountain in Peru. A ski run was built in Goshen. The enrollees from the Rochester camp built about four miles of ski trails in the Breadloaf area of the forest.

Road and Bridge Work

Forest Road #40, a major road and bridge project extending 15 miles from Danby camp to the highway near Landgrove, was completed by enrollees working on both ends. This project had many bridges and culverts and was done by the enrollees from the Peru and Weston camps. The enrollees from the Rochester camp reconstructed portions of the Bingo road which leaves State Rte. #73 about three miles west of Talcville. The youths from the Rochester camp also constructed about six-tenths of a mile of road into the Texas Falls Recreation Area. The Rochester camp also worked on the Michigan road which failed to reach within six-tenths of a mile of State Rte. #73. Other road work included 3.3 miles of road by the Weston Camp into the Greendale area. Peru enrollees built the Mad Tom truck trail, which opened up an extensive area of National Forest timber for harvesting. The CCC cooperated with the ERA in the construction of .5 miles of access road to the White Rocks picnic areas near Wallingford.

Forestry

In addition to the work mentioned above, much work was executed by the CCC in thinning forest stands, planting open lands with forest seedlings, fire hazard reduction, minor truck trails and general forest improvement.*

* J. Allen Taylor.

Civilian Conservation Corps
James J. McEntee, Director

Summary of certain phases of the CCC Program
United States & Possessions from April 5, 1933-June 30, 1942.

The Task
The Civilian Conservation Corps made an outstanding record in the conservation of human and natural resources. Jobs and health and work training were given to about 3,000,000 young men, war veterans, Indians and territorials. The CCC advanced natural resources conservation in such fields as reforestation and erosion control by from 25 to 35 years, completing work on an estimated present and potential value of more than $1,750,000,000. In addition to training the idle young men and advancing conservation, the CCC demonstrated its greatest usefulness as a training and national preparedness agency. Graduates of the CCC made splendid soldier material and excellent war production workers. The work completed materially strengthened the nation economically.

Men
Total enrollment (some individuals enrolled more than once) 3,465,766
    This includes:
        Juniors, veterans and Indian enrollees 2,876,638
        Territorial enrollees, (Est.) 50,000
        Non-enrolled personnel, camp officers, work
        supervisors, educational advisers, etc.) 263,755
Aggregate number of individuals receiving employment 3,190,393

Camps
The average number of barrack camps operating in the
United States during the life of the Corps 1,643
Total number of different camps operated 4,500

Work Done
The CCC work program was nationwide in scope. Enrollees worked in virtually all the national forests and parks, in state forest and park areas, on farm lands, on the public domain, in wildlife refuges, along stream beds and in the arid areas of the west. Major work items and accomplishments include:

Forest Trees planted, number 2,356,000,000
Trails and minor roads constructed 126,000
Telephone lines laid, miles 89,000
Man-days expended fighting fires 6,459,000
Erosion control, check dams, number 6,660,000
Acreage covered in trees, plant disease and pest control 21,000,000

Money Spent
Total Obligations (Est.) $2,969,000,000
    Includes obligations for food, shelter, construction
    of camps, transportation, personal services
    Allotments to dependents by enrollees (Est.) . . . . $ 662,895,000

APPENDIX A

[PUBLIC—NO. 5—73D CONGRESS]

[S. 598]

An act for the relief of unemployment through the performance of useful public work, and for other purposes

Be it enacted by the Senate and House of Representatives of the United States of America in Congress assembled, That for the purpose of relieving the acute condition of widespread distress and unemployment now existing in the United States, and in order to provide for the restoration of the country's depleted natural resources and the advancement of an orderly program of useful public works, the President is authorized, under such rules and regulations as he may prescribe and by utilizing such existing departments or agencies as he may designate, to provide for employing citizens of the United States who are unemployed, in the construction, maintenance and carrying on of works of a public nature in connection with the forestation of lands belonging to the United States or to the several States which are suitable for timber production, the prevention of forest fires, floods and soil erosion, plant pest and disease control, the construction, maintenance or repair of paths, trails, and fire-lanes in the national parks and national forests, and such other work on the public domain, national and State, and Government reservations incidental to or necessary in connection with any projects of the character enumerated, as the President may determine to be desirable: *Provided*, That the President may in his discretion extend the provisions of this act to lands owned by counties and municipalities and lands in private ownership, but only for the purpose of doing thereon such kinds of cooperative work as are now provided for by acts of Congress in preventing and controlling forest fires and the attacks of forest-tree pests and diseases and such work as is necessary in the public interest to control floods. The President is further authorized, by regulation, to provide for housing the persons so employed and for furnishing them with such subsistence, clothing, medical attendance and hospitalization, and cash allowance, as may be necessary, during the period they are so employed, and, in his discretion, to provide for the transportation of such persons to and from the places of employment. That in employing citizens for the purposes of this act no discrimination shall be made on account of race, color, or creed; and no person under conviction for crime and serving sentence therefor shall be employed under the provisions of this act. The President is further authorized to allocate funds available for the purposes of this act, for forest research, including forest products investigations by the Forest Products Laboratory.

Sec. 2. For the purpose of carrying out the provisions of this act the President is authorized to enter into such contracts or agreements with States as may be necessary, including provisions for utilization of existing State administrative agencies, and the President, or the head of any department or agency authorized by him to construct any project or to carry on any such public works, shall be authorized to acquire real property by purchase, donation, condemnation, or otherwise, but the provisions of section 355 of the Revised Statutes shall not apply to any property so acquired.

Sec. 3. Insofar as applicable, the benefits of the act entitled "An act to provide compensation for employees of the United States suffering injuries while in the performance of their duties, and for other purposes", approved September 7, 1916, as amended, shall extend to persons given employment under the provisions of this act.

Sec. 4. For the purpose of carrying out the provisions of this act, there is hereby authorized to be expended, under the direction of the President, out of any unobligated moneys heretofore appropriated for public works (except for projects on which actual construction has been commenced or may be commenced within ninety days, and except maintenance funds for river and harbor improvements already allocated), such sums as may be necessary; and an amount equal to the amount so expended is hereby authorized to be appropriated for the same purposes for which such moneys were originally appropriated.

Sec. 5. That the unexpended and unallotted balance of the sum of $300,000,000 made available under the terms and conditions of the act approved July 21, 1932, entitled "An act to relieve destitution", and so forth, may be made available, or any portion thereof, to any State or Territory or States or Territories without regard to the limitation of 15 per centum or other limitations as to per centum.

Sec. 6. The authority of the President under this act shall continue for the period of two years next after the date of the passage hereof and no longer.

Approved March 31st, 1933.

APPENDIX B

EXECUTIVE ORDER

Relief of unemployment through the performance of useful public work

By virtue of the authority vested in me by the act of Congress entitled "An act for the relief of unemployment through the performance of useful public work, and for other purposes", approved March 31, 1933 (Public No. 5, 73d Congress), it is hereby ordered that:

(1) For the purpose of carrying out the provisions of said act, Robert Fechner is hereby appointed Director of Emergency Conservation Work at an annual rate of compensation of $12,000, less the reduction prescribed in subparagraph (b), section 2, title II, of the act of Congress entitled "An act to maintain the credit of the United States Government" (Public No. 2, 73d Congress), approved March 20, 1933.

(2) The Secretary of War, the Secretary of Agriculture, the Secretary of the Interior, and the Secretary of Labor each shall appoint a representative, and said representatives shall constitute an advisory council to the Director of Emergency Conservation Work.

(3) There is hereby established in the Treasury a fund of $10,000,000 by the transfer of an equal amount from the unobligated balances of the appropriation for emergency construction of public buildings contained in the act approved July 21, 1932, as authorized by section 4 of the said act of March 31, 1933, which fund shall be subject to requisition by the said Robert Fechner, as Director of Emergency Conservation Work, on the approval of the President.

(4) Subject to direction by the President, supplies and materials of the several departments or establishments shall be furnished on the requisition of the Director of Emergency Conservation Work, and the departments and establishments furnishing such supplies and materials shall be reimbursed therefor in accordance with instructions of the President.

(5) Reimbursement, if any, to the departments or establishments for other services rendered shall be made in accordance with instructions of the President.

Franklin D. Roosevelt.

The White House,
April 5, 1933.

APPENDIX C

CIVILIAN CONSERVATION CORPS

(CCC)

AN ACT

To establish a Civilian Conservation Corps, and for other purposes

Be it enacted by the Senate and House of Representatives of the United States of America in Congress assembled, That there is hereby established the Civilian Conservation Corps, hereinafter called the Corps, for the purpose of providing employment, as well as vocational training, for youthful citizens of the United States who are unemployed and in need of employment, and to a limited extent as hereinafter set out, for war veterans and Indians, through the performance of useful public work in connection with the conservation and development of the natural resources of the United States, its Territories, and insular possession: *Provided,* That at least 10 hours each week may be devoted to general educational and vocational training: *Provided,* That the provisions of this Act shall continue for the period of 3 years after July 1, 1937, and no longer.

Sec. 2. The President, by and with the advice and consent of the Senate, is authorized to appoint a director at a salary of $10,000 per annum. The director shall have complete and final authority in the functioning of the Corps, including the allotment of funds to cooperating Federal departments and agencies, subject to such rules and regulations as may be prescribed by the President in accordance with the provisions of this Act.

Sec. 3. In order to carry out the purposes of this Act, the director is authorized to provide for the employment of the Corps and its facilities on works of public interest or utility for the protection, restoration, regeneration, improvement, development, utilization, maintenance, or enjoyment of the natural resources of lands and waters, and the products thereof, including forests, fish and wildlife on lands or interest in lands (including historical and archeological sites), belonging to, or under the jurisdiction or control of, the United States, its Territories, and insular possessions, and the several States: *Provided,* That the President may, in his discretion, authorize the director to undertake projects on lands belonging to or under the jurisdiction or control of counties, and municipalities, and on lands in private ownership, but only for the purpose of doing thereon such kinds of cooperative work as are or may be provided for by Acts of Congress, including the prevention and control of forest fires, forest tree pests and diseases, soil erosion, and floods: *Provided further*, That no projects shall be undertaken on lands or interests in lands, other than those belonging to or under the jurisdiction or control of the United States, unless adequate provisions are made by the cooperating agencies for the maintenance, operation, and utilization of such projects after completion.

Sec. 4. There are hereby transferred to the Corps all enrolled personnel, records, papers, property, funds, and obligations of the Emergency Conservation Work established under the Act of March 31, 1933 (48 Stat. 22), as amended; and the Corps shall take over the institution of the camp exchange heretofore established and maintained, under supervision of the War Department, in connection with and aiding in administration of Civilian Conservation Corps work camps conducted under the authority of said Act as amended: *Provided*, That such camp exchange shall not sell to persons not connected with the operation of the Civilian Conservation Corps.

Sec. 5. The director and, under his supervision, the heads of other Federal departments or agencies cooperating in the work of the Corps, are authorized within the limit of the allotments of funds therefor, to appoint such civilian personnel as may be deemed necessary for the efficient and economical discharge of the functions of the Corps without regard to the civil-service laws and regulations.

Sec. 6. The President may order Reserve officers of the Army and officers of the Naval and Marine Reserves and warrant officers of the Coast Guard to active duty with the Corps under the provisions of section 37a of the National Defense Act and the Act of February 28, 1925, respectively.

Sec. 7. The director is authorized to have enrolled not to exceed 300,000 men at any one time, of which not more than 30,000 may be war veterans: *Provided*, That in addition thereto camps or facilities may be established for not to exceed 10,000 additional Indian enrollees and 5,000 additional territorial and insular possession enrollees.

Sec. 8. The enrollees in the Corps (other than war veterans, enrollees in the Territories and insular possessions, Indians, not to exceed one mess steward, three cooks, and one leader per each company) shall be unmarried male citizens of the United States between the ages of 17 and 23 years, both inclusive, and shall at the time of enrollment be unemployed and in need of employment: *Provided*, That the director may exclude from enrollment such classes of persons as he may consider detrimental to the well-being or welfare of the Corps, except that no person shall be excluded on account of race, color, or creed: *Provided further*, That enrollments shall be for a period of not less than 6 months and reenrollments (except in the case of one mess steward, three cooks, and one leader, in each company, and War Veterans) shall not exceed a total term of 2 years: *Provided further*, That in the discretion of the director continuous service by the enrollee during his period of enrollment shall not be required in any case where the enrollee attends an educational institution of his choice during his leave of absence: *Provided further*, That the director shall be authorized to issue certificates of proficiency and merit to enrollees under such rules and regulations as he may provide.

Sec. 9. The compensation of enrollees shall be in accordance with schedules approved by the President, and enrollees with dependent member or members of their families shall be required under such regulations as may be prescribed by the director, to make allotments of pay to such dependents. Other enrollees may make deposits of pay in amounts specified by the director with the Chief of Finance, War Department, to be repaid in case of an emergency or upon completion of or release from enrollment and to receive the balance of their pay in cash monthly: *Provided*, That Indians may be excluded from these regulations: *Provided further*, That the pay of enrollees shall not exceed $30 per month, except for not more than 10 per centum who may be designated as assistant leaders and who shall receive not more than $36 per month: *Provided further*, That not to exceed an additional 6 per centum of such enrollees who may be designated as leaders and may receive not more than $45 per month as such leaders.

Sec. 10. Enrollees shall be provided, in addition to the monthly rates of pay, with such quarters, subsistence, and clothing, or commutation in lieu thereof, medical attention, hospitalization, and transportation as the director may deem necessary: *Provided*, That burial, embalming, and transportation expenses of deceased enrolled members of the Corps, regardless of the cause and place of death, shall be paid in accordance with regulations of the Employees' Compensation Commission: *Provided further*, That the provisions of the Act of February 15, 1934 (U.S.C., 1934 ed., title 5, sec. 796), relating to disability or death compensation and benefits shall apply to the enrolled personnel of the Corps.

Sec. 11. The Chief of Finance, War Department, is hereby designated, empowered, and directed, until otherwise ordered by the President, to act as the fiscal agent of the director in carrying out the provisions of this Act: *Provided*, That funds allocated to Government agencies for obligation under this Act may be expended in accordance with the laws, rules, and regulations governing the usual work of such agency, except as otherwise stipulated in this Act: *Provided further*, That in incurring expenditures, the provisions of section 3709, Revised Statutes (U.S.C., 1934 ed., title 41, sec. 5), shall not apply to any purchase or service when the aggregate amount involved does not exceed the sum of $300.

Sec. 12. The President is hereby authorized to utilize the services and facilities of such departments or agencies of the Government as he may deem necessary for carrying out the purposes of this Act.

Sec. 13. The director and, under his supervision, the cooperating departments and agencies of the Federal Government are authorized to enter into such cooperative agreements with States and civil divisions as may be necessary for the purpose of utilizing the services and facilities thereof.

Sec. 14. The director may authorize the expenditure of such amounts as he may deem necessary for supplies, materials, and equipment for enrollees to be used in connection with their work, instruction, recreation, health, and welfare, and may also authorize expenditures for the transportation and subsistence of selected applicants for enrollment and of discharged enrollees while en route upon discharge to their homes.

Sec. 15. That personal property as defined in the Act of May 29, 1935 (49 Stat. 311), belonging to the Corps and declared surplus by the director, shall be disposed of by the Procurement Division, Treasury Department, in accordance with the provisions of said Act: *Provided*, That unserviceable property in the custody of any department shall be disposed of under the regulations of that department.

Sec. 16. The director and, under his supervision, the heads of cooperating departments and agencies are authorized to consider, ascertain, adjust, determine, and pay from the funds appropriated by Congress to carry out the provisions of this Act any claim arising out of operations authorized by the Act accruing after the effective date thereof on account of damage to or loss of property or on account of personal injury to persons not provided for by section 10 of this Act, caused by the negligence of any enrollee or employee of the Corps while acting within the scope of his employment: *Provided*, That the amount allowed on account of personal injury shall be limited to necessary medical and hospital expenses: *Provided further*, That this section shall not apply to any claim on account of personal injury for which a remedy is provided by section 10 of this Act: *Provided further*, That no claim shall be considered hereunder which is in excess of $500, or which is not presented in writing within one year from the date of accrual thereof: *Provided further*, That acceptance by an claimant of the amount allowed on account of his claim shall be deemed to be in full settlement thereof, and the action of the director or of the head of a cooperating department or agency upon such claim so accepted by the claimant shall be conclusive.

Sec. 17. There is hereby authorized to be appropriated, out of any money in the Treasury not otherwise appropriated, such sums as may be necessary for the purpose of carrying out the purposes of this Act: *Provided*, That no part of any such appropriation shall be used in any way to pay any expense in connection with the conduct, operation, or management of any camp exchange, save and except such camp exchanges as are established and operated, in accordance with regulations to be prescribed by the director, at such camps as may be designated by him, for real assistance and convenience to enrollees in supplying them and their supervising personnel on duty at any such camp with articles of ordinary use and consumption not furnished by the Government: *Provided further*, That the person in charge of any such camp exchange shall certify, monthly, that during the preceding calendar month such exchange was operated in compliance therewith.

Sec. 18. This Act, except as otherwise provided, shall take effect July 1, 1937.

Approved, June 28, 1937.

APPENDIX D

Enrollment, Civilian Conservation Corps, fiscal year 1937

State	Juniors[1]	Veterans[2]	Total
Alabama	6,101	409	6,510
Arizona	750	145	895
Arkansas	8,090	515	8,605
California	5,890	1,439	7,329
Colorado	2,722	231	2,953
Connecticut	2,254	198	2,452
Delaware	194	42	236
District of Columbia	713	145	858
Florida	4,467	314	4,781
Georgia	7,637	436	8,073
Idaho	814	121	935
Illinois	12,241	1,931	14,172
Indiana	5,148	373	5,521
Iowa	3,281	503	3,784
Kansas	3,287	378	3,665
Kentucky	12,695	399	13,094
Louisiana	4,465	181	4,646
Maine	1,461	130	1,591
Maryland	1,692	330	2,022
Massachusetts	10,828	811	11,639
Michigan	6,347	710	7,057
Minnesota	10,667	700	11,367
Mississippi	4,500	216	4,716
Missouri	10,816	773	11,589
Montana	2,452	135	2,587
Nebraska	2,729	200	2,929
Nevada	144	28	172
New Hampshire	567	48	615
New Jersey	7,383	421	7,804
New Mexico	2,290	104	2,394
New York	11,829	2,044	13,873
North Carolina	5,878	419	6,297
North Dakota	6,235	235	6,470
Ohio	12,352	1,222	13,574
Oklahoma	14,041	680	14,721
Oregon	1,021	158	1,179
Pennsylvania	7,554	1,667	9,221
Rhode Island	1,876	80	1,956
South Carolina	5,161	268	5,429
South Dakota	2,411	157	2,568
Tennessee	5,458	298	5,756
Texas	16,535	1,163	17,698
Utah	742	108	850
Vermont	515	20	535
Virginia	5,168	214	5,382
Washington	2,892	435	3,327
West Virginia	5,857	286	6,143
Wisconsin	6,304	641	6,945
Wyoming	1,189	66	1,255
Total	255,643	22,527	278,170

[1] Reported by Labor Department. Includes juniors aged 17-28.
[2] Reported by Veterans' Administration. Includes war veterans.

APPENDIX E

STATE SELECTING AGENCIES FOR 1ST PERIOD
(Selected men 18 to 25 years of age and experienced men only)

Alabama . . . . Thad Holt . . . . Executive Director, Alabama Relief Administration, 1204 First National Bank Building, Montgomery, Ala.

Arizona . . . . Stuart M. Bailey . . . . Secretary, State Board of Public Welfare, Capitol Building, Phoenix, Ariz.

Arkansas . . . . W.A. Rooksbery. . . . . Assistant Director, State of Arkansas Unemployment Relief, State House, Little Rock, Ark.

California . . . . R.C. Branion. . . . . Special Assistant to the Governor, Emergency Relief Administrator, State of California, 133 State Capitol Building, Sacramento, Calif.

Colorado . . . . Miss Jessie I. Lumis . . . . Assistant to Administrator and Director of Field Service, Official Colorado State Relief Committee, 108 State Museum Building, Denver, Colo.

Connecticut . . . . James W. Hook . . . . President, Unemployment Commission of the State of Connecticut, Blake and Valley Streets, New Haven, Conn.

Delaware . . . . Everett G. Ackart . . . . Temporary Emergency Relief Commission of the State of Delaware, Delaware Trust Building, Wilmington, Del.

District of Columbia. . Leroy A. Halbert. . . . . Supervisor, Emergency Relief Division, Board of Public Welfare of the District of Columbia, John Marshall Place and C Street, NW., Washington, D.C.

Florida. . . . . J.C. Huskisson . . . . Director of Relief, Florida Emergency Relief Administration, P.O. Box, 904 Tallahassee, Fla.

Georgia . . . . H.P. De La Perriere . . . . Director, Georgia Relief Administration, State Capitol, Atlanta, Ga.

Idaho . . . . Parker P. Carver. . . . . Chairman, Idaho State Relief Committee, Governor's Office, Boise, Idaho.

Illinois . . . . Wilfred S. Reynolds . . . . Executive Secretary, Illinois Emergency Relief Commission, 10 South LaSalle Street, Chicago, Ill.

Indiana. . . . . Fred Hoke . . . . Governor's Commission on Unemployment Relief, 206 State House, Indianapolis, Ind.

Iowa. . . . . E.H. Mulock. . . . . Chairman, State Emergency Relief Committee, State House, Des Moines, Iowa.

Kansas . . . . D.E. Ackers. . . . . Director, Kansas Federal Relief Committee, Topeka, Kans.

Kentucky . . . . Harper Gatton. . . . . Director, Kentucky Relief Commission, Fifth and Jefferson Streets, Louisville, Ky.

Louisiana. . . . . G.A. Stair . . . . General Chairman, Unemployment Committee of Louisiana, Canal Bank Building, New Orleans, La.

Maine. . . . . George W. Leadbetter . . . . . . Commissioner, Department of Health and Welfare, State Capitol, Augusta, Maine.

Maryland. . . . . Paul Beisser . . . . Secretary, Advisory Unemployment Relief Commission, 31 South Calvert Street, Baltimore, Md.

Massachusetts . . . . Richard K. Conant . . . . Commissioner, State of Massachusetts Department of Public Welfare, Room 37, State House, Boston, Mass.

Michigan . . . . W.S. Carpenter. . . . . Director, State Welfare Board of Michigan, Capitol Building, Lansing, Mich.

Minnesota . . . . Frank M. Rarig, Jr. . . . . Supervisor of Relief, Minnesota State Board of Control, Room 229, State Office Building, St. Paul, Minn.

Mississippi . . . . George B. Power . . . . Director, State Board of Public Welfare of Mississippi, State Capitol, Jackson, Miss.

Missouri . . . . Walter Burr . . . . Director of Relief and Reconstruction, Missouri Relief and Reconstruction Committee, 407 State House, Jefferson City, Mo.

Montana . . . . T.C. Spaulding . . . . Director of Relief, State of Montana, State Capitol, Helena, Mont.

Nebraska . . . . W.H. Smith . . . . State Tax Commissioner, State Capitol, Lincoln, Nebr.

Nevada . . . . Cecil W. Creel . . . . Secretary, State Emergency Relief and Construction Committee, University of Nevada, Reno, Nev.

New Hampshire . . . . . Eunice E. Patch . . . . Secretary, New Hampshire State Unemployment Relief Commission, State House, Concord, N.H.

New Jersey . . . . Col. Joseph D. Sears . . . . Assistant Director, Emergency Relief Administration, 540 Broad Street, Newark, N.J.

New Mexico . . . . Margaret Reeves . . . . Director, New Mexico State Bureau of Child Welfare, State Capitol, Santa Fe, N.Mex.

New York . . . . Frederick I. Daniels . . . . Executive Director, Temporary Emergency Relief Administration of New York State, 124 East Twenty-eighth Street, New York, N.Y.

North Carolina . . . . . . Ronald B. Wilson . . . . Executive Assistant to the Director of Relief, Revenue Building, Raleigh, N.C.

North Dakota . . . . R.A. Kinzer . . . . Director, State Relief Committee, Bismarck, N.Dak.

Ohio . . . . Major E.O. Braught . . . . Executive Secretary, Ohio State Relief Commission, Wyandotte Building, Columbus, Ohio

Oklahoma . . . . C.H. Scroggin . . . . State Director of Federal Relief, Governor's Office, State House, Oklahoma City, Okla.

Oregon . . . . Raymond B. Wilcox . . . . Chairman, Oregon State Relief Commission, Wilcox Building, Portland, Oreg.

Pennsylvania . . . . F. Richard Stilwell . . . . Pennsylvania State Emergency Relief Board, State Museum Building, Harrisburg, Pa.

Rhode Island . . . . Henry T. Samson . . . . Secretary, Rhode Island Unemployment Relief Commission, State House, Providence, R.I.

South Carolina . . . . . . Alan Johnstone . . . . Director of Relief, South Carolina Relief Council, 4 South Carolina National Bank Building, Columbia, S.C.

South Dakota . . . . W.L. Eales . . . . Director, South Dakota State Relief Committee, Pierre, S.Dak.

Tennessee . . . . George Morris . . . . Chairman, the State Committee of the Reconstruction Finance Corporation, State Capitol, Nashville, Tenn.

Texas . . . . Lawrence Westbrook . . . . Director, Texas Relief Commission, Austin, Tex.

Utah . . . . T.L. Holman . . . . Chairman, the Governor's Central Committee on Emergency Relief for Utah, 505 Felt Building, Salt Lake City, Utah

Vermont . . . . Perry H. Merrill . . . . Commissioner of Forestry of the State of Vermont, Montpelier, Vt.

Virginia . . . . Arthur W. James . . . . Chairman, Virginia State Emergency Relief Committee, State House, Richmond, Va.

Washington .... Charles F. Ernst .... Director, Washington State Emergency Relief Administration, Room 210, Old Capitol Building, Olympia, Wash.

West Virginia........ Maj. Francis Turner .... Director, Unemployment Relief Administration, Department of Public Welfare, State Capitol, Charleston, W.Va.

Wisconsin .... Florence Peterson .... Supervisor, Wisconsin State Unemployment Relief, Capitol Office Building, Madison, Wis.

Wyoming .... James Morgan............. Chairman, Governor's State Emergency Unemployment Relief Committee, Mine Workers' Building, (box 904), Cheyenne, Wyo.

APPENDIX F

Ages of CCC Enrollees

The following figures were collected from a survey taken in January 1937.

Number of CCC enrollees classified according to age groups (continental United States)

Age (last birthday basis)	Number of enrollees	Age (last birthday basis)	Number of enrollees
All ages	350,350	27 years	5,696
		28 years	3,743
17 years	36,240	29 to 34 years	5,585
18 years	53,454	35 to 39 years	6,806
19 years	48,750	40 to 44 years	14,163
20 years	45,185	45 to 49 years	9,381
21 years	35,209	50 to 54 years	3,187
22 years	26,431	55 to 59 years	1,519
23 years	19,441	60 to 64 years	835
24 years	14,667	65 years and over	426
25 years	10,736	Age not reported	194
26 years	8,702		

APPENDIX G

Average number of CCC camps, by States, by services, fiscal year 1940-41

State	War Dept. Army Reservation	Interior: General Land Office	Interior: Bureau of Reclamation	Interior: National Parks and Monuments	Interior: State parks	Interior: County parks	Interior: Metropolitan areas	Interior: Recreational dem. project	Interior: TVA (S.P.)	Interior: Fish and Wildlife Service	Interior: Grazing Service	Interior: Recreational dem. areas	Total Dept. of the Interior	Agr.: National forest	Agr.: State forest	Agr.: Private forest	Agr.: TVA (S.F.)	Agr.: Animal Industry	Agr.: Plant Industry	Agr.: National Agricultural Research Center	Agr.: Soil Conservation Service	Total Dept. of Agriculture	All services
Alabama					7					1			8	4		6					13	23	31
Arizona			2	4			1			1	5		13	12			4				3	15	28
Arkansas				1	4								6	12		4					12	28	34
California			4	14	7		2			2	8		31	36	7						8	51	82
Colorado			4	6	7		2			1	8		20	10							12	22	42
Connecticut						1	2								9	7						9	9
Delaware													3										3
District of Columbia				2									2						1			1	3
Florida					5	1				1			7	5		5					9	10	17
Georgia				3	4								12	5		1					4	19	31
Idaho	3		4		9						10		12	28							24	36	51
Illinois					7	12				1			21	4	3						20	29	50
Indiana					5								8	2	1						13	21	29
Iowa					1								15		3						12	13	28
Kansas					2					1												24	14
Kentucky				3	2				1				1			4					16	25	31
Louisiana					2					1		3	7	4		3						4	28
Maine					1										6	1						15	8
Maryland					2	2							4		6					3		12	21
Massachusetts				1	8					1			6		11	1					9	37	20
Michigan					4					3			8	23	12						11	34	46
Minnesota					4								9	15	10							22	42
Mississippi				2	5					1			8	7		4	1				21	33	29
Missouri				2	6					1			7	9	3							16	29
Montana			4	4	1					1	5	3	10	13	1							15	31
Nebraska			3										15	1	3						11	14	18
Nevada			2	2							17		3	1	10	1					1	8	37
New Hampshire					4								23	2	10	2						29	9
New Jersey					2	1				2			1	6	27	2					11	22	36
New Mexico			4	1							10		7	9							6	11	43
New York				3	14	2		1		3		1	21	8	2	5					15	32	29
North Carolina				6	3			1				1	18		5	5					17	21	45
North Dakota					2								13	2								1	7
Ohio					6	2	4			1			6	2	2						17	21	25
Oklahoma					3		1			3			4	18	32	2					21	56	64
Oregon		5	6	1	6					1	9		28	3	1	7					7	30	58
Pennsylvania					1					1		1	6		1	1					4	1	16
Rhode Island					3											1						1	3
South Carolina				1	2					1		2	6	6	4	6					10	26	32
South Dakota			1		4					2			4	7							4	11	15
Tennessee				4	8				2	1			6	6	4	4	11				6	41	32
Texas			1	2	8		4			2	14		4	6							27	13	58
Utah			1	3			1			3			11	2	1						5	9	34
Vermont					3								17	2							1	36	9
Virginia				14	3	2				1			21	10		2	2					13	58
Washington			3	5	5					2			3	15	12	10					10	36	50
West Virginia					4					1			22	5		3					6	39	18
Wisconsin					4	2				3			11	12					1		6	14	32
Wyoming		1	5	4	1						9		4	9							13	25	29
Total	**3**	**6**	**45**	**91**	**155**	**23**	**16**	**1**	**3**	**36**	**89**	**24**	**492**	**329**	**175**	**96**	**18**	**1**	**2**	**3**	**392**	**1,016**	**1,508**

NATIONAL ASSOCIATION OF CIVILIAN CONSERVATION CORPS ALUMNI (NACCCA)

The National Association of Civilian Conservation Corps Alumni, known as NACCCA for short, was established in August, 1977, and incorporated by the California Secretary of State on the 16th of August, 1977. Membership is open to any individual associated, in any capacity, with the Civilian Conservation Corps (1933-1942). This includes enrollees, military personnel, state forestry personnel, educational advisors, hospital personnel, district headquarters personnel, civilian personnel and all associated with the CCC. Headquarters was originally established at Carmichael, California.

When ten or more members express a desire for formation of a chapter, and the necessary initiative and leadership are present, chapters are encouraged and supported. The membership of NACCCA at present is over 6,000 with 40 chapters in the different parts of the United States.

Each member of NACCCA has the opportunity to promote and contribute to an organization which promotes resource projects relating to renewable energy and is dedicated to the wellbeing of all its members and which provides each individual:

1. The opportunity to participate in a movement to conserve the natural resources of his country,
2. To help the youth of America with their problems much as they were helped forty years ago,
3. To participate in, and contribute to an organized effort to solve the mutual problems of Senior Americans,
4. The opportunity to locate old friends and relive and recall the days of their youth with those who shared them, and
5. To become active as an interested contributor to life in America today, rather than become a statistic in another file of retired do-nothing older citizens.

For information about membership, you should write to NACCCA, 7900 Sudley Road, Suite 418, Manassas, Virginia 22110